MASS MEDIA And SOCIETY

JMC-02

For

Post Graduate Diploma in Journalism and Mass Communication (PGJMC)

Useful For

IGNOU, Rai Technology University, KSOU (Karnataka), NIILM University, Bihar University (Muzaffarpur), Nalanda University, Jamia Millia Islamia, Vardhman Mahaveer Open University (Kota), Uttarakhand Open University, Kurukshetra University, Himachal Pradesh University, Seva Sadan's College of Education (Maharashtra), Lalit Narayan Mithila University, Andhra University, Pt. Sunderlal Sharma (Open) University (Bilaspur), Annamalai University, Bangalore University, Bharathiar University, Bharathidasan University, Centre for distance and open learning, Kakatiya University (Andhra Pradesh), KOU (Rajasthan), MPBOU (MP), MDU (Haryana), Punjab University, Tamilnadu Open University, Sri Padmavati Mahila Visvavidyalayam (Andhra Pradesh), Sri Venkateswara University (Andhra Pradesh), UCSDE (Kerala), University of Jammu, YCMOU, Rajasthan University, UPRTOU, Kalyani University, Banaras Hindu University (BHU) and all other Indian Universities.

Closer to Nature We use Recycled Paper

GULLYBABA PUBLISHING HOUSE PVT. LTD.

ISO 9001 & ISO 14001 CERTIFIED CO.

Published by:
GullyBaba Publishing House Pvt. Ltd.

Regd. Office:
2525/193, 1st Floor, Onkar Nagar-A,
Delhi-110035
(From Kanhaiya Nagar Metro Station Towards Old Bus Stand)
Ph. 011-27387998, 27384836, 27385249
+919350849407

Branch Office:
1A/2A, 20, Hari Sadan, Tri Nagar,
Ansari Road, Daryaganj,
New Delhi-110002
Ph. 011-45794768

New Edition

Price:
Author: GullyBaba.Com Panel
ISBN: 978-93-83921-33-1

PREFACE

Modern mass media, has brought about a profound change in our society. This transition has not been easy. Initially the print media, followed by radio, film and TV, have provided impetus to development efforts in India after independence. Media has Indian Society into two classes-the information "haves" and "have-nots". 'These two classes have parallel existence in our society. Information on health, family planning, education and eradication of social evils like drugs, smoking, alcoholism, and dowry, are being successfully projected by mass media. The freedom of the Press has a constitutional right to function freely and without fetters. But, at the same time, it must exercise this right within the framework of certain reasonable restrictions laid down in various laws otherwise it can be punished. Today media become a part of everyone's life. Media plays a major role in today's society, now media become food to strengthen or weaken society. The best of modern communication technology has to be tempered by the wisdom of the Indian traditional values.

This GPH book ***'Mass Media and Society (JMC-02)'*** clears these concepts for better understanding of students. It also throw light on role of media on issues related to women and focuses on the point that media does not present actual condition of women.

The book is written especially in question & answer format to provide students the instant gratification of a correct answer. In this book, we have tried to solve all possible questions from the exams' point of view. Solutions of previous years' question papers have also been included to help students to understand the unique examination structure.

We hope that this book would not be only a favourite study material for the students but also can be a nice resource for teaching. An attempt has been carefully made to present this book more useful and meet the requirements and challenges of the course prescribed by Indian Universities. We wish you a successful and rewarding career ahead. Feedback in this regard is solicited.

– GPH Panel of Experts

Acknowledgements

Our compliments go to the **GullyBaba Publishing House Pvt. Ltd.,** and its meticulous team who have been enthusiastically working towards the perfection of the book.

Their teamwork, initiative and research have been very encouraging. Had it not been for their unflagging support, this work wouldn't have been possible. The creative freedom provided by them along with their aim of presenting the best to the reader has been a major source of inspiration in this work. Hope that this book would be successful.

– GPH Panel of Experts

Publisher's Note

The present book JMC-02 is targeted for examination purpose as well as enrichment. With the advent of technology and the Internet, there has been no dearth of information available to all; however, finding the relevant and qualitative information, which is focussed, is an uphill task.

We at **GullyBaba Publishing House Pvt. Ltd.,** have taken this step to provide quality material which can accentuate in-depth knowledge about the subject. GPH books are a pioneer in the effort of providing unique and quality material to its readers. With our books, you are sure to attain success by making use of this powerful study material. Provided book is just a reference book based on the syllabus of particular University/Board. For a profound information, see the textbooks recommended by the University/Board.

Our site **gullybaba.com** is a vital resource for your examination. The publisher wishes to acknowledge the significant contribution of the Team Members and our experts in bringing out this publication and highly thankful to Almighty God, without His blessings, this endeavor wouldn't have been successful.

– Publisher

Topics Covered

CONTENTS

QUESTION PAPERS

1 RELATION BETWEEN MASS MEDIA AND SOCIETY

INTRODUCTION

We have divided Indian history into three periods: The Ancient, The Medieval and The Modem. In the ancient period the Hindu religion played a significant role in the development of Indian culture and tradition. In the Medieval period Islam had relatively strong influence in our culture and tradition. Later on, during the Modem period the British culture 'and literature brought about a reform in our religious traditions and beliefs. Technology, guided by consumerism, and sustained by the modern mass media, has brought about a profound change in our society. Indian Communication system has its roots in the age-old Sadharanikaran, evolved by Bharata Muni in his Natya Shastra. The best of modern Communication technology has to be tempered by the wisdom of tile Indian traditional values. Communication media have become vital for the supply of information, education, entertainment and socialisation all around the world. various Communication obstacles faced by the masses due to the present mode of functioning of the mass media. There have been frequent calls for enunciating an explicit media policy for the country. Communication policy is a set of principles to tackle action-oriented problems effectively.

Q1. Describe the evolution and growth of Indian culture.

Ans. The Indian culture, often labelled as an amalgamation of several cultures, spans across the Indian subcontinent and includes traditions that are several centuries old. India has a rich cultural history and continues to preserve it beautifully. India has accepted gracefully the good qualities of different religions which led to the rise of many different cultures in this mystical sub-continent. Different rulers and empires came here and ruled and left behind a rich legacy of their cultural heritage. Every state in India has a culture of its own and even then they all stand unified and form one single culture of India.

The understanding of the social structure, institutions, the beliefs, the vision and the perceptions of the Indian mind is necessary to grasp the relationship between Indian society and mass media. Mass media do not operate in isolation. They are shaped by the people and in truth influences the people. Hence, it is imperative to understand the social context, the social milieus and the environment in which human beings share communication.

The Indian civilisation can best be traced back to the Indus Valley civilisation (Harappan culture) in 2300 BC. The antecedents of the Harappan culture were the most extensive of ancient civilisations were spread over in the Indus plain covering Punjab, Sindh and also Rajasthan and Kathiawar region of Gujarat. It is not known who the builders of the Indus civilisation were. In all probability they were a Mediterranean race, allied to the Dravidians of India, the latter being the original inhabitants of the Indo-Gangetic Plains. With the ingress of the Aryans, the Dravidians crossed the Satpura range into peninsular India. Archeological excavations reveal that Harappans were Phallus worshippers reflecting many elements of the religion of the Dravidian Inhabitants of India. The citadels of Harappa and Mohenjodaro stand even today as symbols of a highly developed urban culture, revealing the deep knowledge of the inhabitants in town planning and management of excellent drainage system.

The Indus people were also the earliest people to develop farming. They cultivated wheat and barley and produced cotton and wore cloth. The alloy of bronze mixing cooper with tin was introduced by the Harappans. The people of Harappa and Mohenjodaro invented the potter's wheel. The Harappan used an atypical scripts which had no resemblance to the early Egyptian or Mesopotamian scripts of the contemporary period. Evidences of trade links both within the northern and western areas of the subcontinent, as well as between people of Indus valley and those of Sumeria (Persian Gulf) and Mesopotamia exist.

The Aryans brought a distinct culture with them. This culture enriched the local culture. And slowly the unique culture, customs and traditions of India evolved.

Q2. How the Aryans and Dravidians came to India and settled down? Also, describe the advent of the Vedas, Jainism and Buddhism in India.

Ans. About 1500 BC, new migrating people arrived in India that soon changed the country's history. They called themselves Aryans, the noble ones. They were a part of the great Indo-European explosion of men and women seeking new homes in Asia and Europe. Originally settling in the lands between the Caspian and Black Seas, they poured into Iran, giving their name to that country. Most continued into India.

The Aryans lived in the areas east of the Alps, in the region known as Eurasia. They spoke Indo-European languages, which are still used with some variations throughout Europe, Iran, and a major part of the Indian sub-continent including Pakistan, and the Northern and Western regions of India. The people of northern India speak Indo-Aryan languages (Punjabi, Hindi, Urdu and Bengali) and are of predominantly Mediterranean (Europoid) racial stock. Indian population is polygenetic and is a confusing mixture of racial strains. Very few can claim to belong to any particular racial stock.

The arrival of the Dravidians in India was undoubtedly anterior to the arrival of the Aryans, but there is some difficulty in determining whether the Dravidians were identical with the Scythian aborigines whom the Aryans found in possession of the northern provinces, and to whom the vernacular languages of Northern India are indebted for their Un-Sanskrit element, or whether they were a distinct and more ancient race.

They were spread over the whole of India prior to the advent of the Aryans. The latter encountered the highly civilised Indus valley with its big towns. The Indus valley people were essentially city people, the Aryans were a pastoral race. The earliest Aryans settled in the area covered by Eastern Punjab, Afghanistan and Western Uttar Pradesh. As migrants, Aryans came in several waves and clashed with the local inhabitants, to establish their supremacy. The success of Aryan invasion in India is attributed to their possession of trained horses, horse-drawn chariots, and better weaponry. The Aryans were also very knowledgeable about climate and agricultural operations like ploughing, sowing, harvesting and threshing.

- The group of Indo-Europeans who moved to Persia and India are known as Aryans.
- The Aryans are the original inhabitants of Central Asia.
- They arrived in India around 1500 BC, though there is an ongoing debate.
- The region where the Aryans settled in India was called Sapta Sindhu (also referred to as the Brahmavarta)
- The Aryans established themselves in India by defeating the natives whom they called Dasas or Dasyus.
- The period when the Aryans first settled in India, is known as Early Vedic Period (1500 BC to 1000 BC).
- The Aryans spread to Indo-Gangetic plains in the later Vedic Period and this region came to be known as Aryavarta (1000 BC to 600 BC).
- The Aryans were the first people in India to get to know the use of iron and brought horses along with them.

Dravidians

- It is believed that before the coming of the Aryans in India, the greater part of Northern and North-Western India was inhabited by a group of people known as Dravidians.
- On arrival of the Aryans, when unable to meet their challenge, they gradually moved southwards.
- Perhaps, in India, they were first to use rivers for navigation and irrigation.

In about 1500 BC, groups of warlike people left their homes in central Asia, possibly near the Caucasus Mountains, and came to India. These people called themselves arya (kinsmen or nobles). They are now known as the Aryans. The Aryans came to India in several waves. They came into conflict with the indigenous inhabitants called the Dravidians mentioned as dasa or dasyus in Rig Veda. The Rig Veda mentions the defeat of

Sambara by Divodasa, who belonged to the Bharata clan. Possibly the dasyus in the Rig Veda represent the original inhabitants of the country, and an Aryan chief who overpowered them was called Trasadvasyu. The Aryan chief was soft towards the dasas, but strongly hostile to the dasyus. The term dasyuhatya, slaughter of the dasyus, is repeatedly mentioned in the Rig Veda.

Some of the chief tribes of the period were Yadu, Turvasu, Druhyu, Anu Puru, Kuru, Panchala, Bharata and Tritsu. Among the inter-tribal conflicts the most important was the 'Battle of the Ten Kings.'

Advent of the Vedas: The Vedas form our main source for this period. The Rig Veda informs us that the early Aryan settlements extended in the valleys of the five rivers of the Punjab, i.e. the Indus and its tributaries, otherwise called the Sapta-Sindhu region. This region was so rich and fertile that the Aryans referred to it as the Brahmavarta or 'Land of the Gods'.

The Rig Veda which is considered to the oldest of the four vedas (Sama Veda, Yajur Veda, Atharva Veda are the three later additions) is a collection of prayers in Sanskrit language offered by the Aryans to Gods of fire and rain. Rig Veda is believed to have been composed around 1500 B.C. The Rig Veda also mentions artisan communities like those of the carpenter, the weaver, the potter and the leather-worker.

- **Social Distinctions:** Varna in the Rig Veda essentially denotes skin colour and Aryans were described as fair complexioned, while the native inhabitants were stated to be dark. This colour distinction seems have contributed to the creation of social divisions. The Dasas and Dasis conquered by the Aryans were treated as slaves and sudras. The society was divided into four principal groups- priests, warriors, traders and the common people.
- **Later Vedic Period:** For purposes of singing, the prayers of Rig Veda were set to music and this modified collection was known as Sama Veda. The Yajur Veda contains not only hymns but also rituals which have to accompany their recitation. These reflect vividly the sociopolitical milieu in which the post-Rig Vedic Aryans lived. The Atharva Veda elaborates on the weapons and also deals with charms and spells to ward off

evils and diseases. An elaborate description of non-Aryan modes of worship is given in the Atharva Veda.

In ancient India, the people used to communicate through oral tradition. The dominant form of worshipping gods was through the recitation of prayers and offer of ritual sacrifices. Both individual and collective prayers were recited loudly. The prayers were offered to gods in chorus by all the members belonging to individual tribes.

- **Atharva Veda:** The later vedic texts have been compiled during 1000-600 BC. The two epics, Ramayana and Mahabharata are concerned with the events which took place in India between 1000 and 700 BC. The Mahabharata as it survives today is the longest single poem in the world. The epic is held in high esteem by all Hindus for its message of Dharma.

  The events described in the Ramayana are believed to have occurred at a much later date in Eastern Uttar Pradesh and Bihar. The Ramayana also reflects the Aryan penetration beyond the Vindhya Mountains into peninsular India and the conflict with the local Dravidian communities to establish Aryan supremacy. The later vedas, the Brahmanas, the Aranyakas and the Upanishads are important contributions to Sanskrit literature. In the Upanishads we have the Hindu philosophical thought in its developed form. The doctrines of Karma, Maya, Punnarjanma, Mukti and other special features of Hindu thought are fully elaborated in the Upanishads. These teachings have taken deep root in the minds of Indians.

  The most important social doctrine propounded during this period was Varnashrama Dharma. The concept of varna stands for the division of society into occupational groups. The doctrine of the four castes: the Brahmins (the learned and the guides), the Kshatriya (warrior), the Vaishya (the trader) and the Sudras (the common man, the tiller, the worker) came into being. The fifth category–the panchamas–was added at a much later stage.

- **Sangam Age: Literary Contributions:** The Sangam age is considered to be a landmark in the history of South India. An academy of Tamil poets and bards flourished at Madurai between 500 BC. and 300 AD. This academy produced classical literary works in Tamil language under the patronage of Chola, Chera and Pandyan kings.

Advent of Jainism and Buddhism: Jainism is also a non-Brahminical religion, founded as a result of revolt against the Brahmanism of the sixth century BC. Some sources place Jainism as one of the oldest religions, belonging to the era of Rig Veda. Jainism rejects the Vedas and condemns the caste system.

The Varna system generated many tensions specifically in the areas of Hindu religion. The ruling and trading communities reacted to the domination of the priestly class of Brahmins. It is in this context we observe the introduction of Jainism as a distinct religion by Mahaveera during the 5th century BC. He preached liberation from worldly bonds and adoption of the path of non-violence (Ahimsa) for acquiring such liberation. Gautama Buddha, who was a contemporary of Mahaveera, also preached and propagated the simple, puritan, ascetic life. Buddhism appealed to the masses who suffered due to the social inequalities and the supremacy of higher castes. Thus, the monarchies in eastern UP, Bihar and foothills of Himalayas (Magedh, Kosala and Kausambi) adopted Buddhism and made sincere efforts to spread the religion of equality and a classless society based on love and respect for all creatures. The Pali (a variant of Sanskrit language) which was the spoken language of the common people contributed a lot to the spread of Buddhism. But, Buddhism could not survive for long in India because the Buddhist monks at a later stage became corrupt and accumulated wealth which Gautama Buddha had condemned. However, Buddhism had spread into Sri Lanka, China, Japan, the far-east, Laos, and Cambodia.

Q3. Discuss the various external invasions of India and impact of Muslim rule.

Ans. Around the 5th century BC several principalities fought among themselves in North-Western region. Taking advantage of this disunity and political chaos, the rulers of Persia expended their empire penetrating into North-west India. In 360 BC Darius, annexed and ruled Punjab and Sindh as provinces of the Persian empire till Alexander's invasion in 331 BC. Alexander conquered Asia minor, Iraq, and Iran and finally reached India through Kabul and Khyber pass into Punjab, defeating Purushottam (Porus) in 326 BC.

The Greek invasion provided the occasion for ancient Europe to come into closer contact with ancient India. Alexander added to his empire a vast Indian territory much larger than Persia. His invasion opened up land and sea routes to India and paved the way for Greek merchants, craftsmen to extend their trade. In 321 BC, Chandragupta Maurya, under the guidance of his mentor Chanakya, annexed Punjab driving away the Greeks. Subsequently, he extended his empire to Magadha, Gujarat and South India. Chanakya's treatise Arthasastra is considered to be a valuable contribution on politics and economic administration. The most significant contribution of the Mauryan period, was made by Ashoka, the grandson of Chandragupta, who in 274 BC embraced Buddhism and propagated the doctrines of social equality, justice and non-violence.

A series of invasions from various foreign powers along the north-west frontier took place from 200 BC onwards. The first to cross the Hindukush were the Indo-Greeks. They contributed to the growth of Sanskrit and Prakrit languages. The Parthenians who originally lived in Persia, then penetrated western India. The Parthenians were followed by the Kushan-from Central Asia. The Kushan king Kanishka built a large empire extending from Central Asia to Uttar Pradesh.

During the first century AD the Christianity came to India through trading sailors from the west. St. Thomas is believed to have arrived in Malabar in about 52 AD. The relationship was mainly confined to trade. However, some Indian embrasec Islam religion. Attracted by the wealth of India, Arabs organised a number of military expeditions from the north-western frontier of Indian kingdoms after the 7th century AD. Those expeditions were mainly to plunder the country's rich stock of gold and other valuable assets and not aimed at territorial expansion. The attacks were confined to sindh and upper Indus region.

Impact of Muslim Rule: The mingling of the Hindu and Muslim cultures led to the growth of new religious movements, and new styles in arts, architecture and music.Urdu language, an amalgam of Persian words and Indo-Aryan grammar, became the court language of the Moghuls. The Bhakti movement, propagated by the exponents like Meerabai, Chaitanya, Ramanuja, Vallabhacharya, Kabir and Guru Nanak, was greatly influenced by Islam. It emphasised simple devotion and faith and protested against the domination of priests and upper castes. While the compositions of Kabir are a great contribution to Hindi literature,

Guru Nanak preached in the Punjabi language and Meera Bai's Bhajans are in Brij bhasha of Mathura. Bengali literature was enriched by Chaitanya and his followers of the Vaishanava cult. The Indo-Islamic architecture had got amply reflected in the monuments like Qutub Minar and the exquisite forts of the Mughal emperors.

Q4. Discuss the salient features of the Indian Society and analyse the impact of caste system in our society.

Ans. India is a vast country and it has a long history. It's society has evolved through the ages and has also been affected by foreign influences giving it extreme diversity and made unity amidst diversity and characteristic of the Indian society. However, to understand the process, we need to understand the meaning of three kinds of plurality. These are as follows:

- **Ethnic Plurality:** Ethnological studies reveal the existence of six main racial stocks in India. The earliest was the Negrito, who are found even today in Andaman and Nicobar islands and in some of the primitive tribal groups of South India. They were followed by the Proto-Australoids, the Alpine, the Mongoloid and the Mediterraneans whose skeletal remains were even found in the Harappan sites. The last to come were the Aryans. The proto-Australoids constitute the basis element of the Indian population and they are found in many of the tribal communities in Central India, Eastern India, Bihar and Orissa. The Mediterranean race is associated with the Dravidian culture. The concentration of the Mongoloid people is in the North-Eastern and Northern fringes of India.
- **Linguistic Plurality:** Four major languages are identified in India: Dravidian, Austric, Sino-Tibetan and Indo-Aryan. The Indo Aryan language was originally the archaic Sanskrit introduced by the early Aryans. This has great similarities with Latin and German languages. Prakrit, which was allied to but different from Vedic Sanskrit, became popular as the spoken language of the Aryans. The alphabets of many of the Indian languages were actually derived from Brahmi script, which came into being during 4th century BC.

  Telugu, Kannada, Tamil and Malayalam, which constitute the Dravidian group of languages, are purely of Indian origin.

Some of the allied Dravidian languages are spoken by the tribals like Todas, Kotas and Kodugus of South India and Gondi, Kui, Naiki of M.P. and Malto and Kurukh (Oroan) of Bengal or Bihar. The Austric languages are: Mundari, Kol, Santal, Korku and Khasi. These language are spoken by the tribal in Central India, Eastern India and parts of North-Eastern region. The Sino-Tibetan languages are spoken by the tribals Nagaland, Arunachal Pradesh, Mizoram and the people in Himalayan ranges.

The Indian constitution now recognises eighteen major languages but as many as 1650 mother tongues are spoken throughout the country. Despite this great linguistic diversity, all Indians feel that they share together the rich literary and cultural heritage of Sanskrit.

- **Religious Plurality:** Religious pluralism is a belief that one can overcome religious differences between different religions and conflicts within the same religion. Indian society is composed of diverse cultures and peoples, languages and religions. India is the home of a majority of the religions of the world, such as Hinduism, Islam, Christianity, Buddhism, Jainism, Sikhism, Judaism and Zorostrianism could flourish without much interruption in the country. Contemporary Indian thinkers and saints have pointed out the contributions of each great religion to humanity and emphasised their underlying unity of thought. Spirituality and Sadhana constitute two distinct dimensions of Indian culture, enabled the Indian culture to retain its originality and uniqueness.

Caste System in India: In India, a caste system organises division of labour and money in human society. It is a system of social stratification and a basis for affirmative action. Historically, it defined communities into thousands of endogamous hereditary groups called Jātis. The Jātis were grouped by the Brahminical texts under the four well-known caste categories (the varnas): viz Brahmins, Kshatriyas, Vaishyas and Shudras. Certain people were excluded altogether, ostracised by all other castes and treated as untouchables. Caste is commonly thought of as an ancient fact of Hindu life, but various contemporary scholars have argued that the caste system was constructed by the British colonial regime.

(1) Varnas: The ancient culture of India was based upon a system of social diversification according to spiritual development. Varna is from the root 'vri' which means choice according to inherent traits. Varna seems to have been the division of the society in the Rig Vedic times when there were four classes. These classes were Brahmin, Kshatriya, Vaishya and Sudra. It is found from the Vedic literature that Varna meant the color of the skin according to which society was divided into four classes. These classes were based on the distinction and differences between the white or the Aryans and the black or the Dravidians.

The post-vedic period, reflects a very rigid stratification of the varnas. Each varna was regarded as a distinct unit, almost complete in itself for its social life. It may be noted in this context that while the varna system is uniform throughout the country, the caste (jati) system evolved gradually with many regional variations.

The development of caste system is generally attributed to two doctrines: (i) doctrine of the religious unity of the family; and (ii) doctrine of Svakarma and Svadharma, enjoining a way of life to be pursued by the individual according to the community/caste in which one is born.

Caste is defined by noted sociologist M.N. Srinivas as a hereditary, endogamous, usually localised group, having a traditional association with an occupation, and a particular position in the local hierarchy of castes. Relations between castes are governed, among other things, by the concepts of pollution and purity and generally maximum commonality occurs within the castes.

(2) Jajmani System: To most people, the "jajmani system" represents a conception of Indian village economy determined by ritual rules laid down 2,500 years ago in the Dharma Sastras. The term jajmani itself comes from the Hindi term "jajman," which derives from the Sanskrit term yajamana, "the one who provides the sacrifice." It stands in semantic opposition to the term purohita, "one who performs the sacrifice."

Tradition, customs and rules of behaviour differ from one caste group to the other: but each caste tries to maintain its influence over it's members and regulates inte-rcaste and intracaste social interactions. Although different castes are arranged in hierarchical order and social distances are maintained, there are many situations in which one caste secures services from the members belonging to other castes.

Under the Jajmani system, each caste group within a village provides certain social, religious and economic services to the other castes members. For illustration, the brahmin performs various religious and ceremonial rituals like marriages, death ceremonies, etc., for other castes. In return for his services, the brahmin is paid in cash and kind. Similarly, other service castes like carpenter, blacksmith, barber, washerman, cobbler, etc., perform their caste-based occupational services for the members of the other communities.

One of the distinctive aspects of the Jajmani system is that service relations between the Jajman (Producer) and the Prajan (Client) are regulated on a hereditary basis, according to the law of inheritance. The payment for the service is based on the barter system (in terms of grain at the harvest time); and cash is seldom paid. But the relation between the patron-client is not like the master-servant relation. The jajman is expected to meet the needs of his dependent and look after his family. Thus, the system provides security of occupation for sustenance.

The system, however, suffers from the evils perpetuated by the caste system. It has led to the exploitation of the lower castes by the elite land-owning higher castes. In spite of this weakness, the Jajmani system continues to have a stronger hold in rural India, where the social interactions are mostly governed by caste rules.

Despite the high degree of interdependence at the village level, different caste groups function as distinct socio-cultural entities. The caste system, in the recent past, has been exploited for (acquired) political patronage leading to caste rivalries and social tensions. In view of this, the social diversity projects an image of a broken society. However, at the conglomerate level, many of these diversities become submerged to reflect in united society, bound by common ethos, values and beliefs.

(3) Tribal Communities: 'Tribe', commonly called 'scheduled tribe', in the Indian context is an administrative and legal term to label some ethnic groups–based on their socio-economic status, and religious and cultural customs – in order to give special attention to them as mandated by the constitution.

Most of them live in remote areas, particularly in the forest and hill tracts. A minority of them, however, are settled in industrial belts, tea-gardens, mines and collieries as non-agricultural labourers. Among the states, a very high concentration of the tribal is found in Madhya Pradesh, Orissa, Bihar and Maharashtra while the states of Punjab, Haryana,

Jammu and Kashmir have a very low per cent of tribal population. In the North-eastern region, in states like Nagaland and Meghalaya, we find a high concentration of tribals accounting for more than three-fourths of their total population, Similarly, Tripura, Manipur and Sikkim also have a very high concentration of tribal people.

(4) Unity in Diversity: India, a land of varied cultures, different languages and dialects, various religions and their innumerable sects, and different living style; provides the best example of unity in diversity. This particular phenomenon is limited to India only and this makes our nation a cut above from all other nations in the world.

India is a vast country with nearly 1.252 Billion (2013) people. It has a land frontier of 15,200 km and a coastline of 7,517 km. Despite its spread, the country reflects unity in diversity. The Indianness of the people is exhibited clearly irrespective of the region to which they belong-from Kashmir in the North to Kanyakumari in the South, from Gujarat in the West to Manipur in the East. The Indian way of looking at life-the psyche of the people-is deep rooted in the Dharma and Karma doctrines propounded by the ancient scriptures and sages. Another distinct quality of Indian culture is manifested in the sacredness of the bonds of family life. People of all regions, irrespective of caste and creed, respect age and wisdom. Variety, in fact, contributes to the richness of Indian culture. The ethos though rooted in diverse ecologies, religious ideas and values, yet reflects the underlying unity of the Indian people.

Another important contributing factor for diversity of life pattern is the striking difference between the prosperous elite and the deprived poor. In terms of material living as well as social development, the mass of the common people living mostly in villages, exhibit a different image from the elite. The rural-urban dichotomy conspicuously persists despite the initiatives taken by the government for bridging the gulf between the rich and the poor.

(5) Little and Great Traditions: The process of change in traditional societies due to urbanisation and industrialisation has received the attention of many scholars who tried to analyse the dynamics of change in social institutions, organisations, and human relations. Robert Redfield, who pioneered studies in social change among traditional societies, postulated the theory of Folk-Urban continuum. According to Redfield, each society experiencing change reflects a set of traditions: (i) the Little

Tradition of the illiterate and semi-literate folk community, mostly shared in oral tradition; and (ii) the Great Tradition of the urbanised community which is formally articulated. Scholars like Milton Singer and Mackim Marriott, who studied the process of social change in India, also observed such continuity and coexistence of the Little Tradition of the rural and tribal communities and the Great Tradition of the more urbanised communities. Such cultural continuity is attributed to the basic similarities in the Indian ethos and beliefs. However, Indian social scientists like S.C. Dube do not agree with this theory of dichotomous division of Indian culture into Little and Great traditions.

Q5. Highlight the Status of women in Indian Society.

Ans. The position of the women community has been a fluctuating subject since the early ages. With the ups and downs in the Hindu Society, the status of women has been affected. The worth of a civilisation can be judged from the position that it gives to women. Of the several factors that justify the greatness of India's ancient culture, one of the greatest is the honoured place ascribed to women. Manu, the great law-giver, said long ago, 'where women are honoured there reside the gods'. According to ancient Hindu scriptures no religious rite can be performed with perfection by a man without the participation of his wife. Wife's participation is essential to any religious right. Married men along with their wives are allowed to perform sacred rites on the occasion of various important festivals. Wives are thus, befittingly called 'Ardhangani' (betterhalf). They are given not only important but equal position with men.

Even in early Buddhist period we come across women who were highly respected for their achievements in education and contributions to Buddhist literature. Sanghamitra, the sister of Ashoka was sent to Sri Lanka to spread Buddhism.

During the medieval period, the position of women further deteriorated due to the introduction of Purdah and greater prevalence of polygamy among the kings and chieftains. The revival of Sati, making it obligatory for the women to die on the funeral pyre of the husband, worsened the position of women and reduced their status to the level of helpless dependents. The complete neglect of education of girls and the advocacy of child marriages contributed to further degradation of the status of woman. Social reformers, like Rammohan Roy, Ishwar Chandra

Vidyasagar and Dayanand Saraswati, took great pains during 19th century to create mass awareness and bring about significant changes in the sphere of education as well as social legislation for the improvement of the position of women in India.

Spiritual leaders like swami Vivekananda provided tremendous support to the social upliftment of women. The call of Mahatma Gandhi facilitated many women to come out of seclusion and participate in the political movement during the freedom struggle. There is greater commitment at politico-administrative levels to provide more opportunities for women to assert their equality with men so that they can contribute to the enrichment of the society.

But in the later period the position of women went on deteriorating due to Muslim influence. During the Muslim period of history they were deprived of their rights of equality with men. They were compelled to keep themselves within the four walls of their houses with a long veil on their faces. This was definitely due to Islamic influence. Even today in some Islamic countries women are not allowed to go out freely. The conservative regimes of Iran and Pakistan, for example, have withdrawn the liberties given to women folk by the previous liberal governments. Even in India the Muslim women are far more backward than their Hindu, Christian and Sikh counterparts. The sight of Muslim women walking with long 'Burkas' (veils) on their face is very rare. The women are, as a matter of fact, regarded as captive and saleable commodities in Muslim families. One man is allowed to have so many wives with the easiest provision of divorce. The husband can divorce a wife just by saying 'I divorce you' under the provision of Muslim laws. This is what the emperors did hundred years back and the men are doing it even now in almost all Islamic countries. Even in this last phase of the twentieth century, rich and prosperous men of Islamic countries keep scores of wives in their harems. It was natural outcome of the Muslim subjugation of India that woman was relegated to a plaything of man, an ornament to decorate the drawing room. Serving, knitting, painting and music were her pastimes and cooking and cleaning her business.

In the wake of Raja Ram Mohan Roy's movement against women's subjugation to men and British influence on Indian culture and civilisation the position of women had once again undergone a change. However, it was only under the enlightened leadership of Mahatma

Gandhi that they re-asserted their equality with men. In response to the call of Gandhi they discarded their veil and came out of the four walls of their houses to fight the battle of freedom shoulder to shoulder with their brothers. The result is that the Indian Constitution today has given to women the equal status with men. There is no discrimination between men and women. All professions are open to both of them with merit as the only criterion of selection.

As a result of their newly gained freedom Indian woman have distinguished themselves in various spheres of life as politicians, orators, lawyers, doctors, administrators and diplomats. They are not only entrusted with work of responsibility but also they perform their duties very honestly and sincerely. There is hardly any sphere of life in which Indian women have not taken part and shown their worth. Women exercise their right to vote, contest for Parliament and Assembly, seek appointment in public office and compete in other spheres of life with men. This shows that women in India enjoy today more liberty and equality than before. They have acquired more liberty to participate in the affairs of the country. They have been given equality with men in shaping their future and sharing responsibilities for themselves, their family and their country.

Another job in which Indian women are doing so well is that of teachers. In country like India where millions are groping in the darkness of illiteracy and ignorance efficient teaching to the children is most urgently needed. Small children in the kindergarten schools get motherly affection from the lady teachers.

Women have been serving India admirably as doctors and nurses. Lady doctors have been found to perform efficient surgery by virtue of their soft and accurate fingers. They have monopolised as nurses in the hospitals and nursing homes. It is thus natural tendency found in women which motivated Florence Nightingale to make nursing popular among the women of the upper classes in England and in Europe.

But all this should not lead us to conclude that the women should look down upon domestic life. The main sphere of action for them who have not taken up jobs outside should be essentially a happy home which is their real kingdom and where their sweet manners and mature advices as wife, mother, sister and daughter make tremendous effects on the male members of the family. Recently The Hindu Code Bill has given the daughter and the son equal share of the property. The Marriage Act no longer regards woman as the property of man. Marriage is now considered to be a personal affair and if a partner feels dissatisfied she or he has the right of divorce.

Q6. Discuss and analyse the evolution and growth of communication in India.

Ans. Communication has originated and evolved in the West, particularly in the United States of America. With the development of technologies, the communication methods also developed. The methods became complex and sophisticated. But the concept of 'communication' has been with us since the creation of man. The methods and the process is differ from region to region, country to country. Even now, with the idea of 'global village' becoming a reality, we differ as far as methods and process of communication are concerned.

The Upanishads, the Gita, the Sangeet Ratnakara, the Natya Shastra, Mannu Smriti, Sanskrit literature, works on Vaishnavism, Bhakti, the medieval saints and Sufism did communicate and are still communicating valuable thoughts to us on the subject. Some experts say as a result of exposures to foreign television programmes, our values and culture may be damaged beyond repair. The negative influence of such telecasts may prove detrimental to the development of the nation.

Religion and Philosophy: 'Communication' is a word coined in the recent past to explain a particular area of study. Therefore, in our ancient literature this view was not dealt with separately. But, a lot has been said on the process and methods of communication in our literature. Communication does not exist in a vacuum. Communication is an integral part of our socio-political and cultural life. It was as important then as it is now. It worked according to the social and cultural norms. At present, we must ensure that it works as per the cultural ethos of our nation. Otherwise, the fabric of the nation may be disturbed.

Mysticism and Intrapersonal Communication: Mysticism is a cryptic concept that seemingly both captures the imagination in some individual and stimulates loathing and trepidation in others. Mysticism has given birth to a new method of communicating one's deep realisation and understanding of God and the Universe. Mysticism is centered on oneself. It is a process by which one plunges into the deepest core of one's heart or self. A profound communication takes place in one's innermost care. This communication process can be termed as intrapersonal communication-'communication with oneself. Mira Bai and Kabir communicated so much in a very easy way because their realisation was clear. We have not explored this mystical process. This mystical approach possibly can help us to communicate with our people more effectively.

Intrapersonal Communication enriched interpersonal communication. This area of communication has not been sufficiently explored. Some enthusiastic communication professional take a parochial view and try desperately to invent a communication theory or a model which existed in the ancient times.

Accounts of Vedanta, Bhakti, Vaishnavism and Sufism speak volumes on communication. To be effective in our communication we should be able to establish their relevance to the people of modern India. This Indian orientation will help us to recast and reframe the whole outlook towards communication concepts norms and beliefs.

Q7. Describe the Indian Heritage and Communication Values.

Ans. Culture and its preservation matters a great deal to Indians, at least in rhetoric. The Government of India has even formulated a “Cultural Policy” which lays out three major objectives as preserving the cultural heritage of India, inculcating Indian art consciousness amongst Indians and promoting high standards in creative and performing arts. Unfortunately, it seems the advent of mass media has made the cultural policy redundant, as performing arts seem to have virtually disappeared for the masses of India.

In India, communication is inextricably linked with philosophy and religion. Sarvapalli Radhakrishanan says, "The pursuit of philosophy is deemed a religious vocation. Therefore, in order to come to terms with the cultural ideal that animates Indian society, we need to examine, brief though they may be, the outlines of Indian philosophy".

(1) Jain and Buddhist Values: With the passage of time, a number of non-Vedic philosophical traditions sprang up. The Charvakas placed heavy emphasis on the material world and discarded all notions of transcendentality. Jainism was tradition of philosophy which was non-Vedic in character. It maintained that both the animate and the inanimate world were eternal and independent. Therefore, one has to be tolerant to all that exists on earth.

Buddhism, another non-vedic philosophy constituted a powerful reaction against the ritualism that characterised the Vedas and the transcendentalism that was associated with the Upanishads. The individual, according to Buddhism, should diligently work out his salvation, from pain and suffering.

(2) Indian Schools of Philosophy: Indian Philosophy (or, in Sankrit, Darshanas), refers to any of several traditions of philosophical thought that originated in the Indian subcontinent, including Hindu philosophy, Buddhist philosophy and Jain philosophy. It is considered by Indian thinkers to be a practical discipline, and its goal should always be to improve human life.

The Indian schools of philosophy originated from the Vedas; two schools are Vedic-the Mimamsa and the Vedanta; the four-Samkhya, Yoga, Vaisesika, and Nyaya-have their base in the Vedas. Therefore, these six schools are classed as Vedic or Astika. The two schools of Buddhism and Jainism are called Nastika as they do not accept Vedic authority. These eight schools are products of the great thought that characterised the post-Vedic age.

Each school of philosophy is called a Darsana, meaning a view or a vision of the truth. The aims and aspirations of life are not only the pursuit of material gains (Artha) and pleasure (Kama) but also virtue and morality which chasten life (Dharma) and spiritual enlightment and freedom (Moksa).

Each school is associated with a sage (Rishi) as its first Promulgator-Samkhya with Kapila, Yoga with Paanjali, Vaisesika with Kanada, Nayaya with Gautama, Mimamsa with Jaimini and Vedanta with Badarayana-Vyasa. Because of their mutual relationship, these six schools fall into three groups of allied systems, Samanatantras. Samkhya and Yoga go together; the philosophical framework of Samkhya is accepted by Yoga, with the addition of God as the omniscient first Teacher. The speciality of Yoga is the practical aspect of the methods of mental control by which the philosophical ideal of the Samkhya, namely, the isolation (Kaivalya) of the Spirit from Matter is achieved. But Yoga as a Sadhana or preparatory discipline and means came to be accepted by all schools. Today, it has, with the help of science, grown in strength and gained a worldwide vogue. The vaisesika doctrines form the basis of Nyaya, both being schools of realism and pluralism. The Mimamsa and Vedanta go together because of their common Vedic basis but otherwise they differ fundamentally. The former is concerned with Karma and Dharma, the performance of ordained duty, but the latter to the opposite of Karma, namely, renunciation from activity; according to Vedanta, knowledge (Jnana) is the means of salvation (Moksa). Mimamsa is thus related to the Karma-kanda (Samhita and the Brahman Portion of the Vedas), and Vedanta to the Upanishads. The Mimamsa also made a valuable contribution to the science of interpreting texts; it came to be known therefore as Vakya Sastra (the rules of constructing a sentence). The words coined in various philosophical and theological books are still being used by us to convey the same meaning. Thus, to communicate meaningfully, we must be well grounded in this rich heritage.

Q8. What are the implications for an Indian perspective of communication theory?

Ans. On the basis of philosophical tents. We can construct a workable model of communication for the Indian situation. This may differ substantially from models found in the Western countries. Each culture may have models of communication of its own. What is essential is that any communication model must be based on a cultural context. Otherwise the meaning conveyed may differ from the intended meaning to be conveyed in a communication. Many times, we may fail to communicate if we do not take this cultural context into consideration.

In India, generally the primary focus of interest in communication is how does the receiver make sense of the stimuli that he receives, so as to deepen his self-awareness. In the Western models, the basic questions that present themselves are how does the communicator affect/influence/ manipulate the receiver and how does the communicator and receiver share information and enter into a two-way relationship. According to traditional Indian views, meaning should necessarily lead to self-awareness. Hence the Indian definition of communication would be that it is an inward search for meaning-a process of intra-personal communication.

In the West, communication is seen as the transference of meaning with the intention of influencing the receiver. But in India meaning brings enlightenment. Meaning, according to traditional Indian thought, was seen as a process which leads to self-awareness, then to freedom, and finally to truth. Here, by freedom we mean the liberation of persons from ignorance, from illusion of the world, and the web of the artificial categories constructed all around us. Another significant point of divergence between the Indian and the Western ways is that the Indian way focuses attention on the intra-personal dimension as opposed to the inter-personal dimension. In western ways, intrapersonal communication leads to interpersonal communication, but in the Indian way interpersonal communication is secondary to intrapersonal communication.

The Western way is expression-oriented but the Indian way is interpretation oriented. The Indian way seems to suggest that what is important in human communication is to find out how a receiver makes sense of the verbal stimuli that are received by him and engages in a search for meaning. This search is an inward one. The traditional authorities maintain that the reality is indeed within man. To know it is to be. In other words, distinction between the knower and the known narrows down considerably. The realisation of truth is facilitated neither by language nor by logic and rationality. To know is to be; to know is to become aware of the artificial categorisation imposed on the world by language and logic. It is only through an intuitive process that man will be able to lift himself out of the illusory world, which, according to the Indian viewpoint, is indeed the aim of communication. People may differ with this view. But in India realisation dawns when we internalise the communication. It needs to be pointed out that one may not understand the current development in communication society in the light of this model. We are living in a world where the border lines between countries are disappearing very fast. We do know and feel at one with the happenings in other parts of the globe. We are passing through a phase civilisation which could be termed, at best, the transition, and 'chaotic' at worst.

Q9. Discuss the concept of 'Sadharanikaran' as the basis of Indian communication theory.

Or

What is Sadharanikaran? How did Sadharanikaran help to build the rigid caste system?

Or

Explain 'Rasa' and 'Bhava'.

Or

In a communication context, how does the source and receiver in a Western model differ from that of the Eastern Model?

Or

What is sadharanikaran? Is it still relevant in today's times of technological interventions? Justify your answer. [June-2019, Q.No.-1]

Ans. Sadharanikaran is a proposed form of communication from eastern perspective that implies on Hindu prospect of a communication process. The term sadharanikaran is derived from the Sanskrit word sadharan; and has been translated into English as "generalised presentation", "simplification" and "universalisation". This word (Sadharanikara) is equivalent to the Latin word communis that is communication or sharing knowledge or information. This word was coined in India as early as 500 BC, in Bharat muni's Natyasastra (theory of dance). Sadharanikaran is described as that point in the climax of a drama or any performing art when the audience becomes one with the actor who shares an episode and leaves that experience through his acting on the stage. In this process, the individual in the audience identifies himself with the actor and the episode on the stage and becomes emotional in that character. As such, Sadharanikaran creates commonness of experience in full form between the communicator (actor) and the receiver (audience). This clearly indicates the fact that Indian public information heritage is much older than the Western communication heritage. The entire superstructure of Indian aesthetics centres on the act of sadharanikaran through rasa swadan.

Rasa has been explained thus: man in his essential characteristics is a bundle of bhawa (moods) that constitute his being and form part of his total consciousness. These have been categorised as 50 in number. Of these nine are described as Sthai bhawa (permanent moods), 33 as Vyabhicari bhawa (secondary moods) and the remaining as Satwik bhawa (wholesome mood). Bharata, after an intensive study of these moods, has grouped them under one all encompassing expression bhawa (moods) for purposes of establishing Sadharanikaran.

Coomaraswamy describes 'bhawa' as springing from aesthetic emotion of a person who derives its existence from sensory experience. Each mood is capable of arousing a relevant state of feeling/quality of response.

A Bhava is the first reaction or sensation caused in the sympathetic mind by a stimulus called Vibhavas song, a bird, a picture. A sustained Bhava (emotion) that leads to Rasa is the Sthayee Bhava (for example: seasons). An Anubhava is the physical manifestation that takes place immediately as a Bhava (emotion) registers itself in the mind. (examples: Glance, lifting of eye, smile, etc.) The Sthayee Bhava is stimulated by the Vibhava in the mind and is heightened by Anubhavas and Sanchari Bhavas. In this state, the mind will be highly receptive to the Rasa experience.

Rasa can be understood only by the Sahridaya, the person who alone is capable of rasawadan (partaking of the flavour). Sahridaya is a person in a state of emotional intensity i.e. a quality of emotional dimension coequal to that of the sender the message or communicator. Both must be sahridayas.

In India, communication lays great stress on the communicator and the one who receives communication belonging to the same cultural group. The same cultural context will help the communicator and the receiver to communicate effectively. The sender and receiver of a communication belonging to the same culture, would be able to communicate more effectively.

In Western societies, sources and receivers at least in principle, communicate as equals, but in Indian society, it is not the case. The source is viewed as higher and the receiver as lower in status. The relationship is a hierarchical one of dominance and subordination. The hierarchical aspect of Sadharanikaran contributed to the blossoming of Indian civilisation through efficient communication. This was, however, later taken to the level of absurdity, resulting in a highly rigid and hierarchical society. To some extent, it made Indian society into a more or less closed system and thereby contributed towards its stagnancy and decay. It is true Natyashastra was written by Bharat Muni to simplify the complex vedas for the benefit of the common man and thereby bridge the gap between the elites, the priests, the nobles and sudras. However, with the passage of time, Sadharanikaran resulted in divisions within society. Later, with institutionalisation of difference the society became stagnant. Sadharanikaran, through communication, between unequal over a period of time, contributed toward the development of more or less permanent and rigid hierarchical social relationships, as reflected in the caste system.

The caste system influences communication patterns, particularly in

Indian villages. Within a village community, far more communication takes place among the members of a caste than between castes because of the highly stratified and hierarchical nature of the caste system. People of "high" and "low" castes accept their position as natural. The asymmetrical relationship between "high" and "low" caste members is hereditary and is accepted by those who are in a disadvantageous position.

In India many sages and saints, in different times, launched reform movements against social inequalities. They attempted to further simplify and reinterpret Indian philosophy for the benefit of the common people and thereby bridge the gap between elites and commoners.

Apart from the academic exercise, there is a use of studying of the Indian view on communication. It is necessary and the need is urgent. Some of the reasons are as follow:

- The Indian view of communication takes into consideration the man and his environment as a healthy unit as against the mechanical and quantitative view of man.
- The use of technology has added a new dimension to the use of words as a tool of communication. The printing press, radio, TV and satellite have multiplied words and their use to an immeasurable extent. The knowledge of Indian view of communication may help in minimising the use of words to create a greater effect with the aid of visuals.
- The emergence and use of a large number of words has resulted in the distortion of the meaning of words. Words, however, would continue to occupy primacy in human communication in future despite the expansion of electronic media.

  "Better than a collection of a thousand meaningless words is one word full of meaning on hearing which one becomes peaceful", says the Dhammapada.
- The sadharanikaran theory underlines the role of communication. It is total communication and communication at its best. It is a more integrated approach to communication because it seeks to affect the behaviour of human beings by arousing emotional and physical response simultaneously.

Q10. Discuss the impact of communication on Indian Society.

Ans. India, with over one billion population, is a land of contrasts, a plural and a multi-lingual society. It has a wide range of communication media, extending from oral communication, to inter-personal methods of communication to satellite broadcasting, from a two-page broad sheet in a regional language printed on a treadle so common in small towns and villages even now, to multi-edition dailies printed through facsimile printing process.

Indian society is often characterised as one of "unity in diversity" and its villages as "independent republics". These characterisations have important implications for the patterns of human communication in India.

In ancient India, cultures blossomed in different parts of the subcontinent. These were unique and independent of each other. These cultures derived strength and inspirations from each other. The merits of cultures were communicated through the long established oral tradition.

The roving saints and sufies performed the task of communicating messages. They propagated the gospels of truth enshrined in the Vedas, Puranas, epic stories like Ramayana and Mahabharata and other scriptures. They reinterpreted these messages as per the realities prevailing in the society. In the process, they succeeded in communicating the norms and values proper for decent social living.

At the community level, known as a class of knowledgeable people, Brahmins enjoyed the highest social status. They played an effective role as "link persons" between the common man of their own community and persons from outside the community. Each community had strong and extensive cultural links with other communities beyond the neighbouring villages and towns.

Administrative contacts were minimal, largely confined to revenue collections. Even this task was performed through intermediaries such as the Nawabs, Zamindars and Lambardars. Thus, in ancient or traditional India, there existed effective systems of communication which were both local and pan-Indian in character. Such communication provided meaning and justification for the social order. It inculcated the spirit of devotion, love and faith.

Indian society was highly stratified and hierarchical. Communication tended to flow from persons of higher status to persons of lower status. In any communication situation, the relationship between the source and the receiver was that of dominance and subordination. In spite of this, there was some dialogue between the two. Both shared a common frame of reference which made communication smooth and effective.

Q11. State the emergence of modern mass media.

Ans. With the arrival of British rule in India, there was an increase in the administrative links and physical mobility was encouraged through rails and roads. A new philosophy and culture spread by Macaulay's education system started making inroads into traditional Indian society and culture. The two were incompatible in many ways. However, the communication of foreign concepts, ideas, and philosophies was successful as a lot of Indians accepted them. At the same time, the conflict between the Indian and British ways of life became evident. As a consequence, there were upheavals, and turmoils, which ultimately led to the birth of independent India.

Free India has adopted democracy based on universal adult franchise as a form of government. As a welfare state it has opted for planned development. The technological growth and developments, huge development in communication, and increases in the scale of economic activities have enlarged the range of choices. The philosophy of equality, irrespective of caste, creed, and religion, and the compulsions of democratic elections at all levels-village panchayats to the Parliament help to minimise the disadvantages of the traditional social and political relationships.

Assumptions about Mass Society and Media: Societal conditions have given rise to various mass media. It is normally assumed that technology has been necessary for the reproduction of communications for mass audiences. Industrialisation, with the division of labour and urbanisation, has created mass and heterogenous audiences. The proponents of this idea also hold that "in the pre-industrial period: the communication system was restricted to direct face-to-face communication between individuals."

These assumptions, as far as India is concerned, are not wholly true. First, despite passing from the from the First Information and Communication revolution (printing) to the second Information and Communication Revolution (electronics and computers), the India society has largely retained the traditions of oral and interpersonal communication. Therefore, when we consider the distinguishing features of modern society, it is not the 'mass' of people (numbers) that constitutes 'a mass society', but the relationships between the members. The western concept of mass society explain its heterogeneous nature due to its being alienated by technology, socially differentiated due to occupation and physically separated through expansion of urbanisation. Thus, the need to reach out to this highly "impersonalised" mass society requires various "mass media" not only to bring together its members into the mainstream, but also, to seek their consent for social action.

(2) India and the West: A Comparison: There has been a tendency to transplant communication models from the West to developing countries. They have transplanted the idea that rational, independent messages beamed at "individual" will lead to motivation and attitude change. This is basically the advertising and marketing model of a society believing in perfect competition. Although, Sadhranikaran model is much more scientific than the Aristotle model. This model is non-linear communicative approach.

We are now beginning to realise that there is another model of society in which the individual drives his legitimacy from the system. In such a society, the role of "communication" is quite different. Therefore, attempts to inform, educated and motivate the individual in many a times do not succeed. However, messages with symbols appealing to the "collective" consciousness many times do succeed. The Indian society, with its unique concept of the "collective" nature of interpersonal networks, affirms that while we keep our windows open to the world, our feet are rooted in the innate wisdom that has come down to us over the last 5000 years. It is within these parameters, that India's transition from the oral to the modern mass media-based society has to be perceived.

Q12. Describe the impact of media on Indian society.

Ans. As the freedom struggle gained momentum, newspapers were published from the main centres of the agitation like Delhi, Lahore, Lucknow and Kanpur. Other newspaper centres were concentrated in the princely states of Mysore, Hyderabad, Bhopal and Baroda. These cities also had their own radio stations.

After independence the print medium emerged its pre-colonial past and spread into the semi urban and rural areas. Advanced technology, better roads and transport helped the press to move into semi urban centres, but they were still rooted in the cities. The advertising world-the backbone of newspaper-hitched its wagon to the highly-circulated newspapers and magazines, fuelling the growing difference big and small newspapers and magazines. The power of the print media attracted big industrialists to invest in the newspaper industry. Today we have chain-newspapers controlled by business tycoons who run them purely on commercial lines.

Newspaper have become a class medium, catering only to the rich and the powerful. However, the language newspapers do cater to the lower levels of society. But their reach and access are linked to literacy and capacity to purchase. A wide gulf has been created between the "information-rich" and "information-poor. Instead of a democratising and bringing equity, the newspapers have helped to perpetuate a class structure in society.

The broadcasting media (TV and Radio), though under government control, have the capacity to reach out to the people in every nook and corner of the country. While both are highly capital-intensive, it is their capacity to reach out to millions that makes them a people's medium. The development of Akashwani and Doordarshan in India has had its ups and downs. Both AIR and Doordarshan have not been found wanting. While "news" has been accepted as the important segment in their programme content, other aspects like development and education have been given adequate attention. However, entertainment has become synonymous with these two corporations. AIR has opened various channels for entertainment; but has failed to evoke the same kind of audience response to other development-oriented programmes as to entertainment. Doordarshan has fared no better. The criticism levelled against AIR also applies to Doordarshan. The criticism levelled against Doordarshan is sometimes more severe as the policy formulated for it says that it should serve the development aspirations of the majority. DD largely depends on films and film-based programmes to fill in its telecast time. Criticism about lack of professionalism, creativity and production skills, have been levelled against DD.

People do say that TV is an "idiot box" and has harmful effects on children. But TV is a tool of learning also and so far, has been well-received. Further, information on health, family planning and eradication of social evils like drugs, smoking, alcoholism, and dowry, have all been successfully projected over Doordarshan.

Films: Films are the important mass medium communication source.

Films can be produce on almost all subjects of human interest and include, broadly speaking, feature films, documentaries and newsreels. The themes may encompass such diverse subjects as industry, agriculture, development, education, environment and vital national issues like family welfare, national integration and untouchability. A large number of films are not commercial in the usual sense.

Films seek to attract the audience by providing rather glib and naive entertainment in order to convert people's childishness into cash. For the majority of the viewers, a film is a day-dreaming device in which they forget their worries and get lost in a world of fantasy-full of melodramatic sentiments, songs and dance, violence and sex. The Indian film stars have exerted such a hypnotic hold on the masses that they have made a place for themselves in public life, politics and even influenced the living style of the people. Exceptional Indian Films, with their intense realism and abiding concern for the common man, have found their way to international acclaim. The emergence of the new cinema as a movement, presenting a modern humanistic approach, offered a refreshing contrast to the commercial cinema.

Video: Video has grown to be a very popular mass medium within a remarkably short times. It has endless possibilities for entertainment and education. Video in India is largely perceived as an alternative source of entertainment. However, video news magazine has caught the popular fancy and many leading newspapers have come forward to launch news magazines in audio-visual form. Public sector companies have utilised the video medium for bringing out house journals. But video has also come to occupy an important place in political and poll campaigns in India.

Satellite Communication: Satellites have changed the way news is distributed and received around the world. A Satellite Communication is a man-made platform launched into space; it remains relatively stationary over the earth. It serves as a platform for radio relay stations which receive radio signals beamed to it from the earth and relays those signals back to other locations on earth. Satellite communication greatly benefitted the newspaper industry. It made possible fascimiles of newspaper pages to be sent electronically via satellite to a receiving station anywhere in the world where printing facilities may be located.

The satellite distribution systems give the newspapers a flexibility hitherto not possible. Satellites now link news bureaus all over the country and can instantly transmit news reports to any station. Computers can automatically set the stories into type and start the process rolling. The cable TV system can receive programmes through satellite and deliver them by cable to subscribers' sets. In another form of transmission, called Direct Broadcast Satellite (DBS), television programmes are directly received by the antenna at home, totally bypassing the cable system.

But the strongest impact of TV comes through the Hong Kong-based STAR-TV, CNN, the BBC, and Pakistan TV, using satellites to beam programmes right into our homes. There has been a furore over the role of these foreign satellite broadcasts, referred to as post-colonial cultural imperialism. They have made serious inroads into DD viewership. DD replied to this "invasion from the sky" by opening the 5 Metro channels to Indian viewers from August 15, 1993. It has been observed that large majority of TV viewers seem to be convinced that the foreign-based TV channels, though better produced, are not culturally conducive to a large number of viewers.

Q13. Write a short note on "future of communication in India".

Ans. The Communication Industry in India is one of the fastest developing sectors in the country and is estimated to become the second biggest international telecom market in the next few years. As per the report published by the Telecom Regulatory Authority of India (TRAI), the total number of telephone users in India crossed 806.13 million in January 2011 as compared to 787.28 million in the previous year during the same period.

It should be obvious by now that for an Indian approach to communication a sound knowledge of its philosophical, cultural and linguistic traditions is necessary. It is also necessary to go to Sanskrit, as it may provide us with a lot of materials on communication which could be of use to communicate to our people properly and effectively. It is only by undertaking such kind of studies and by relating these to the demands of modern life that we will be able to re-cast and reframe our whole outlook towards communication concepts, norms and beliefs.

In this connection, we have to look at the trends in characteristics of the highly industrialised west and particularly of the USA. There, the art and science of communication have been mastered, but because of a highly materialistic focus, who are losing the true purpose of communication is lost sight of in their eagerness to consume more, and provide themselves with more free time and leisure, the listener has unleashed a Frankensteinian unstoppable momentum to the growth of sophisticated technology. The wisdom of the East, from India and China, may help them to reframe their communication priorities.

It is a matter of concern, that the lure of technology is creating a wide gap among various communities and classes in Indian society. We require to prioritise our use of technology, particularly those needs related to the socio-cultural and linguistic demands. According to many scholars, catering to this large number of people with diverse needs has become a problem. Faced with the spectre of proliferating communication technology, India is on the threshold of a giant leap forward.

Indian has used a lot of communication technology in almost five decades since Independence. But the increase in the use of modern technology for development did not make our communication better. Analysis reveals that during this process of modernisation, very powerful political and economic forces have gained control over the communication system. This is turn has led to either distortion, discrimination or even total obstruction of the communication flow from and to the grassroot level. Indian with its teeming millions cannot afford to sustain an imbalanced system of communication. We have communicated with our people for so long through the oral tradition, now, let us not destroy this tradition.

Q14. Discuss how communication is an integral part of human civilisation and culture.

Ans. Culture is an integral part of human nature. Marshall McLuhan, one of the foremost authority on mass communication says that a "global village has been created in the recent times". His words were no doubt true and we are therefore living in an era of melting pot of various cultures. Culture however is a complex whole that includes traditional preserve.

Communication is important to human civilisation and culture, because without it civilisation could not exist. Unlike many species of animals, humans can pass down information for more than one generation.

Human civilisation is passing through a crucial phase of its existence and survival. Mass media as purveyors of news and views, have a decisive role of preparing the human race for the 21st century. Due to the primacy accorded to information as a social input, many developed societies have become information societies. The rest are on the verge of becoming so. With the growing importance of communication, the societies are racing against time to be in the mainstream of the communication revolution.

The process of communication started with travellers and letters, but due to various reasons such as physical inaccessibility, restrictions imposed by kings and emperors it was often incomplete or distorted. The kings and the emperors permitted only such information which helped them. Governments of the day deliberately encouraged preservation of the traditions of social systems that adhered to fatalism and submission since it suited them. The transformation in European societies following the Renaissance, Reformation and Industrial Revolution, resulted in a sea change and the modernisation process began spreading to newer areas beyond Europe.

The process of communication was fast and receipts of communication and the feedback were ensured. After World War II there was a tremendous growth and development of communication technologies which changed the very nature of our society. Mass media today have become the product of technologies operating directly in our society. We cannot imagine our life without newspaper, radio, TV, telephone and probably fax machine. Mass media and communication technologies have become integral parts of our life and our society.

Q15. Distinguish traditional and modern system of communication.

Ans. Both traditional and modern communication are systems of communication. The former is simple while the latter is complex and sophisticated.

The mass media can address the communication needs of diverse audience within a short period. They preserve and refine the trado modes of communication with a view to addressing the entertainment and education needs of the people. The mass media can initiate social change in the society using any of the forms of traditional communication in a globalised manner.

The mass media overcome the challenges of trado-communication by opening 24-hour vistas of communication to anonymous, heterogeneous and large audience across national frontiers.

Both the trado-communication and the mass media can re-engineer the society depending on how they are used. The mass media are wider in concept, sophisticated in the process and dynamic in operations. The reverse is almost the case in traditional communication.

Q16. Explain the functions of the mass media.

Or

Discuss traditional or conventional functions of the mass media.

Or

Outline the main functions of mass media.

Ans. Traditional/Conventional Functions of the Mass Media: The mass media perform some traditional or conventional functions which include:

- **Education:** Media provide education and information side by side. It provides education in different subjects to the people of all levels. They try to educate people directly or indirectly using different forms of content. Distance education program, for example, is a direct approach. Dramas, documentaries, interviews, feature stories and many other programs are prepared to educate people indirectly. Especially in the developing country, mass media is used as an effective tool for mass awareness. It can be said therefore, that the mass media is a school of its own. The overall human development is directly related to education. Media enable the spread of education through conventional as well as unconventional methods.

  An educated or literate person will read books, journals, magazines, newspaper etc. This increase in consumption of media product is related to their availability and easy access to them. Normally, an educated man is not satisfied with access to only one medium. He may become a consumer of other media as well. This desire to have access to media increases the level of education and knowledge among the population.

- **Economical Growth:** The demand for information has boosted the media hardware production causing an unprecedented growth in the economy. This, in turn, has stimulated the expansion of communications industry including media industries. It is said that the level of media use is an indicator of the overall national development. According to experts, levels of efficiency will increase with increased media use in the service sector in particular.

- **Entertainment:** Another important function of the mass media is entertainment. The media can make the people laugh and forget their sorrows. Mass media fulfill this function by providing amusement and assist in reducing tension to large degree. Newspaper and magazines, radio, television and online medium offer stories, films, serials, and comics to entertain their audience. Sports, news, film review, columns on art and fashion are other instances. It makes audience recreational and leisure time more enjoyable.
- **Public Watchdog:** Mass media have also played a leading role in shaping, guiding and reflecting the public opinion. These functions of media help to establish democracy. Use of media in a democratic polity creates critical awareness among the people, and so it becomes an essential component of mass vigilance to keep authorities tenterhooks. The media may not be able to perform these functions unless the access to them is ensured to a large section of our population.
- **Information:** Dissemination of information is the major function of mass media. Information provided by mass media can be opinionated, objective, subjective, primary and secondary. Informative functions of mass media also lets the audience knows about the happening around them and come to the truth. Media disseminates information mostly through news broadcast on radio, TV, as well as columns of the newspaper or magazines. Moreover, advertisements are also mainly for information purpose.
- **Safeguarding Democracy:** Media access is important in the political sphere. Access to media is access to public opinion, so essential to protect and preserve democratic institutions. It is advantageous to both the leaders and masses. Leaders can address masses depending upon their convenience. They reach widely dispersed masses simultaneously, through the electronic media in particular. One of the chief advantages of media access is that it helps correct distortions in facts, views

and attitudes. For radio and TV, distance is not a barrier. For instance, the Press conference address by the UN Secretary-General in New York can be watched by the Indian people through satellite.

- **'Access to Media' and 'Access for Media':** The former relates to the availability of media to audiences and the access that various audience segments have to media. However, the latter term denotes media's access to news sources, to people, places and stored information not easily available.

In the Indian context it has to be understood with reference to the reach that the media have in making themselves available to the audience. Here, the interplay of various factors like illiteracy, poverty, unemployment, caste, occupation, economic hierarchy, political socialisation, all have a direct bearing on the kind of access people have to the media.

Other Functions of the Mass Media: Apart from the traditional or conventional functions of the mass media, i.e to inform, educate and entertain, the mass media also perform other numerous functions. Harrold Lasswell identifies the following functions of the mass media:

- **Surveillance:** This means keeping close watch over someone or something. In the context of mass communication, surveillance means that the mass media is to inform and provide information to the society by keeping watch on the activities of government and correcting uncomplimentary occurrences. Lasswell describe the surveillance role of the media as the "watchman function". The surveillance function often corresponds to what is generally called news handling. This includes the collection and distribution of information about events in the environment, both outside and within any particular society.
- **Transmission of Cultural Heritage:** This function of the mass media focuses on the transmission of knowledge, values and social norms from one generation to another or from members of a group to newcomers.

  The existence of a community depends on the ability of its members to share common values and to agree on what constitute acceptable behaviours. Also, the continued existence of the society depends on the ability of its members to transmit the values and norms of the society from one generation to another. This can be done through songs and preservation of certain artifacts.

- **Status Conferral:** Another function of the mass media is the bestowal of prestige on people who attempt to remain well informed about events in their community. In Nigeria, for instance, being well informed about what is going on in government and society generally is a source of prestige. People who are well connected are looked upon as opinion leaders. The function of status conferral comes from being the subject of news reports. The mass media have the power to make instant celebrities of hitherto unknown persons either for good or bad.

  The electronic media, most especially, have conferral effect on the audience. People or organisations that are featured in the media tend to acquire some level of importance above the ordinary.

- **Interpretation and Prescription of News:** The chief function of interpretation and prescription is to prevent such undesirable consequences of the mass communication of news. The selection, evaluation and interpretation of news – focusing on what is most important in the environment, according to Sambe (2004) tend to prevent over stimulation and over mobilisation of the population.

  Like surveillance, he observed that the activities of news interpretation and presentation for behaviour, when performed as mass communication can also be dysfunctional both at the societal and individual level. On the societal level, experts believe that some activities can impede social change and enhance social disorder in a society. At the individual level, the dysfunctional role of the mass media is believed to create panic among individual members of the society.

  Another important function of the mass media in modern society is the agenda setting function. The agenda setting function of the mass media presupposes the fact that the media can lead members of the public in taking very sensitive decisions on issues of public significance be it politics, economic and social standings. The agenda setting function of the media is predicated on the fact that the mass media can influence a thinking of members of the public through its court of public opinion.

In addition to the aforementioned functions of the mass media, Folarin added national integration; social-economic modernisation; and cultural creativity as functions of journalism.

Q17. Discuss the concept of media availability and media participation.

Ans. Modern society is participatory in nature. Consensus is its hallmark. Individuals make their own decisions on public issues and the public expression collection of common individual decisions is necessary for stability and common governance.

Media availability is an indispensable element for a participant people to shape and express their opinions. By using mass media for such expression, the participants believe that their opinions do matter in decision making and policy formulation. Such a reciprocal relationship is required for societal development.

Some experts say that there are three vital areas of development. These are literacy, urbanisation and media participation. The interrelated development these three aspects help to achieve better living conditions. The mutual impact between literacy and media participation is interesting as the increase in literacy level leads to the increase in media participation. Urbanisation, at the outset, helps the growth of literacy and media participation. The literates, on their part, support and develop mass media and in turn, media help the growth of literacy.

Media participation in simple words means the number of people buying newspapers, owning radio and television sets and watching movies. In the communication market, literacy and media participation have supply-demand reciprocity that is directly connected with the web of desires and satisfactions of the public. We are well aware that modernisation prompts mobility. Mass media provide the participants with new experiences and insights into new skills. Naturally, the curiosity of the people is aroused which can be quenched only through greater access to media. It means that media must have greater access to information to meet the participants' needs. As a corollary, greater access generates greater participation in a democratic society. The increased participation is sustained by making media available and it accelerates supply and demand for media products. Pocket radios, portable TV sets and roadside news-stands have provided greater media availability. Increase in media participation and access to information will increase participation in all sectors off the social system.

Q18. Describe the concept of right to free expression.

Or

What do you mean by free access to media and social change?

Ans. When we speak of freedom of expression, we focus on freedom from abridgment by the government. This is because the First Amendment provides that Congress is the agent that is forbidden to abridge freedom of speech and press. The freedom to communicate not only is threatened by government action, but also is inhibited by a number of private actors including employers, property owners, corporations, community members and even neighbours. Nevertheless, the discussions in Supreme Court have focused on freedom from government sanctions on expression. There have been a limited number of cases involving private restrictions on expression and the Court has been reluctant to find that the First Amendment prohibits such constraints.

An ideal relation between a citizen and the government is found in the media system. In the seventeenth and eighteenth century, in Europe earlier days, much emphasis was placed on freedom of 'thoughts and opinions'. This Libertarian was a sequel concept to the licensing system of the press in the West by the Church as well as the rulers. John Milton, Isaac Newton, John Locke, William Blackstone, Lord Mansfield, John Stuart Mill, Oliver Wendell Holmes, and a host of others espoused the cause of freedom of the press, which has now been equated with the right to communicate.

As technological innovations improved, as the spread and reach of the press expanded, attention was focused on diffusion of information upholding the right of the public to the freedom of information. Originally freedom of information meant the people's right to information. New information technology has posed new dangers to the freedom of media person as well as media consumers. In theory, everybody enjoys the right to freedom of expression, but the huge capital needed for investment in new media of mass communication, for example radio and television, has negated the whole concept since only the very-well-to-do, the elite, can afford to launch media ventures. Others in the race are left behind. Since they have control over enormous public funds, governments wish to harness the new technologies for their own purposes. The freedom of expression that has ultimately been redesignated as right to information, has acquired sharp political, social and economic overtones. A stunning paradox is the demand for information by the ever-burgeoning audiences on one side and the concentration of media control either with the governments or few elite individuals, on the other.

Free Access to Media and Social Change: Mass media are a mode of social interaction. They facilitate interaction among individuals, between individuals and institutions and finally among institutions themselves. Social interaction of any type is characterised by transfer of meanings, customs, beliefs and values. The media are also products of social ethos and orders. They reflect both these elements in their functions and contents. Media also belong to social institutions. In the normal course of interaction, media influence other cultural institutions and get influenced by them in return. Wittingly or unwittingly, the dominant social institutions will make use of the media, to stabilise the existing social order.

Mass media are supposed to act as agents of social change, especially in developing countries like India. Social change is a process that demands alterations in structure and functions of society. Media normally reinforce the existing values and beliefs in a given system. Access to information may, on the other hand, alter the social structure. Hence, this dual of contradictory interaction occurring between media and society. Several institutions and factors can, with the help of mass media, bring about changes. For instance, the creation of mandal, panchayats, invention of new industrial technology, improvement in the public transport system and even the formation of a ministry can be responsible for effecting social change. Social change and economic change are linked, because economic development programmes, such as improved methods in agriculture, health, industry and education are all aimed to induce changes in a specific social structure. The mass media aid this process of economic advancement directed towards social change.

Q19. Discuss the Indian situation with regard to mass media access.

Or

Write a short note on media access. [June-2019, Q.No.-10 (a)]

Ans. India is the world's largest democracy. Its mass media culture, a system that has evolved over centuries, is comprised of a complex framework. Modernisation has transformed this into a communication network that sustains the pulse of a democracy of about 1.1 billion people. Certain media are allowed in the private sector while others are controlled by the Government. For example, the print media and feature film production are in the private sector while radio and television are wholly owned by the Central Government. When the government made allegations against some industrial tycoons for monopolising the press in India, well known Journalist, Frank Moraes, countered by accusing the Central Government of having the monopoly over electronic media. He challenged the right of the government to call others monopolistic when the government itself was a monopolist.

Newspapers in India have traditionally uphold the freedom of the press. From the day of the appearance of the first newspaper in 1970 the Bengal Gazette published by James Augustus Hickey, the Indian press has been fighting against the government control. The Indian press during the freedom struggle was up the forefront. The sacrifices made by journalists of eminence for a free press and the liberty of the country is worthy of emulation. The Indian press has traditionally been in the private sector, being a powerful tool of free expression of opinion. Before Independence, the press was pre-occupied with political views and the trend continued even after independence. The electronic medium of radio was under the control of the British Government which made use of it for propaganda purposes during World War-II.

Indian newspapers, in the real sense of the term, are not mass newspapers for the following reasons:

- The newspapers are largely published from urban centers, making them an urban phenomenon. This is evident from the fact that the largest circulated newspapers and magazines are situated in metropolitan cities or State capitals. The rural hinterland is thus denied the availability of the newspapers.
- The question of widespread illiteracy, with the rural populace having at many places less than 20-30 per cent literacy, has

made newspapers totally irrelevant. Just 15% of our total population of 873 million people read newspapers.

- The stark poverty of the rural illiterate masses prevents them from buying a newspaper whose cost has escalated 200% over the last 20 years.
- It is for these reasons that it would be a misnomer to call newspaper a mass medium.

The newspapers are owned mostly by the elite business tycoons and political interests take precedence over any other human interest. Professionals have debated the issue, but a solution has eluded them. Even the Second Press Commission has pointed out this anomalise trend. A study conducted by the Indian Institute of Public Administration, Delhi revealed that out of 54 dailies selected, 27 newspapers were owned either partially or totally by business and industrial houses and controlled about 50 per cent of the total circulation. For the purpose of unbiased and objective performance, delinking the ownership of newspapers from large industrial houses was suggested.

However, with all drawbacks it has, the performance of the Indian press since independence has been claimed that it enjoys credibility with reading audiences. This superiority of print media over the electronic media is attributed to the former being more influenced by a critical reading public while the latter provide only the liteny of the government views. Public opinion is reflected either in the editorial or letters to the editor published in newspaper, it is claimed.

Government controlled electronic media are anathema to the very concept of an open society. Frequent political interference has eroded the credibility of both AIR and Doordarshan. Added to this, bureaucratisation has affected professional aspects of their functioning. Several Committees and study groups that went into the question suggested autonomy for the electronic media in order to make them more accessible to the public. These two powerful media that can cross the barriers of illiteracy are destined to become partners in developing Indian society. The reach of electronic media is the reason why political authorities keep a stranglehold on them. The government monopoly will not so easily be replaced by autonomy even though Parliament has approved the Prasar Bharathi Bill for setting up an independent and autonomous authority for the electronic media. We should remember here that where there is a monopoly neither any evaluation of performance nor accountability is possible. To be accountable to the public, the latter's access to electronic media is doubly essential. A comprehensive communication policy to allow unhindered public access is the need of the hour. Public access leads to public scrutiny. In turn, it will lead to professional excellence and standardisation.

Q20. Define the difference between Media Control Vs Media Access.

Ans. Media control not only determines the character of ownership, information slant and selection, but also the extent of access that its consumers enjoy. In the case of media, the question arises whether the control should only be on the management or on the principles and output of these media organisations? On the other hand, Media access is the method by which individual stations determine when they are permitted to transmit, or "use" the media.

Control also determines the pattern of growth of a medium. Government control over television has resulted in a highly centralised bureaucratic setup. Control also determines the choice of technology. The establishment of High Power Transmitters (HPTs) in a few selected places, and relay centres in the form of Low Power Transmitters (LPTs), is a function of control. The case of newspapers, though different from that of television, also serves to highlight the overriding importance of proprietary control. To illustrate publishing of a chain of newspapers by leading newspaper houses not only standardises editorial opinion but also acts as a deterrent in fostering local intellectual creativity. In other words, a level of technology that enabled the nation to develop a sense of unity, has now recoiled on it to perpetuate unanimity. Diversity has been the first casualty of the national endeavour to import latest technology.

Q21. Describe the concept of 'Media Reach.'

Or

Describe the expansion of Media Reach.

Ans. The term "Media reach" is used to describe the number of individuals or homes exposed a specific medium or a combination of media within a particular time frame. It can be expressed either in numerical frequencies or percentages. Duplication in assessing the reach of a particular medium is different to avoid. If it is television, generally the number of households owning television set are taken into account.

The vast geographical reach at the command of mass media has made it possible for them to envelop urban and remote rural areas, in addition to national and regional centres owing to the diversity of audiences. The expansion has changed the nature of the message transmitted by the media. The geographical and demographic reach of TV has forced the press and radio to re-orient their contents. Unfortunately, in India the growth of TV has been at the expense of the radio. Unless the trend is checked by introducing innovative programmes. All India Radio stands to lose its traditional pre-eminent position.

Psychological Penetration: The expansion of mass media has added a new dimension to the art of persuasion. As carriers of commercial messages in the form of advertisements, mass media have made the technique more sleek and sophisticated. Mass production of goods for mass consumption necessitated the trend towards persuasive sales. Mass media have not only survived but have also become stronger because of incoming revenue from advertisements. Another area of psychological penetration has to do with stimulating the faculty of cultural awareness among the public. The opinion impact is in the form of editorialisation through analysis, interpretation and inference.

The psychological penetration of media messages depends on individual responses rooted in social attitudes, needs, values and other personal as well as collective factors. People do not generally accept any information which seeks to challenge their opinions and values. They tend to select and retain what agrees with their own views and avoid what does not agree with their values and opinions. Stonewalling of any persuasive information is not uncommon. In fact, personal contact has a stronger influence than do mass media in matters relating to politics, shopping, fashion, etc. Many studies have found that mass media can utilise the services of those people who can influence the opinions of others. Such people are called Opinion Leaders. They can mould the mindsets of people. Personal contact mitigate resistance. A link between mass media and interpersonal network is essential for acceptable psychological impact.

Feedback Facility: The functions of communicators are complete only upon obtaining reactions to their efforts. The audience reaction is known as 'feedback'. It may be manifest in any form such as reporters informing their original news source; or editors to reporters; or members of the audience to editors, reporters, new sources, or even among themselves. Feedback is quick and discernible in person-to-person communication, helping the communicator to modify the message to make it more convincing. Feedback is slightly delayed in mass media communication. It will generally be in the form of letters or talk-back as the case may be. Many communication research studies have been conducted on audience feedback. A communicator who understands the audience feedback can make appropriate changes in the message for its eventual acceptance. Thus, receipt of audience reactions and consequent replies create a broader public access to mass media.

Q22. What is community participation? How is the participation of the ordinary people restricted in Television?

Ans. A community is an assembly of people in an identified geographical area. Every community consists of groups with adverse backgrounds of social class, economic status and political or religious affiliations. Community participation typically increases with age, education, income, employment, church attendance, general sociability and personality strength. Community media operate within a geographically based community or social group, or a sector of public who have common or specific interests. The media should be transmitting within a given location and serving a community or a particular interest which intends to reach all members of that interest group. They carry, advertise or air programs on specific needs such as health, education, employment, marketing, gender, peace and environment. With community media, there has to be active community participation. A community's development hinges on effective communication. Media can be used for negative purpose also. At the community level, many issues need media attention or intervention for immediate solutions. Issues like community development, sanitation, public health, literacy, the welfare of women and children etc., can be resolved through local participation.

Mass media generally seek to attract large group concentrated in big cities and towns. However, their reach amongst the people in small communities and their reactions to it are equally important for effective communication. For the purpose, more emphasis is now laid on small media and local issues. In some countries, the small media are neglected in favour of big media resulting in the wastage of limited resources besides the usage of inappropriate channels to reach a distant audience. The remedy is to combine big media with small media. In the changing scenarios, the top-down model of media communication is being replaced by a multiplex model in which communities participate vigorously in framing policies, and plans, and in implementing them. This model has helped familiarise to the audiences.

The increased use of local media makes communication a vital input of every community development programme. Community particular in media programmes accentuates free flow of information. Consequently, the democratic process acquires more meaning and relevance. The involvement of independent groups, voluntary organisations and non-governmental agencies in the community programme stimulates socialisation and makes it more purposeful. Community involvement in mass media has a tremendous bearing on social decisions. We must note that several organisations like political parties, religious groups, labour unions, and youth and women's organisations, besides professional associations, are a permanent feature of any given community. These groups generate and promote action for changes in the law, protection of the media, besides other activities on their agenda.

Community participation in mass media can be both at the level of decision-making and management. It can also mean the setting-up of regional or local radio stations, decentralised programme production centres and launching of Cable TV. Several recent examples highlight the increased community participation in mass media. A television station in Germany encourages social groups to make films about themselves which are then telecast. In former Yugoslavia, information centres at the community and regional levels published newspapers and broadcast radio programmes reporting local events. In some countries radio and television stations publish programme proposals for audience scrutiny and the consequent feedback is transmitted to the programme councils.

Restrictions: Media laws that prescribe specific dos and don'ts, have adversely affected people's participation. Moreover, the proliferation of media networks and concentration of multimedia ownership have brought uniformity of control. To be precise, networking technology has effectively blocked the community participation in programme preparation. National advertising, national news and national hook-ups have contributed to diminished media access.

In India, the network of low power relay transmitters linked by satellite to the central station of Doordarshan at Delhi, has made community participation in any manner impossible. It has resulted in one-sided vertical communication. The regional services, with their limited durations, are not of much help in this respect.

If you are interersted in this aspect, then you may watch Doordarshan and AIR programmes for a week or so. Assess for yourself the element of community participation in them. People in power decide for the rest of the country both the content and the form of the programme. Do the Nagas, the Keralites, the Kashmiris indentify themselves with their programmes?

Unchecked professionalisation and pre-set standards of excellence have obstructed community participation in media programming. It is particularly true in the case of Indian TV which, instead of democratising programming, has bureaucratised it furthermore.

Over-bureaucratisation breeds red tape, inefficiency and corruption and in a very short period affects negatively the creativity and talent available among the residents of a community. Experience in many Asian and African countries shows that governments have deliberately ignored the particularly aspect, and manipulated the media messages, to the detriment of their own interests. In effect, community participation promotes liberal attitudes in the long run.

Q23. Write the psychological, official and legal limitations of Media.

Or

What do you mean by psychological, official and legal limitations of media? Also, Explain The Official Secrets Act.

Ans. The media impact on an audience is limited it is generally exaggerated. Media can only be hidden persuaders. The process of impact starts with perception. Media influence depends upon the perception of the message by the audience. Individuals have their own perceptions of persons, events and environment. Cultural institutions, peer groups and the social public of which they are members influence their perceptions. Thus, individual perceptions vary and are limited. When different groups and institutions vie with each other to influence individuals in society, the impact of mass media is reduced. Studies have found that peer groups, opinion leaders and, on occasions, even religious institutions, have more influence over individuals than mass media. In reality, attitudes of the people towards media are influenced by these groups. The audience has a tendency to accept the message according to individual needs and affiliations. The next psychological stage is of retention. Here too the retention is selective.

Media must exercise care while attempting to influence the beliefs, customs and attitudes of individuals. If strongly held beliefs, customs and attitudes are challenged. The rejection of media message is outright. Media can influence only those who are receptive and willing to change. Loosely held beliefs and attitudes can be, at the most, channelised. Several psychologists have recognised the importance of gratification as an influential factor. Reward, whether delayed or immediate, decides the acceptance of media messages.

Another curious psychological phenomenon that affects media is the 'sleeper effect'. Repetition of the message is resorted to by communicators to have a positive impact on the audience. But data on the frequency of repetitions is not available. Advertisers in particular are a harried lot in this regard since over-repetition may prove counter-productive. Another psychological limitation is that interpersonal networks have more credibility than mass media in traditional societies.

Legal limitations generally originate from the government. History provides us with a lot of examples of intolerance of independent opinions. Free expression of opinion is the main worry of all governments. Dissent is a bugbear for authorities and, in order to retain power devoid of public consternation, the government attempt vigorously to stifle the counter viewpoints.

Nonetheless, governments are responsible for ensuring media accessibility and for channelising communication for collective welfare. However, direct control of mass media is a much-debated issue. Government control may check the effects of commercialism, but its record in providing access to balanced information is not enthusing. The flow of information is filtered and transmission norms are one-sided-favourable only to the party in power.

Censorship is a powerful restriction to curtail independent opinion. Physical violence and threats against media persons are evident forms of restrictions. Governments resort either to censorship or repressive statutes and sometimes in both. Particularly in the case of the press, the circulation of printed copies is either banned or confiscated. Not only the executive, but even the legislature and the judiciary can curtail media.

The Officials Secrets Act can be a real threat to media persons. The sweeping powers sunder this statute are such that their detention under any pretext is possible. Besides these limitations, official pressure for suppression of views can be in the form of patronisation. Distribution of government ads as largesse is a common practice in several states of India since state governments are the largest advertisers. The carrot and stick policy is being diligently practised by authorities to keep the press at a distance.

Q24. Identify the communication needs of the people.

Or

Explain the communication system.

Ans. A considerable part of our communication activities take place through the media. Communication technology has equipped us to overcome constraints of distance and time. It enables us to interact with each other without being in 'face to face' situations. In addition, mediated communication exposes us to varied experiences and makes us aware of new people, things and events.

In contemporary society, there are communication systems such as the postal and telecommunication agencies, radio and television, news wire services and newspapers, archives and libraries, information and extension services and other organised networks.

The Mass Media are a very important component of society. Their use in a developing country like India is considered most crucial in the challenge to mobilise people for development activities. Therefore, there must be a communication policy, and more specifically a mass media policy in each country. The policy should give direction to the programmes which are channeled through various mass media networks.

Q25. Describe the problems of communication.

Or

"Society has equipped itself with useful tools to communicate better". Explain.

Ans. The concept of "noise" creates problems of miscommunication or even lack of communication. To minimise the effects of communication problems in our social transactions, society has equipped itself with useful tools. In order to communicate better, people have made use of timely inventions. The first major invention which helped to cope with communication related problems was language, in both its oral and written forms. Then came special tools and materials for recording messages about material objects, and for transferring these messages from one person to another. Besides, there were ways to convey messages through signals, to communicate across distances. The second major invention was the printing press. Finally, in a surge of recent inventions, powerful acoustic, optical and electronic communication instruments have been developed within a very short period.

A communication and mass media policy would have to explore the following problems:

- **Technology-oriented Problem:** The mass media systems may fail to perform their functions when unplanned use of such technology creates problems. For instance, communication resources can be concentrated in a few centres alone. The mass media may be misused by the owners to exercise their power, or the media content may be manipulated to give as a result' of the communicators biases. Guided by past experience, all these problem will have to be foreseen and reasonable solutions formulated for a viable communication policy. If the policy itself becomes outdated in the face of technological developments, it will have to be suitably changed. A mass media policy should contain directions for our media personnel to make correct use of the media technology. From the installation of equipment to its maintenance and from media ownership to its mode of operation, every decision that is taken should be part of the policy.
- **Problems of Research:** Traditionally, communications research in India has shown a remarkable orientation towards social problems. Studies on propaganda techniques, attitude change, effects of mass media, personal influence, diffusion of innovations, communication and development, flow of information, media uses and gratifications, organisational and management structure of the media and the economics of communication have been motivated by practical problem faced in society. These studies focus on the need to understand

the role of communication in those problems and the desire to apply the knowledge gained from research to solve them.

In spite of a great deal of empirical research, no systematic knowledge about the nature, frequency and origin of communication problems in India is available. However, the situation is beginning to change now. Dissatisfaction is being expressed at the conventional way of using communication resources, the defining of functions and jurisdictions of the media systems and the regulation of communication. Demands are being made for improving existing regulations, resource allocation principles, institutional arrangements and defining the rights and responsibilities of professional communicators, commercial communication organisations, and the bureaucracies. These factors are forcing communications researchers, practitioners and policy makers to take a fresh look at the nature of communication problems and their relationship with other social problem. A communication policy must give importance to these issues. The policy, in effect, is built on the body of knowledge developed by research.

Q26. Define communication policy and underline its importance in the process of development and change. [Dec-2019, Q.No.-5]

Ans. Communication policy refers to the guidelines on ownership, distribution and utilisation of communication resources; define the role of communication in society; define the relationship between media, government and business; provide the framework by which the present structures may be transformed so that they can support the goals of building a just and humane society.

Communication policy can be described as action-oriented principles, outlining objectives and means of achieving objectives, focusing on what needs to be done and what is to be avoided in dealing with current and anticipated communication problems in society. The policies are formulated as authoritative guidelines, by legitimate bodies, for developing, maintaining, utilising, regulating, and changing the mass media systems.

A social policy would facilitate the framing and implementation of action programmes to solve social problems. In the same way, a communication policy is formulated in response to the challenges of new communication technologies. Policy making is a complex, dynamic process involving different kinds of inputs: scientific knowledge from theoretical and empirical research; social wisdom expressed by philosophers, scholars, and leaders engaged in different areas of social activities; and valid opinions expressed by the public. It is obvious that to be effective, the policy making process needs to dealt with a large volume of information from different sources, mostly processed and integrated for immediate use. This is possible only when the society has a well organised communication system.

Role of Communication Policy: Communication policy aims at ensuring that all households, businesses and organisations have well-functioning and reliable data connections and services. The operating environment for communication policy is, alongside technological development, strongly shaped by the global character of the sector, changing user habits and the challenges related to the reliability and safety of activities.

The objective of communications policy is to ensure that basic services of high-quality and affordable price are available to everyone. The level of basic services is guaranteed by means of legislation. If necessary, the basic services are ensured by public funding.

It would be based on society's goals and expectations about the structures, functions needs, and resources of communication. It would take into account the problems that crop up when using communication in varied activities.

Objectives of Communication Policy: The manifest objective of the communication policy of developed countries is to safeguard the free and open flow of information the world over and to ensure the public's access to varied points of view.

While the developing nations seek to safeguard their societies from economic, cultural and communication invasion by the developed nations, one major objective of their communication policy is to eliminate the vestiges of colonial dependency. The governments of developing countries demand balanced trade as well as news flow with the developed countries. A major thrust area of the communication policy of developing countries is the implementation of viable alternatives to the one-way flow of information into their societies. The communication networks of developing countries are devoted to affirming and preserving the diverse cultural identities, and reinforcing the ideology of national integration.

Most of the developing countries however, are busy waging a constant battle against poverty, malnutrition, illiteracy, and indebtedness. Thus, communication development receives scarce priority in their national objectives. The chance to build a strong communication network depends on the availability of foreign aid. Under the circumstances, communication policy debates centre around the acceptance or rejection of financial and other assistance from developed countries.

The main issues are not just the mobilising of financial resources, transfer of technology, and development of the human resources for communication. There are more fundamental issues concerned with the basic role of communication in society, such as:

- The role of government,
- The mode of financing communication services,
- Basic access to communication-independent of the economic ability to pay for essential services.
- Protection of the rights of the poor and disadvantaged,
- Regulation of commercialism in communication, and
- Harnessing of cultural resources through mediated communication on the mass media networks.

Q27. Discuss India's attempts to formulate a mass media policy.

Ans. Mass media can and often do, play a critical role in policymaking. The typical view of media is that they matter in the early stages of the policy process — that media can help to set an agenda, which is then adopted and dealt with by politicians, policymakers and other actors. The impact of media is rarely so constrained, however. Our argument here, in short, is that media matter, not just at the beginning but throughout the policy process.

The mass media can be tools of cultural enrichment; national cohesion and advancement; and understanding and peace among people, through a "truer and more perfect knowledge of each other's lives". Or they can become the "new opiate of the masses", the debasers of standards and the instruments of cultural domination. Either way, the result depends on the applications of the media. The applications depend on policy deliberations based on research findings.

The media policy makers in India have to first bridge the gap between ground realities and ideal situations. Certain paradoxes exist in the field of communication which need to be considered by policy makers, planners and researchers. some of these realities are elucidated here:

- There is misappropriation of the mass media for commercial and political purposes, when the need of the hour is to apply the media to task of propagating culture, education, information and leisure time entertainment.
- There is predominant use of the media to impose foreign values instead of giving due importance to reflecting the values and norms that are inherent in a particular society.
- The communications generally create a rapport with the audience by taking into consideration the feedback received from them. But in India the communicators do not desire to find out the reactions of the audience to their programmes. This mentality hampers the qualitive growth and improvement of the programmes over a period.
- The increase in the number of channels of information is not matched by any corresponding increase in the standard of programming.
- While communication satellites and such other new technologies remove the barriers to information and education across national boundaries all over the world, the same technologies pave the way for phenomena such as 'new communication colonialism' and 'cultural imperialism'. This is expectedly a by-product of the current one-way flow of information.

Q28. Examine the recommendations of some of the Committees appointed by the Central Government to advise it on the form, structure, ownership and content of broadcasting in India.

Or

Evaluate various commissions and committees on the media.

Or

Write a short note on Verghese Committee. [Dec-2019, Q.No.-10 (b)]

Ans. Necessity of Expert Committees: There is an oft-repeated charge that the government, for reasons best known to itself, is not interested in framing a communication policy. Through policies have been announced in other sectors like agriculture, industry, education, health and even tourism, the same has not been done in the case of mass media.

Chanda Committee: During Mrs. Iildira Gandhi's tenure as the Union Minister for information and Broadcasting, the A.K. Chanda Comnittee was appointed in 1964 which submitted its report in 1966, which was tabled in Parliament only in 1970. It recommended the liberation of Radio and from rigid government control by converting them into separate corporations. It took another six years to separate 'Doordarshan' from 'Akashwani' to create Akashwani and Doordarshan in 1976. though both function under the same administrative and financial procedures with common engineering and programne staff cadres.

Kuldip Nayar Committee: On the constitutional legal fronts, the 1975-77 emergency and the Janata Party rule during 1977-79, heralded a fresh look at the media issues like the restructuring of the, national news agencies and the granting of automatically to the broadcasting media.

The four national news agencies-PTI and UNI (English) and Hindustan Samachar and Samachar Bllarati (Hindi) were merged on February 1, 1976, and one news agency "Samachar" was formed. After the Emergeacy, the Kuldip Nayar Committe was appointed in March 1977., It recommended the dissolution of samachar and suggested the creation of two news agencies-Varta in Hindi and other Indian languages and Sandesh in English, plus an international news agency News India. But the Kuldip Nayyar Committe report was rejected.

Verghese Committee: The Working group on Autonomy for Akashvani and Doordarshan, popularly known as the Verghese Committee, was constituted in the wake of the stranglehold of the Government on the media during the Emergency. Public opinion asserted itself in favour of creation of an independent professional body, protected from the day-to-day incursions of politics and free from the rigid regimen of rules and regulations of the Government.

Prasar Bharti: After it assumed power in 1989, the National Front government came out first with a Cabinet Paper and then introduced the Prasar Bharati Bill in December 1989. According to P. Upendra, the Minister for Information and Broadcasting, the Bill borrowed from the Prasar Bharati Bill of 1979 and took into account the changed circumstances and the present ethos. Many, however, felt that the bill was put before the nation in a hurry. A national debate was initiated, in many cases with the active encouragement of the government to arrive at a consensus on the framework and the modalities of media autonomy. The Bill, after incorporating some amendments, was unanimously passed in both Houses of Parliament. But following a clrange of government in October 1990, the lack of political good will to translate the concept into a working proposition was apparent. While there was no official pronouncement, the interim government headed by Chandrasekhar continued to maintain the status quo. The dissolution of the Lok Sabha in April 1991 signed the warrant of the Paras Bharati Bill, which then had needed only the Presidential assent for becoming Law. The death of Rajiv Gandhi and the advent of Congress rule in June 1991, under P.V. Narasimha Rao, put an end to any hopes about the issue. Meanwhile, the question of broadcasting autonomy has become irrelevant as other sources of information and entertainment viz., STAR TV, CNN and BBC have burst into view in the wake of the Gulf War. The invasion from the skies has begun.

Q29. Enumerate the performance of the Indian Press.

Ans. The Indian press is more than two centuries old. Its strengths have largely been shaped by its historical experience and, in particular, by its association with the freedom struggle as well as movements for social emancipation, reform and amelioration.

The press in a democratic country plays a vital role in creating, moulding, and reflecting public opinion. It is a fundamental institution of our society. Though the press in India is free but it suffers from many ills. There are a few in-built handicaps such as vast geographical area, illiteracy, poverty, multiplicity of languages, and absence of adequate communication facilities.

There are some other bottlenecks like:

- The linking of ownership of newspapers with other industrial or commercial enterprises.
- Limited newspaper ownership with closely held 'share interest'.
- Urban-oriented expansion of newspapers leaving the vast country side population untouched.
- Inadequate and expensive newsprint.

- The lack of local advertisement support.

Q30. What do you understand by second press commission?

Ans. The Second Press Commission was set up in May 1978 with Justice P.C. Goswami as the Chairman: however, Justice Goswami and the members of the Commission resigned in January 1980. The Commission was reconstituted in April 1980 with Justice K. K. Mathew as its Chairman.

The appointment of Second Press Commission became necessary since the press has undergone major changes and had acquired added significance with the continuously expanding readership base.

The Commission redefined the role, status and functioning of the press in a democratic set-up, particularly in view of the experience of the press during the Emergency. The Commission enquired into the growth and the status of the press since the First Press Commission submitted its report in 1954.

The terms of references of the Commission included:

- role of press in a developing and democratic society;
- present constitutional guarantee regarding freedom of speech and expression;
- means of safeguarding the independence of press against economic and political pressures from proprietors and management;
- role of the press and the responsibilities it should assume in development policies;
- ownership patterns, management practices and financial structures of the press;
- chain newspapers; links with industry, their effect on competition and on the readers' right to objective news and free comments; and
- economics of newspaper industry.

The Commission said: "The press as a medium of communication is a modern phenomenon. It has immense power to advance or thwart the progress of civilisation. Its freedom can be used to create a brave new world or to bring about universal catastrophe."

The Commission made concrete suggestions to curb the influence of foreign money on the press and suggested enactment of necessary changes in laws for the purpose. It recommended the following five steps:

- There should be legal provision, under which no newspaper undertaking should have any foreign ownership either in the form of shares or in the form of loans,
- Advertisements as well as printing contracts from foreign sources should be on terms no different from those applicable to similar work done for others,
- Advertisement rates must be published each year and on every revision, and there should be no discrimination in their application to foreign advertisers,
- Once a year every newspaper should publish its profit and loss account with separate information about foreign and Indian sources,
- Every newspaper undertaking must submit with its annual account the following information to the Press Council.

Q31. Discuss the future trends in mass media policy.

Ans. The government plays an important role in making the mass media truly effective vehicles of culture, creativity and expression. Whatever the nature of media ownership-whether government, public corporation, or private enterprise-it is the government which is ultimately responsible for ensuring the use of broadcasting frequencies in the public interest.

Programme content is based on the objectives of the medium, These objectives form the basis for media policies. In our country, the Ministry of information and Broadcasting monitors the content of the print and electronic media to ensure that all the mass media serve their noble purpose; to be tolls in the process of development and change, The improvement and expansion of the media network is directly linked to this goal. From time to time various Committees and commission have been set up for the purpose of evaluating the working of the communication network. Attempts have been made to formulate a mass media policy based on their recommendations, Whether or not these suggestions will be incorporated to the working of the media system depends on the authorities. In response to some of the policy considerations the government may decide to make resources available through direct budgets, or grants or provided fiscal advantages to quality productions, or offer preferential customs duties when importing hardware or software, etc. Alternatively, the media policy its& may be the outcome of such decisions and regulations. Public participation in the formulation of national mass media policies may .be achieved by setting up Mass Media Policy Council, with representatives from among media professionals and others concerned with the role of communication in society. To implement policy initiatives, institutions may be started or existing ones improved for training and research in the media of film, radio and television broadcasting, printing and book production, etc. It is of utmost importance to chalk out a detailed communication policy to guide the growth of the communication networks. Piecemeal initiatives only harm the functioning of the media system. A comprehensive policy would help bring about more effective and purposeful communication.

2 MASS MEDIA AND DEVELOPMENT

INTRODUCTION

Development is a process or increase in the standard of living accompanied by structural and Institutional chases embracing social, political as well as economic factors. One of the widely used measures of development is the per capita GNP. There are alternative paradigms of development, which explain the process of development or underdevelopment. which are grouped. All these paradigms are grouped into two world views, viz., unilinear and non-unilinear. There are some problems in development like poverty, inequality, unemployment and illiteracy, which have been persistent in most of the less developed countries. Communication is an important input in development. The four principle elements are a communication source, a message, a channel or medium and a receiver or audience. It becomes the process of affecting or influencing behaviour of individuals or groups towards certain desired goals and objectives, necessarily for the benefit of the entire society. Development Support Communication is applied to agriculture and other related areas of the rural sector. DSC can help in implementing: the programmes in population, education, and environment successfully. These disciplines have attained in relation to be overall development of the country.

Q1. Explain in brief the concept of development.

Or

Describe the limitations of measurement of development and the characteristics of developing countries.

Ans. The process of development involves not only changes in the economic structure, but is interlinked with the entire social, political and cultural fabric of society. It is necessary to note that development does not mean mere increase in the per capita income or mere industrialisation, but "a process involving a number of qualitative changes", nothing less than the "upward movement of the entire social system." Some may interpret development as "attainment of a number of modernisation ideals, such as rise in productivity, social and economic equalisation, modem knowledge, and improved institutions and attitudes " hoper and adequate development is not done by dislodging people from their roots, culture or environments. Proper development always helps people to be self-sufficient and self-reliant. Development also means reducing unemployment, mitigation of inequality and eradication of poverty," According to this 'concept, a country may not be called developed, if it has poverty and high degree of Concept of Development, unemployment and inequality.

Measurement of Development: The Economists have, traditionally, measured economic development by the level of per capita Gross National Product (GNP), which, in simple terms, means the total national income divided by the population. This measure was adopted by the United Nations, in 1950, when it classified all countries with a per capita income of less than $ 200 as less developed countries (LM3). This was a rough but convenient measure for the UN to identify the less-developed countries for the purpose of providing economic aid.

However, the limitations of the per capita GNP as a measure of development are well known.

- It is based on national income statistics, which does not include major portions of real income, like the contribution of work done in the household. This will seriously undermine the value of the real per capita income of countries like India, where household work provides substantial proportion -of goods and services.

- It is an average and does not say much about the structure of production or distribution of the national income. For example, Kuwait's per capita income, in 1990, was $ 32,680, the highest in the world, and that of the United Arab Emirates was $ 19,860. It does not mean that these counties are developed, and that is why the UN has categorised them as developing countries.
- Progress in a narrow sector, like natural resource-exports, oil, minerals, timber might show high per capita income as in Kuwait and the UAE, Trinidad and Tobaggo, ($3,610), Gabon ($3,330). But, by no stretch of imagination, can these countries be considered ten times more developed than India with a per capita income of $350 in 1990. Also the purchasing power of local currency is higher than the dollar in the US or other countries. Kuwait, Brunai, the UAE etc. are rich in non-renewable resources. Once these resources are consumed, the development process in these countries might cease. Therefore, this kind of development is hollow and temporary.
- The per capita income may increase even in the face of increasing unemployment. For instance, today we see that the gross national income of the USA has increased. The normal process and assumption is that with the growth of per capita income unemployment diminishes. However, in societies which use high technologies, i.e., labour-displacing or capital-intensive societies, the per capita income may rise with the rise of unemployment. For example, computerisation or the use of robots might cause a rise in the unemployment rate.

Characteristics of Developing Countries vis-a-vis Development: There are many textbooks which try to present underdevelopment in terms of certain common characteristics of the developing countries. These include:

- low levels of living,
- low levels of productivity,
- high rates of population growth,
- high and rising levels of unemployment,
- underemployment, and
- high dependence on agriculture and other primary production.

Development, in contrast, is associated with some of the characteristics of the developed capitalist countries. These include:

- the opposite of the characteristics mentioned above, and include
- high levels of living,
- high levels of productivity,
- low or no population growth, and
- the predominance of industrial or non-agricultural activities.

Q2. What do you mean by Theories and Paradigms of Development?

Or

Differentiate between Unilinear and Non- Unilinear World-view of Development.

Ans. The process of depending on the aims over and over again till its refined. In other words, the process with its various trials becomes a theory. The development processes emanate from some philosophy. Therefore, a particular philosophy can have a group of developmental processes. In easy understanding, we might call these theories as paradigms.

Unilinear World View of Development: The unilinear world view of development simply means that underdevelopment is a condition preceding development. All developed countries are late comers to the process of development, which had already taken place in the developed West. The Western developed countries followed some kinds of processes, and, they have achieved a kind of standard of living. The people of these countries enjoy certain consumer items, which are not easily available for the common men living in other parts of the world, at an affordable cost. It suggests, that development is becoming more like the West or like the already developed countries.

Types of Unilinear Theories

(1) Mainstream Paradigm: Of those paradigms, which project development as becoming more like the West and developing countries as late-comers to the process, with certain initial conditions, which should be overcome to experience transition to development, the more familiar is what could be described as the 'Mainstream paradigm'.

The most important resource for development is savings or

accumulation of capital. The transition from underdevelopment to development is essentially a process of moving from low savings ratio of about 5% of the GNP to a high savings ratio of about 12% or more. "Development is a process of transforming an economy, which is predominantly agriculture-based and other related primary activities, towards predominance of industry and non-primary activities."

Therefore, these theories describe the initial conditions or barriers responsible for the low savings, and suggest strategies to overcome those hurdles, which would put the underdeveloped countries on the path of development like the West.

Once the low savings syndrome is overcome, then aid or foreign investments help in a sustained development, either through balanced investment or investment in the unbalanced sectors, that would set up inducements and pressures.

(2) Counter-revolution Paradigm: According to this paradigm, the state intervention through licensing and regulation leads to 'directly unproductive profit seeking', corruption, and red tape. Minimising the state's role, and allowing the market to play the role in allocation of resources, would improve efficiency, competitiveness, and rapid growth. This paradigm has gained some popularity only in the 1980s, by which time there was widespread disenchantment with the interventionist policies. In recent years, this paradigm is at the basis of the package of liberalisation that is recommended by the World Bank and the International Monetary Fund.

(3) The Structural Paradigm: There are two variants of the structuralist paradigm, one referring to the distortions in internal structure, and the other pointing to the global or international structure, It is the 'international structuralism' of the Rural Prebisch that is more familiar. According to the paradigm, the world is divided into the developed capitalist countries forming the core of 'the Centre', and the underdeveloped countries forming 'the Periphery' Over the years, there emerged a division of labour with the Centre producing and exporting manufactured goods and the Periphery depending on the production and export of the primary products. While the income elasticity of demand for high technology and high productivity-based manufactures is high, it is low for the primary products. As a result, while the demand for the manufactured goods increased faster, ensuring higher prices for their exports, the demand for the primary products increased slowly, and the export prices did not keep pace with the rise in the prices of imported manufactured goods. There was, in the long-run, deterioration in the terms of trade of the primary exports from the less-developed countries. All the benefits, technical progress and productivity flowed to the developed centre, keeping the periphery in a continued state of underdevelopment.

(4) Orthodox Marxist Paradigm: The familiar marxist concept of development is associated with the five epochs or stages: (i) Primitive Communism, (ii) Ancient Slave State, (iii) Feudalism, (iv) Capitalism, and (v) Socialism. Each of these epochs is marked by a corresponding mode of production. Development, in this framework, may be viewed as one of transitions from feudalism to capitalism.

The Orthodox Marxist theory also visualised the future of the underdeveloped countries, entirely in terms of the developed capitalist countries. Karl Marx wrote that "the country that is more developed, industrially, only shows to the less developed the image of its own future."

It is such an image of development that led Marx and Engels to believe that the capitalist colonial expansion would result in the spread of development of capitalism in the countries.

Non-Unilinear World - view of Development: The Unilinear paradigms do not have a systematic nature.

Types of Non-Unilinear Theories

(1) Populist Paradigm: The term "populist" is used here in the absence of any other term that is adequate to describe this approach. Tine theories under the "Populist" approach question either the need or possibility of the less-developed counties developing on the lines of already developed capitalist countries.

Populist paradigm is discussed as an alternative strategy by not housed by any less-developed country. This is partly because of the dominance of the mainstream paradigm in the initial stages of independence, and the creation of an impression among the people that development means becoming like the West. Most of the less developed countries hold on to the "mainstream" paradigm, its failures notwithstanding.

(2) Neo-Marxist Paradigm: A serious challenge to the unilinear world-view of development did not arise until the emergence of the neo-Marxist paradigm. There are quite a few economists who can be called neo-Marxist, but here, we are concerned with the writings of Paul Baran, A.G. Frank, and the related "dependency theory". An attempt is made here to capture the neo-Marxist paradigm, as far as possible, in terms of the original writings. The essence of the paradigm lies in the fact that, at present, the less developed countries cannot develop like the West. It stresses the interconnectedness of development and underdevelopment, of traditional and modern, and indeed many other social, political and economic factors. It seems many conflicts and clashes of interest in the development process occur, both between nations and between social classes within the underdeveloped countries.

It emphasises the historical factors, especially, the active process of how underdevelopment has come into being in the various Third World countries.

Q3. Explain the development experience of the third world countries.

Ans. After the Second world war, many colonies got independence, and started re-building their nations. The leaders of these newly independent countries were desperate to bring their nations out of the vicious circle of poverty, uneducation, disease, hunger, etc. Thus, 'development' became a key word in most of their speeches. And the meaning of development were as varied as the countries. About three quarters of all humanity, numbering three and a half billion people, living in the developing countries in Asia, Africa and Latin America, spanning two thirds of the earth's land surface, constitute the Third World. A Third World because it belongs neither to the group of industrialised capitalist countries nor the socialist countries, wherever such countries still exit. These Third World countries vary greatly in size, natural resource endowments, in the structure of their economics, in the level of economic, social, and technological development. The diversities are fairly marked, making even the Third World less homogeneous. But the unifying aspect is that, in these countries, the need to overcome poverty and secure a-better life for their people is primary. Yet, it is ironic, by the end of the 1980s, it could be seen that the achievements of the Third World during the post-world War II decades had not fundamentally changed the status of these countries in relation to the world economic system. "They remained poor, subordinate, and powerless. In general, their national self-reliance had not increased, in some countries dependence intensified as they tried to modernise". Poverty persisted and the income gap between the developed countries and Third World widened.

The growth in the Third World rarely removed the structural inequalities and cleavages. On the contrary, the income gap between the rich and poor became wider. As a result, the economic growth brought along with it the problem of growing disparities, tendencies towards disintegration and instability. The social and economic status of women leave much to be desired. And there was growing dependence of these countries on the developed ones. In spite of the fact that any of the developing countries are dependent on international trade, their share of the world trade has dropped from over 30 per cent in the 1950s to about 15 per cent by the end of 1980s. A considerable part of the declining share has been due to the deteriorating terms of trade. These countries are becoming increasingly dependent on aid and borrowings from abroad, resulting in a growing foreign debt. There has been an increase in the participation of the multinational corporations in these countries, and their influence on economic policies has been growing. The Third World accounts for hardly two per cent of investment on research and development, thus leaving these countries technologically dependent. Most often the imported technologies are inappropriate, leaving little scope for expansion of much needed employment opportunities.

Faced with the growing international inequalities in economic power and influence in the existing world economic order, the Third World countries lobbied for a better deal, which resulted in the U.N. Resolution popularly referred to as the New International Economic Order (NIEO), which sought a programme of action towards an equitable world. Some of the important aspects of NIEO were:

- Renegotiating the debts of the developing countries;
- Redefining the terms of trade, and assuring greater access to the developed country markets;
- Reforming the IMF and its decision making process; and
- Attaining the UN official development assistance targets.

Q4. What are the development dichotomies?

Ans. The dichotomies range from the meaning of 'developed' and 'developing' countries, to different approaches and methods of economists and 'policy-makers', to policy issues, such as concentration on heavy capital goods versus 'small is beautiful' approaches.

We shall consider only a few dichotomies like Growth vs. Justice and Rural vs. Urban.

(1) Growth vs. Justice: The mainstream development paradigm as well as the counter--revolution paradigm suggested that economic growth should be given priority, even though it would result in growing disparities in income distribution.

Traditionally, it is believed that unequal distribution of income is a necessary condition for rapid growth. It is argued that growing inequalities in income distribution, by making the rich richer, would provide for more savings, and, therefore, higher growth. If growth is accompanied by more equitable or just distribution, the poor also get more income, but may not have much left for showing, and the consequent low savings will result in slow growth.

Thus, the traditional theory implied a dichotomy between growth and justice, we have a very rich, elite class in India.

Now, many development economists believe that just or equitable distribution of income would actually promote better growth for the following reasons:

(i) The rich in the developing countries appear to be spending much on unproductive activities, imported commodities, and in any case do not seem to save a higher proportion of income than the poor.

(ii) Perpetuation of low levels of income through unequal distribution may affect, not only their purchasing power, but also their health and productivity, both of which affect the growth.

(iii) Raising the income of the poor would increase the demand of indigenous production and, therefore, higher growth.

(2) Rural vs. Urban Dichotomy: There is a widespread feeling that the theories of the unilinear world view would suggest strategies of economic development, which would only result in urban bias. Our metropolices and cities are over-populated.

Unprecedented migration from the rural to the urban areas is taking place. This urban bias would lead to growing neglect of the majority who live in rural areas as well as unmanageable rural to urban migration affecting the quality of life in the urban areas. Alternative strategy based on the theory that development is not becoming like the West, but one of strengthening the investments in the rural sector. Though there are no examples of Gandhian or populist strategy being implemented, the Chinese experience with the Maoist model, a variant of the neo-Marxist paradigm, gives ample evidence of a health development of the rural areas at the same pace as the urban sectors.

Q5. What are the problems of Underdevelopment?

Ans. There are some countries that have increased their per capita income after decades of trial but the changes that took place in the form of increase in the GDP per capita, the basic problems of underdevelopment continue to plague most of the less developed countries including India. These are:

- **Poverty:** It may be defined as the inability to attain a minimal standard of living. The minimal standard of living may be expressed in terms of the expenditure necessary to buy a minimum standard of nutrition and other basic necessities. Such a measure may suffice as a poverty line for a country. The World Development Report, 1990, estimated "that more than one billion in the developing world are living in poverty. Nearly half of the world's poor live in South Asia, and nearly half of them, i.e., about 250 million live in India". In other words, India accounts for about 25 per cent of the poor in the Third World. The poor in these countries are concentrated in the rural areas. A substantial proportion of them live in areas of acute environmental degradation. Much of the deprivation is due to poverty suffered by women and children. In poor households, women shoulder more workload than men, are less educated, and have less access to remunerative activities. Children, particularly girls, suffer disproportionately. Their future quality of life is compromised by inadequate nutrition, health-care, and education. Low life expectancy and educational attainment are common among the poorest households.
- **Inequality:** It refers to disparities in the living standards. Often, it is attributed to unequal distribution of income. Though the majority of people in less developed countries continue to live

in the rural areas, there has been growing disparity between the rural and urban incomes, leaving the rural incomes much behind. It is a burning issue in our country. There have also been growing disparities in the interpersonal income distribution. In other words, the share of the rich is increasing faster, while that of the poor has not been increasing or, if at all, at a very slow rate. Thus, the gap between the rich and the poor is widening. The income disparities in the less developed countries are wider than in the developed countries.

- **Unemployment:** It is one of the most striking problems of the less developed countries. We do experience it in each and every family. It is not only open unemployment, but also under utilisation of all those employed resulting in underemployment that plague these countries, An additional problem is the low productivity of those employed. In many poor countries, open unemployment, especially in the urban areas, affects 10 to 20 per cent of their labour force. The incidence of unemployment is much higher among the young and increasingly more educated in the 15-24 age group. Even more fractions of both the urban and rural labour force are underemployed. One of the major causes for persistence of poverty is the widespread unemployment and underemployment, the solution to which holds the key to the problem of underdevelopment. The unemployment issue occupies a central place in the study of underdevelopment.
- **Literacy:** It is one of the scourges that perpetuates low productivity and prevents mobility to the higher levels of living of the masses in the Third World. Education is not only a lever to improve the productivity, but also a basic need. Progress in education in to be sought mainly as an end in itself. In addition, there is growing evidence that schooling contributes substantially to the overall development. It is shown that one year increase in schooling can increase wages by more than 10 per cent. An additional year of schooling has in some countries, raised farm output by 2 to 5 per cent. Schooling of women has brought down substantially the infant mortality and fertility while raising life expectancy.

Q6. Define the concept of Development Communication.

Ans. According to Nora Quebral (1975), "development communication is the art and science of human communication applied to the speedy transformation of a country and the mass of its people from poverty to a dynamic state of economic growth that makes possible greater social equality and the larger fulfillment of the human potential."

Development communication is 'art', because one has to create his strategy, and programme to communicate to his target audience. Nora calls development communication ' a science', because it follows a process, a system. When she says that it is the art and science of human communication, we have to comprehend it from these perspectives. Development communication is an art and at the same time a science. It works with the human hearts (because it is an art) and brain (because it is a science) to yield a result which can be measured in terms of economical growth.

A famous communication scholar M.Rogers (1983) says, "development communication refers to the uses to which communication is put in order to further development. Such applications are intended to either further development in a general way, such as by increasing the level of the mass media exposure among a nation's citizens, in order to create a favourable 'climate' for development, or to support a specific development programme or project (this type of development communication is often termed as 'development-support communication' DSC").

The application of communication for the development will create an environment or climate. This climate or environment may be of two types: (1) physical climate and (2) psychological climate. When knowledge about something is propagated or disseminated among a large number of people, the users find many relevant things around them, say a special kind of fertiliser. The radio programmes could be heard, the TV programmes could be seen or posters could be seen on the walls of that particular fertiliser. This may be called physical climate.

Now, the disseminated message about the fertiliser works on the psyche of the people. The information acquired through the various communication media create a favourable attitude towards the new fertiliser. In the long run, they might use or adopt it, if possible. But, definitely, resistance from the people in general will be the minimum.

F. Rosario Braid is of the opinion that development communication is "an element of the management process in the overall planning and implementation of development programs".

Development communication is, in a broad sense, "the identification and utilisation of appropriate expertise in the development process that will assist in increasing participating of intended beneficiaries at the grassroots level." Thus, development communication is communication with a social conscience.

Rosario Braid emphasises that development communication is nothing but an element in the process of a project. Generally, it is the decision of the management to utilise communication to disseminate information about their project, if and when they feel it appropriate.

It is really an important segment in the whole scheme of management at the present time.

A good and useful management strategy would always identify the important elements and make the users conscious about them.

Development communication has two primary roles:

(1) A transforming role, as it seeks social change in the direction of the higher quality of life. The higher quality of life can be achieved in various ways. Might be by adopting all the required vaccines for the infants of each family of the society, Some countries might adopt techniques of producing enough food for the citizen. Some countries might systematically and scientifically break all the myths surrounding various religious and social customs. And communication could be a marvelous instrument to achieve these objectives.

(2) A socialising role, by seeking to maintain some of the established values of the society. In playing these roles, development communication seeks to create an atmosphere for change as well as providing innovation through which society may change. Each and every society has some traditional values. These values give the people of each society an identity and a sense of belonging.

The aspirations of a society sometimes are embedded in these values. Now, the values, customs and beliefs of other societies might make inroads into other societies. If, the people are not careful, they might be taken off their ground by the new incoming sets of values. communication can play a very vital role by making the people aware about this pitfall. It can also help immensely by drawing the attention of the members of a society to the richness of their own valued, customs, beliefs and, above all, aspirations.

Q7. Explain the Philosophy of Development communication.

Ans. Development communication can be purposive, positive, pragmatic. Following are the aspects of development communication:

- **Development Communication is Purposive:** The other communication scholars hold that communication is and should be 'ethically' non-purposive. A non-purposive message is one, which is transmitted to a receiver directly or by means of a channel (e.g., mass media) without any intention to influence the receiver. But, in development communication, one looks for specific behavioral objectives, such as getting farmers to go in for a specific variety of seed, pesticide, etc.
- **Development Communication is Positive:** In development communication, positive value is attached to what one communicate about. Take the example of the high yielding variety of seed. Once adopted, the farmers can increase their harvest manifold. This means more income which can be utilised to buy land, cattle or equipments. This is what we mean by positive value attached to development communication.
- **Development Communication is Pragmatic:** In this context, we might define pragmatic as practical and purposeful. In development communication, the purpose of communication is important. Let us assume that we want the farmers to plant a particular rice variety or the so-called miracle rice. The judgment or evaluation of communication does not rest on the mere invention of communication activities performed, such as the number of the press releases issued or the number of farm visits made. Findings have showed that mere increase in the flow of information does not necessarily result in those behavioral changes, which are desired to be achieved.

Q8. What is the role of media in the development communication?

Ans. The role of the media changes in development communication. It plays the following four responsible roles:

- Circulate knowledge that will inform people of significant events, opportunities, dangers and changes in their community, country and the world.

- Provide a forum where issues affecting the national or community life may be aired.
- Teach those ideas, skills and attitudes that people need to achieve for a better life.
- Create and maintain a base of consensus that is needed for the stability of the state.

To perform these roles, the media keeps the development orientation in its perspective. Three approaches have been identified in relating communication to development. These are empathy, diffusion, and multiplying of information. We shall discuss each separately, individually.

- **Empathy:** Daniel Lerner (1958) in his book, Passing of Traditional Society, saw the problem of 'modernising' traditional societies. He saw the spread of literacy resulting from urbanisation as a necessary precondition to more complete modernisation that would include participatory political institutions. Development was largely a matter of increasing productivity. And to increase this productivity one must aspire, and it must begin in the psyche of the people. Hence, it is basically "psychological".

  According to D. Lerner, development failed to occur because peasants were unable to 'empathise' or imaginatively identify with the new role, and a changed and better way of life and so remained fatalistic - unambitious and resistant to change. Every change in society must originate and begin in the hearts of the people. If the people would like to change, only then the development would begin. Lerner saw the media as filling this need of promoting interest among the people for a better life. Not only that, he saw the media as machines, inspiring people for better things in life. He said 'empathy' endows a person with the capacity to imagine himself as proprietor of a big grocery store in a city, to wear nice cloths and live in a nice house, to be interested in "what is going on in the world" and to "get out of his hole."
- **Diffusion:** According to Everett M. Rogers (1983), "the mass communication influence appears to operate by a 'two step flow' process through awareness of the mass media,

development of favourable attitudes and adaptation by inter-personal channels, particularly, "opinion leaders".

It has been found that when a message is propagated, a segment of the population adopts it, and develops a positive attitude towards it. This can happen in the case of a product, fertiliser, seeds, ideas, journals, etc. Then, the people who adopt first, directly or indirectly shape the positive attitude of others who remain indifferent to the message. This is true in places where information and literacy levels are low. Simple people would like to get confirmation from the people living in their proximity.

Magic Multiplier: Wilbur Schramm's (1964) Mass Media and National Development, which was produced for the UNESCO, became almost a blueprint for development communication. While Lerner and others saw all of the media output as having potentially. Mnrur Medh end Development modernising effects, for Schramm it was their content that was the key to their use in development. "Social change of great magnitude is required. To achieve it, people must be informed, persuaded, educated. Information must flow, not only to them but also from them, so that their needs can be known, and they might participate in the acts and decisions of the nation-building; and information must also flow vertically so that decisions may be made.

Works should be organised, and skills should be learned at all levels of society for better utilisation of the resources of society. Here is where the mass communication enters the calculus - the required amount of information and learning is so vast that only by making effective use of the great information multipliers, the mass media, can the developing countries, hope to provide information at the rates their time tables for development demand".

Q9. What are the communication needs and resources?

Or

State the UNESCO guidelines.

Or

State the strategies in development communication.

Ans. In planning communication strategy for development, the most important element is identification of communication needs and resources. Unless one is careful about this, or if one overlooks this elements, communication strategy and plan will not be effective, and all efforts will go in-vain. It is necessary to assess carefully the communication needs of the community and the country. To identify communication needs and resources of a country, the following process has been suggested by the UNESCO (United Nations Education, Scientific, and Culture Organisation):

UNESCO Guidelines

- The collection of basic data and systematic analysis of the country upon such bases as population densities, geographic limitations to communication, variety of social structures, ecology and agriculture transportation, physical communication, mobility of population, electrification, industrial capacity, manpower capacity, etc.
- The production of an inventory of the present communication resources, including the modem and traditional media, and analysis of the variety of present communication structures. Such an inventory should also include the study of the audience, its communication consumption patterns, etc.
- Critical analysis of the present communication politics (or lack of the same), including such considerations as ownership, structures, decision-making, etc.
- Critical analysis of the communication needs of each society, especially, in relation to the existing social and communication structures, and the uses to which communication is put.

Analysis of the communication components in all aspects of the national development plans and programs in order to ascertain the communication requirements of the programs, and the communication capacity which is essential to the execution of the plan. These needs must then be reconciled with the means and capacities that are available.

Strategies in Development Communication: The careful formulation of plans towards achieving a goal is known as strategy. Since development communication is goal oriented, one has to be careful in planning communication strategies. There may be a number of communication strategies for the achievement of particular communication goal.

Since these strategies are formulated in the context of the developing countries, one should give keen consideration to cost-benefit factors before selecting the right strategy. In the modern world, there are number of new technologies, media and techniques, which are available to a communication strategy planner. One has to evaluate these alternatives available to him, using cost-benefit analysis and administrative feasibility. Always, one has to keep in mind the target audience.

Site Project: India's biggest experience in using the mass media for the purpose of development was the Satellite Instructional Television Experiment (SITE) of 1975-76. This one year project was primarily undertaken to telecast special developmental programmes through the satellite communication toxic rural clusters, which included a total of 2330 villages, scattered in 20 districts, spread over six states - Andhra Pradesh, Karnataka, Orissa, Madhya Pradesh, Rajasthan and Gujarat. Its objectives were to:

- improve the rural primary school education, .
- provide training to the teachers,
- improve agriculture, health and hygine, and nutritional practice, and
- contribute to family planning ad national integration

After the completion of the project evaluation studies, the results showed that exposure-to developmental messages through the television had contributed for the widening of horizons of the villagers.

SITE is one of the biggest and technologically most advanced social experiments in the direct broadcasting for education and development. It is also one of the largest Indo-US experiments in communication conducted so far. In this project, the experimenters main objective, was to provide instantaneous information for national development to those who otherwise would have been deprived of such information for many years to come due to technological constraints.

Q10. Explain the development-support communication.

Or

Plan a development support communication campaign for farmers to promote organic farming. [Dec-2019, Q.No.-4]

Ans. The practice of Development Support Communication, DSC, is a multi-sectoral process of information sharing about development agendas and planned actions. It links planners, beneficiaries and implementers of development action, including the donor community. It obligates planners and implementers to provide clear, explicit and intelligible data and information about their goals and roles in development, and explicitly provides opportunities for beneficiaries to participate in shaping development outcomes. It ensures that the donor community is kept constantly aware of the achievements and constraints of development efforts in the field.

The origin of the development support communication is traced to the agricultural extension, which was initiated in the fifties of the present century in many of the developing countries. The study of the diffusion of hybrid corn by Ryan and Cross, in 1942 established the critical role of technological information for increased farm production. Agricultural extension education, as a part of agricultural sciences, branched off as a specialised field to help evolve theory and practice of modern methods of agriculture. In the developing, countries even though, a large majority of the population is engaged in agriculture, the small and marginal farmers are not able to produce adequate food because of the subsistence methods of farming. In our country, the traditional way of tilling the soil and depending on the monsoons are very common. It was, therefore, considered necessary to help these farmers to change their agricultural practices, through extension methods so that they could adopt better practices to increase their output.

This approach, of spreading innovation, new ideas, practices, and technologies in agriculture to the farmers in the developing countries, became very popular as agricultural extension during the 50s. In view of the heavy dependence of agricultural extension of communication techniques and methodologies, in due course, communication applied to agricultural extension came to be known as agricultural communication. This was the time when development communication, as a specialised area of communication, was recognised, and became, very popular. It slowly diversified into rural communication when extension Specialists with knowledge of communication principles, transferred like health, hygiene, nutrition, sanitation, etc. Instead of confining developmental activity to the rural areas alone, the urban section was also included to help the poorer sections living in the slums. Thus, communication theory and practice applied to help stimulate the development process in general, and branched off as the development support communication (DSC).

The DSC was a concept popularised by the UNDP and other UN institutions like FAO, UNICEF etc. The World Bank also supported the DSC. It stands for linking all agencies involved in the planned development work such as political executives, policy planners, development administrators, subject specialists, field workers, opinion leaders, the media representatives, the researchers and beneficiaries who constitute the final delivery points, and the consumers of information. Thus, the routes of communication envisaged are not only vertical from top to bottom and bottom-upwards, but also horizontal between the institutions and personnel connected with the process of development.

Q11. What do you mean by shifting emphasis?

Or

Describe the shifting focus of agriculture.

Or

Explain agriculture development.

Ans. The main objective of Department of agriculture is to give pace to the growth rate of agriculture development and crop production and productivity which will strengthen the economic status of the farmers and uplift their life-style and the ultimate aim of agricultural development is to increase food security.

The communication scholars like Lerner (1958), Pye (1963), and Schramm (1964) recommended that densification of the mass media and an increased exposure to the media would contribute to the process of development. Based on their studies of diffusion of innovation, Rogers and Shoemaker (1971) defined development 'as a type of social change in which new ideas are introduced into a social system in order to produce higher per capita income and the levels of living through more modern methods and improved social organisations'. But, by the 70s, it became clear that such an economic approach to development failed to deliver tangible results. Increase in per capital income did not result in enrichment of human life in terms of equity, social justice, etc. The problem of unemployment and underemployment got aggravated with the poor becoming poorer and the rich becoming richer. The trickle down effects failed to materialise. In 1976, Rogers modified his definition of development, "Development is a widely participating process of social change in society, increasing greater equity, freedom and their valued qualities for the majority of the people through gaining control over environment".

This second approach to development, which became more popular as the new paradigm of development, underpinned income distribution, decentralised planning, labour intensive technology and indigenous and exogenous factors in development. The thrust of the new approach was on improving the quality of life through appropriate technologies, and promoting participation of people in the development process. This shift in the meaning of development was accompanied by a redefinition of the meaning of communication. The old, linear, mechanistic one-way communication model with greater focus on the source (communicator) as replaced by a more dynamic interactive two-way model of communication. The focus in the new approach was on the recipient and the socio-cultural system.

Another approach to development is currently gaining wide recognition. The basic tenet this approach is self-reliance. The advocates of this approach place high premium on in Agriculture integrated rural development, popular participation in the decision-making process, grassroots development, productive use of local resources, fulfillment of basic needs, maintenance of ecological balance, identification of the felt-needs and integrating culture as a mediating force in development This approach discouraged the widespread tendency in the developing countries "to be like the west", to initiate the path of Western countries and pursuing their strategies to catch up. Instead, it urges a radical rethinking of the issues by adopting a culture-specific approach, using local resources for achievement of self-reliance.

Q12. Specify the features of agricultural development.

Or

Explain agricultural development in India.

Or

Explain the theory of diffusion of innovation with the help of examples. Discuss relevance in contemporary times.

[June-2019, Q.No.-3]

Ans. The distinctive characteristics of agriculture such as wide regional disparities in terms of ago-climatic zones, cropping patterns, and levels and productivity; small and dispersed land holdings; cultivation of vast tracts of land in rain-fed conditions; low soil-fertility status and high incidence of pest attack and proneness to flood and drought influence the pattern of development in India.

The strategy adopted for agricultural development has been multi-dimensional and broad based: efforts to introduce extensive land reforms; centre-to-village level administrative machinery to implement development programmes; a nationwide network of agricultural research and education facilities; a number of surface and groundwater irrigation schemes; large scale production of chemical fertilisers; village level co-operative infrastructure to meet the credit and distribution needs; corporate sector to manufacture, process and supply agro-inputs, warehousing and storage facilities.

(1) Agricultural Extension: According to Ensminger (1962), "Extension is a programme and a process of helping village people to help themselves, increase their production, and to raise their general standard of living". Further, he calls it a process of teaching under practical living situations.

The National Commission on Agriculture (Government of India, 1976) has a much broader perspective. Extension, in its view, refers to informal out-of-school education and services for the farming community, to enable them to adopt improved practices in the production, management, conservation and marketing of agricultural and allied activities. Agricultural extension aims at not only imparting knowledge and securing the outlook of the farmer to the point where he will be receptive to innovation on his own initiative, but also continuously seeking means of improving his farm occupation, home, and family life.

(2) Extension Approaches Over the Years: The national extension service of the early fifties, with its broad objective of improving management of the traditional agriculture, envisaged participation of elected representatives of the people, a network of village level functionaries and subject matter specialists, and the greater use of audio-visual aids.

The Intensive Agricultural District Programme (IADP) of the sixties was envisaged to impart knowledge about innovations like improved agronomy practices, better quality seeds, chemical fertilisers, pesticides, implementation, soil and water management practices, and other services like research, information, credit, storage, marketing and related supplies. The approach included technical support to the extension workers, better administrative co-ordination, and establishing a link between education and input. The extension efforts were made goal oriented by concentrating on these activities. By the mid-sixties, a programme on national demonstrations was launched to popularise the superiority of the new technique; through on-farm demonstrations, determine on-farm applicability of research recommendations, give confidence to the extension workers about the suitability of the new practices, and establish a direct link between the scientists and farmers so that the latter could understand the field problems better. The emphasis was on demonstrations and group discussions.

(3) System Approach in Agricultural Communication: The communication support for agricultural development is intended to provide knowledge and skills about improved agricultural technologies so as to induce change in the existing farm practices for increasing agricultural output. In our country, agricultural communication forms a part of the overall agricultural extension strategy. According to K. N. Singh, the agricultural communication follows a system approach, consisting of three different sub-systems: (i) Research System (ii) Extension System and (iii) Client System.

(4) Diffusion of Innovation: Key to Extension: The process of spreading innovation is known as diffusion. The diffusion process is the spread of a new idea from its source of creation to the adopters or users. Hence, the essence of the diffusion process is the human interaction, in which one person communicates a new idea to another person.

An innovation refers to an idea perceived as new by an individual. All innovations need not be new to all people. What is new to one individual may be a known thing for another individual. Hence, the term innovation is applied to an idea which is perceived by an individual or group as something new to that person or to that group. There are four elements in any analysis of the diffusion process: (i) innovation, (ii) communication of one individual to another, (iii) the social system, and (iv) the time taken from the stage of innovation to the stage of adoption.

Stages in the Adoption Process

(i) **Awareness Stage:** There is a broad exposure to the innovation, but the individual does not have sufficient information about the innovation. He is yet to get motivated either to seek further information or to act upon it.

(ii) **Interest Stage:** At the interest stage, the individual shows interest in the new idea, and makes an effort to seek additional information. However, the person is still undecided about its application. The function of the interest stage is mainly to seek and get more information about the idea.

(iii) **Evaluation Stage:** At the evaluation stage, the individual mentally applies the innovation to one's own situation, and then decides whether to try it or not.

(iv) **Trial Stage:** At the trial stage, the individual uses the innovations on a pilot stage to decide about its utility and relevance to one's own situation. It was observed that most persons would not adopt an innovation without trying it on a pilot basis.

(v) **Adoption Stage:** The individual decides to continue the innovation. Adoption implies sustained use of the adoption process: The rejection is, thus a decision not to adopt an innovation.

Information Sources and their Relevance at Various Stages of Adoption: Communication through the mass media like the print, radio, TV and Mass Media and Development film is most effective in providing various options and alternative choices. The mass communication channels are found to be most important in the evaluation stage of the adoption sources. Inter-personal communication, through extension workers, friends, and family members, can influence behaviour and facilitate transfer of ideas. The mass communication channels seldom effect decisions directly, although they operate through an intervening variable to influence behaviour.

Factors affecting the Rate of Adoption of Innovations: Individuals in such a system are very slow and rigid in accepting new ideas, practices and technologies. The rice-eating people show a marked resistance to accepting coarse grain, since it involves a change in the food-habits. Many studies have substantiated that new crop varieties, which give higher yields and better incomes, have been rejected on the ground of taste, fear of ill-health, and unacceptability as food. Thus, cultural incompatibility and mismatch with the existing social system, which are considered to be very strong inhibiting factors in the process of diffusion of innovations. Other important factors identified in this context are: (i) relative advantage of the innovation, (ii) perceived impact of the adoption on social relations, (iii) scope for reversibility in case the innovation is to be rejected, (iv) complexities involved in the acceptance of the innovation on sustainable basis.

Classification of Adopters: Basing on the rate of adoption and the time lag between initial exposure to final adoption.

Diffusion researchers have classified adopters into five distinct categories: (i) venturesome innovators, (ii) early adopters, (iii) early majority, (iv) late majority, and (v) laggards. The venturesome innovators are the most eager members of society to try new ideas and adopt new practices. They are enterprising and willing to take risks. Usually they belong to the cosmopolite category. The innovators, becoming the reference groups for the subsequent late adopters, constitute the early majority and late majority. The laggards are very slow in adoption. They are rigid and hard to be convinced, stick to the old methods, and resist change.

(5) Models of Agricultural Extension in India: A comparative analysis has been presented of the three models of agricultural extension and communication systems that are (i) The Intensive Agricultural Distinct Programme (IADP), (ii) Agricultural Extension under the Panchayat Raj Set-up, and (iii) Agricultural Extension under the Training & Visit System (T & V).

IADP was launched in the early sixties. Initially, the Project Executive Officer (EO) was assisted by a numbex of subject matter specialists (SMS). Later, when the IADFW Programme was renamed as IAAP. Studies conducted by the Development Communication NIRD researchers at Raipur in MP revealed poor linkage between research and the field level in Agriculture functionaries. Similarly, there was no involvement of the field level functionaries in the planning of the agricultural development programme. Due to lack of periodical training, the VLWs and their supervisors (AEAs) did not have adequate knowledge of the important areas of paddy cultivation, which is the staple food in the district. The withdrawal of the SMSs, reduction of field level extension staff like AEOs and VLWs, and lack of regular training have diluted the programme. It gained status as a special programme after the introduction of the

Integrated Rural Development Programme (IRDP), in 1978.

The agricultural extension pattern under the Panchayat Raj System, where the District Agricultural Officer (DAO) at the Zilla Parishad level was responsible for planning and implementation of agricultural schemes, was studied in Amaravati district. The technical competence of the Gram Sevaks, at the village level, was much below the mark, since most of them had no training in agriculture. A significant amount of time of the Agricultural Extension Officer (AEO) and the VLWs was consumed in preparing returns and reports. The VLWs having been made responsible for activities like family planning, health,-sanitation, social welfare, etc., were spending less time on agricultural development.

Information flow from the radio, agro-service centres, and local newspapers was high, and it was rated to be very useful. The credibility of the VLW was found to be low.

The operation of the T & V system, studies in the Kota district of Rajasthan, reflected that the contact of the farmers with the VLWs was limited. It was observed that the extension workers were not working through the contact farmers, as envisaged by the T & V system. The contacts with VLW were almost the same for all types of farmers - both contact and non-contact farmers. The level of knowledge of the farmers about the improved practices relating to the major crops of the area was low. The T & V system did not help the fanners to increase their knowledge. It is necessary to use other effective extension methods like demonstrations.

Q13. Explain the concept of population control and family welfare.

Ans. Population control and family welfare needs hardly any reiteration as it is an integral part of the overall development programmes of the country. Fortunately, communication has been playing a vital role throughout the various developmental phases of the programme by extensively using different communication media and methods, In spite of the large efforts of educating and motivating people for accepting small family norms, changing the health practices of the people, and introducing spacing methods, the achievements of the programme have always fallen short of the expected results.

Some studies have shown that factors such as paucity of resources, the traditional ethos, low education and illiteracy profile, diversity of languages and dialects, lack of coordination between the communication and policy planners and the overall resistance to change, are responsible for the failure of various effort put into this scheme. A deeper analysis, however, shows that the development programmes in any field, where formal resources have been deployed to promote communication, the socio structural factors play a vital role in the reception of new ideas in any community. In other words, factors within the universe of the socio cultural set-up have already been responsible for preventing innovative ideas from being functional and operational at the community level. Most administrators view motivational and educational techniques as a kind of magic, which, when applied any where on anybody, can yield results in the form of acceptance and adoption of the family planning measures. It needs to be recognised that implementing educational and motivational efforts in the community require not only patience, but also capabilities of the workers.

(1) DSC Activities in Population Control: In their eagerness to reach a wider audience many DSC activities in the population control and family welfare are gradually losing their informational components and becoming propaganda.

Such propaganda has naturally a short life, and does more harm than good to the programme. Yet another issue that needs to be mentioned is that the present DSC efforts in the family welfare programmes seldom use the knowledge and the talent available at the local levels. It is becoming more evident that the expensive mass media technology is receiving higher emphasis at the cost of the traditional media. Usage of the traditional media is not only acceptable, and creative but affordable also. The urgency of containing the population did not allow the planners of the communication policy and programmes to pay due attention to the needs of different socio economic and tribal groups, spread in different regions of the country.

Thus, proper attention might not have been given to proper communication planning. It is thought that putting messages in the mass media channels would ensure positive results. The psyche, ethos, economic-social milieu have been given less importance.

(2) New Challenges: The challenges that are at the forefront of the family planning communication policy can be briefly subsumed under the message content, media mix and organisation of media. Decentralisation of media, wider choice of suitable media and development – integrated approach, giving due recognition to the socioeconomic environment of the country also help.

The focus and emphasis of the future DSC strategy in the family welfare programme has to be rural based and addressed to the rural and urban poor as its target audience for a country like India, where the rates of literacy and the level of purchasing power are low, the choice of the media assumes importance for any meaningful strategy.

The purpose of communication in family welfare should be more information-oriented, and it needs to be supplemented by developing messages through which functional and purposeful relationship among people could be developed. This is important, because family planning involves subjective motivation, and the questions relating to it are very personal and delicate in nature. The handling of such questions at the communication strategy level in terms of message content have to be very carefully considered. The present message content has been greatly influenced by the "urban alienating culture", which has infused among people a sense of social isolation, powerlessness and frustration.

(3) Solutions: The most important issue, which merits attention, is to provide linkage between the DSC strategies and different welfare programmes as part and parcel of the larger whole. In philosophy and in principle, this approach has been accepted. But it has always lagged behind in implementation for various reasons. The isolated communication approach has brought in contradictions within the developmental programmes. The family welfare programme has come to a stage where rural people appear to be aware of the benefits of the family welfare, but the socio-economic pressures that confront the rural and urban poor rather than planning strategies vertically for programme acceptance.

Q14. What do you mean by support communication?

Or

Explain the concept of health and development- support communication.

Or

Explain how communication strategies are formulated for development in health sector. [June-2019, Q.No.-4]

Or

Write a short note on Health communication.

[June-2019, Q.No.-10 (e)]

Ans. The practice of Development Support Communication, DSC, is a multi-sectoral process of information sharing about development agendas and planned actions. It links planners, beneficiaries and implementers of development action, including the donor community. Development in one sphere of life leads to development in other spheres. The main purpose of development is to prepare people to lead economically productive and socially satisfying lives. However, social satisfaction and economic productivity is perceived in different ways in different societies. Everywhere, people strive to increase their earnings, leading to increase in the purchasing power, which enables them to get for themselves and their children better and sufficient food, housing, better education, better opportunities of leisure, and, most important of all, better health. Unless people have healthful living, they cannot enjoy the other benefits of life. Therefore, health development is essential for social and economic development.

(1) Health Communication: Health communication is the study and practice of communicating promotional health information, such as in public health campaigns, health education, and between doctor and patient. The purpose of disseminating health information is to influence personal health choices by improving health literacy. Health communication is a unique niche in healthcare that allows professionals to use communication strategies to inform and influence decisions and actions of the public to improve health. In the case of Indian society, the complexity of health behaviour is guided by informal but deep-rooted socio cultural values, the country has adopted such measures which help the people to keep themselves healthy. Thus, the process of motivation of the people is attempted through the mass media and interpersonal communication, based on development-support strategy. The mass media and other communication channels have tremendous effect on every sphere of human life, but we have to accept that its impact is not uniform in all fields, nor can it be predicted universally. Those who hold the view, that mass media is uniformly effective in economic, agricultural, political or health fields, have a reasoning based on the theory of the effort of opinion-leaders. It has been found that the opinion leaders are comparatively more effective in changing the non-health behaviour of an individual. The concept of the two step flow of communication simply implies that the opinion leaders take the basic message, translate it into personal terms, and feed the same to their own influence network in ways that are acceptable and understandable to the target audience. There are evidences that the big landlords were the first to accept changes in the agricultural process and production but not in health including family planning. Not all opinion leaders can influence everyone, but their influence is within relatively restricted spheres. The opinion leaders generally specialises in some fields.

(2) DSC and Health Behaviour: In this communication, word-of-mouth and personal communication from a trusted source is significantly more effective than mass communication from a remote source, however prestigious that source might be. Innumerable studies have established more credibility of interpersonal communication than mass communication.

Health and development support communication are closely interlinked and mutually interdependent. In a country like India, a DSC strategy needs to be developed in a manner that can cater to the needs of the diverse groups based on social and cultural background. Merely by transferring health information to the people through mass communication alone will not bring health development. The goal of achieving health behaviour change should be a central point of the DSC strategy, and it needs to be operated in that spirit. The health communicator should, therefore, pursue the following activities if he aims to achieve behavioural change:

(1) Assess the needs of the community or different target groups.
(2) Assess the local resources available to meet these needs.
(3) Assess the areas of likes and dislikes of the people towards different types of communication.
(4) Generate need for the programme.
(5) Provide scientific, specific and basic information to the policy-makers and decisions-makers.

Q15. Explain the concept of education and society.

Ans. The process of imparting or acquiring knowledge through instruction or study is known as Education.

In education, the greatest emphasis should be placed on the development and growth of a person, both physically and psychologically. The development and growth must be positive, and these must be manifested in daily life.

Types of Education: With the development of society, education has focused on various aspects, such as child education, adult education, technical education in arts and crafts, health education, physical education, and several others. The broad classification of education could be:

- Formal Education,
- Non-formal Education, and
- Extension Education, which will be discussed in succeeding part of this unit.

(1) Formal Education: Formal education is basically an institutional activity, uniform and subject-oriented, full-time, sequential, hierarchically structured, leading to the award of certificates, degrees and diplomas. The schools, colleges and universities fall under this category.

(2) Non Formal education: Non-formal education, is not formal, which means it is:

(i) flexible,
(ii) life, environment and learner-oriented,
(iii) diversified in content and method,
(iv) non-authoritarian,
(v) built on learner-participation,
(vi) helpful in mobilising local resources, and
(vii) an instrument/which enriches human and environmental potential.

Non-formal education processes and programmes should, in the long run, lead to:

(i) creating an awareness in individuals and society, of the prevailing environmental situations and the need for and direction of change,
(ii) cultivating a rational, objective and scientific temper,
(iii) enriching human potential and, thereby, increasing community resources, and promoting individual and group creativity,
(iv) increasing the functional relevance of learning, both to the learners and to the community, achieving a greater degree of

individual, social, cultural and economic development through democratic action and active participation,

(v) building a learning environment in which every individual shall have equal opportunity for continuing self-learning, and

(vi) a better sharing of opportunities and social wealth and, particularly, a more equitable and

(vii) just distribution of knowledge among various sections of society.

(3) Extension or organised face-to-face communication is kept within the scope of the DSC. Extension provides a form of DSC, which might be more effective than the mass media. Extension education has proved very effective in Agriculture, and has since then widely been practised all over the world, especially in the third world countries.

Literacy Programme: The Farmers' Functional Literacy Programme is the biggest on-going country-wide programme of adult education. It is in reality a complex non-formal education system at its initial stage. Its implementation is the responsibility of the Central Government, and the scheme is classified as a Central Sector Programme. The Farmers' Training and Functional Literacy Programme, an inter-ministerial project implemented jointly by the Ministries of Agriculture, Education, and Information and Broadcasting, is an attempt to get a qualified answer to this fundamental challenge. The basic idea behind the project is that there is a direct correlation between the physical and human resources. In other words, this is an integrated approach to a comprehensive rural development programme, to the "Green Revolution". The main goal of the scheme is to support and strengthen one of the basic national objectives: self-sufficiency in food, increase in crop production and growth of agricultural productivity.

Education and DSC: Communication for development purposes should be distinguished from communication for the sake of entertainment, such as chitrahar, or commercial advertising of soap and tooth paste or news dissemination news bulletins, The World This Week, etc. Entertainment-oriented communication also has a powerful social influence and possible effect on the attempt to meet the national objectives.

It was agreed that the development-support communication should be taken to embrace the following:

- the infrastructure (economic, technological, organisational/ administrative);
- the information processing and transfer systems;
- the media the personnel, the communicators;
- the recipients;
- the supporting communication services;
- the contents organised interpersonal communication and extension services;
- the purposes or objectives (recognising that they may vary, but that national development goals an usually central).

It was recognised that the central focus was on mass communication, and that a multi-media approach with inter-media comparisons was necessary.

Uses of Communication for Education: The case for uses of communication for education has been convincingly argued on the following grounds:

- communication helps to enlarge mental horizons;
- it can be used to raise levels of aspirations;
- through communication, attention can be focused on problems having a bearing on the contemporary developmental and educational context;
- it can be effectively employed to build consensus on the new economic and cultural goals;
- through communication, experimentation can be encouraged and knowledge relating to their success and/or failure can be widely disseminated; and
- it can also be utilised to teach specific skills and techniques.

Q16. Discuss the concept of environment and development.

Ans. In 1987, the World Commission on Environment and Development, a United Nations body, published its findings in 'Our Common Future', known as the Brundtland Report. It says that problems of environment and development are interlinked, and that economic interdependence among nations is increasing.' Areas focused on included:

- population and food security;
- the loss of species and genetic resources;

- energy; and
- industry.

It calls for economic growth based upon sustainable development, - meeting the needs of the present without compromising the ability of the future generations to meet their own needs.

The Brundtland Report called for continued economic growth, while emphasising the need to integrate environment and development.

Activities such as the burning of coal and other fossil fuels, and the use of CFCs as aerosol propellants are leading to a build-up of greenhouse gases in the atmosphere, resulting in damage to earth's climate. The Inter-governmental Panel on Climate Change (IPCC), looking at the climate processes, concludes that if there is no change in emissions of greenhouse gases, global mean temperature would rise by about 0.3"C a decade in the 21st century, faster than at any time in the past 10,000 years. An increase in global temperature could, in turn, lead to major problems for mankind.

Economic Growth and the Environment: The environmental problems that countries face vary with their respective stages of development, the structure of their economics, and their environmental policies. Some problems are associated with the lack of economic development, inadequate sanitation and availability of potable water, and indoor air pollution from bio-mass burning. Many types of land degradation are a root cause of poverty in the developing countries. Here, the challenge is to accelerate equitable income growth and promote access to the necessary resources and technologies. But, many other problems are made worse by the growth of economic activity.

Industrial and energy-related pollution (local and global), deforestation caused by commercial logging, and overuse of water are the result of economic expansion that fails to take account of the value of the environment. Here, the challenge is to build the recognition of environmental scarcity into decision-making. With or without development, rapid population growth may make it more difficult to address many environmental problems.

Rapid population growth can worsen the mutually reinforcing effects of poverty environmental damage. The poor are both victims and agents of environmental damage. Since they lack resources and technology, the farmers resort to cultivating hill sides, and move into the tropical forest areas, where crop yields on cleared fields usually drop sharply after a few years. If environmental pollution and degradation were to rise in step with a rise in output, the result would be appalling environmental pollution and damage. Tens of millions of people would become sick or die each year from environmental caused diseases or disasters. Water shortages would be intolerable, and tropical forests and other natural habitats would decline to a fraction of their current sizes. Fortunately, such an outcome need not occur, if sound policies and strong institutional arrangements are put in place.

DSC and Environment: Ignorance is an important cause of environmental damage and a serious impediment to finding solutions. This principle holds true for international negotiations and poor households alike, as is illustrated by the global damage done to the ozone layer by the CFCs and the serious implications of indoor air pollution, like smoking, for family health. Fit, it is necessary, to know the facts; second, to determine values and analyse the benefits and costs of alternative measures; third, to ensure that information is available on the public and private choices.

The DSC regarding environmental issues increases access to information. Many governments encourage involvement of local population in tackling environmental issues. But if such involvement has to be effective, the local people need to be well-informed. Some ways to achieve this are:

- to share/supply information to the local communities at the early stage in identifying a project;
- to discuss local environmental problems with the affected communities;
- to allow public comments on the DSC-inputs; and
- to encourage public comments and discussion on the proposed environmental solutions.

3 MASS MEDIA AND CONTEMPORARY SOCIAL ISSUES

INTRODUCTION

The media play a significant role in the socio-economic development of nations. The stronger and more purposeful the communication channels, the more developed the countries and vice versa. Media, pre-occupied as they are with politics, have not evolved any sustained programming for and about women. Researchers have analyzed that the images of women transmitted by the media are essentially not found in reality. Though Ways to raise the status of women are suggested through the media. Movements of social reform set into motion a positive attitude toward the development of women in India. There is an important role of the media in generating awareness about the environment among the people. The various studies and slants are taken on the same environment issue by different interest groups in the media. There is a close ties between development and environment. The technology of a country has to be environment friendly, or it will have to be discarded. The media educate the masses on an important aspect of their lives--consumerism. More than advertisements, it is the news media which can guide the customers in making purchases. We can say, 'let the media help the buyer to beware'. Media plays an important role in reporting human rights issues. The media can make people aware about various schemes and programmes to improve their general living conditions. The concern over human rights has taken on new dimensions in recent times. When addressing the human rights situation of a country, the media can throw light upon the actions and inactions of the administration. In all likelihood, such exposure will alert everyone involved. This will result in creating a favourable human rights scenario in the country.

Q1 . Explain the women's issue in India.

Ans. Being a girl or woman is not easy. Issues hinder the growth of a country and makes the women feel inferior. Gender discrimination is one of the issues that women are facing in India.

The most common issues faced by women in Indian society are:

- Firstly, Indian parents prefer a male child to a female one, because they assume that daughters will walk away with their dowry and thereafter wash themselves of any responsibility for the care of their parents.
- Secondly, it is generally presumed that a daughter will never prove herself cost effective whereas a soil will later bring in wealth from his bride's family and at the same time faithfully look after his elderly parents for the rest of their lives.

These are the prejudices that women face almost daily. They simultaneously wage a double battle against problems of both kinds: these in common with society and the ones peculiar to women kind.

Women's issues include all those areas which concern women's personal and social well-being. Amenities provided by the state for the comfort of its women citizens, and the steps taken by different organisations for improving the quality of women's lives are women's issues, as much as the prevalent social apathy toward violence against women and the on-going efforts to invite women to participate at various levels of administration.

Improvement in the status of women was a pledge taken by the makers of our constitution. Laws have been passed by the legislature to embody these principles . In the last two decades, the women's Movement has demanded and obtained amendments in existing laws on violence against women, such the Rape Law.

Women activists raised debates about Family Law. Divorce and Maintenance, and so on. Attempts have also been made to introduce programmes for the development of women which would enable them to play an effective role in our national life.

Q2. Discuss the historic status of women in society and culture.

Or

Explain legal, political and economic status of women in India.

Or

Explain the evolution of women in India.

Ans. Women's history is the study of the role that women have played in history and the methods required to do so. It includes the study of the history of the growth of woman's rights throughout recorded history, personal achievement over a period of time, the examination of individual and groups of women of historical significance, and the effect that historical events have had on women. Inherent in the study of women's history is the belief that more traditional recordings of history have minimised or ignored the contributions of women to different fields and the effect that historical events had on women as a whole; in this respect, women's history is often a form of historical revisionism, seeking to challenge or expand the traditional historical consensus.

In the India of the nineteenth century, women suffered from the denial of freedom in their own homes. They were constantly subjected to repression, unnatural indoctrination, and unequal and inferior status within and outside their homes.

It was in such an oppressive scenario that movements for social reform developed within different religions. The most important of these movements developed within the Hindu religion i.e. the Brahmo Samaj, Prarthana Samaj and Arya Samaj. Like the parallel movements among the Hindus. There were movements of reform within the Islamic Community. A progressive movement to make educational opportunities available to women took shape in the latter part of the 19th century. Under the leadership of a few individuals like the Begum of Bhopal, Sir Syed Ahmed in Aligarh and Justice Karamath Hussain in Lucknow, a large number of books and journals were published. They gave ample food for thought to the newly educated Muslim women.

Status of Women: This is a famous quote by Jawaharlal Nehru on women. The status of women depicts the social, economic and mental condition in a nation. Women have been regarded as a symbol of spirituality in our scriptures. Yet, they have been treated badly and unequally to men. Social evils such as dowry, sati-system, child marriage, and female infanticide were widely prevalent in the early ages. The spread of education and self-consciousness among women has led to their progress over the period. Women of today are empowered. Also, women are gaining advancements and success in each and every field.

In early times, the status of women in India was inferior to man in the practical life. However, they had a higher status in scriptures. They are considered as the perfect homemaker in the world.

The socio-cultural setting in which women are born, brought up and live, is the result of several determining factors like, types of social organisations, patterns of hierarchy, kinds of family structures, value attached to women's education, nature of the institution of marriage.

Patriarchy is characteristic of the social structure in India. As a natural corollary, a girl is considered another's 'property', a guest in her parents' home, one who has to be given away and so on. Discrimination between sexes in the allocation of scarce resources such as nutrition, medical attention and education stems from the notion of greater desirability of son and inevitable transferability of daughter. This attitude is internalised by girls quite unintentionally. In her husband's home too, a woman does not acquire rights comparable to the male members. A vicious circle is thus born.

On the work front, women are faced with gender-specific work areas and roles. As homemakers, they bear the entire burden of domestic chores. While their contribution goes unrecognised, is invisible and unpaid for, it is considered their "real" work. In effect, salaried jobs are considered secondary to their domestic roles of wife and mother.

Legal Status of Women in India: According to the Indian constitution, Women are legal citizens of our country. And have equal rights comparing to men. Various aspects related with women can be identified in India, Women are responsible for baring children, yet they are malnourished and in poor health. Most Indian women are uneducated. Although the country's constitution says women have equal status to men. The women of the household are required to take care of household works and handle the daily activities restricted to home.

In India, a series of laws have been enacted to encourage women's participation in different activities of society. Legislations have been enacted to ensure that women get the same rights and privileges as are enjoyed by men. However, discrimination against women continues to exist. Women earn less than men for the same work.

They are not allowed to perform work allotted for males. For instance, we do not often see women bus drivers or even conductors. The prevalence of child marriage in the 18th and early 19th centuries, which often led to untimely widowhood, was curbed in 1856 by the implementation of Hindu Widows' Remarriage Act. As the national movement gained momentum in the early 20th century. A few legislations, to improve the plight of women, were passed. The plight of widows without any means of their own, led to the passing of the Hindu Women's Right to Property Act in 1929. This was later amended in 1937.

The Hindu Code Bill of 1955 prohibited Hindus from contracting a bigamous marriage and outlawed polygamy. It gave a wife the right to divorce under certain circumstances. The Special Marriage Act of 1954, amended in 1976, treated men and women as equal in matters pertaining to property and inheritance. This is applicable to civil marriages The Hindu Succession Act of 1956 gave women equal rights to succeed to all property of their parents on par with their brothers. The Dowry Prohibition (Amendment) Act of 1984 was passed ostensibly to curb the evil of taking dowry. This act had been initially passed in 1961.

Legal Rights of Women as Portrayed on Indian Television Today Doordarshan telecast a programme a few years ago, entitled Adhiktar dealing with several legal issues. The various episodes dealt with issues ranging from property rights of women, widowhood, maintenance law for divorcees, dowry deaths, equal remuneration for equal work, and bigamy.

A serial titled Humrahi was telecast recently. Its theme revolved around the life of a deserted women fighting for her rights. Humrahi was specially designed to communicate messages on women's development and equality. It focused on issues such as women's education, the evils of child marriage. The importance of health care and nutrition and the status of women in family and society. The women play non-traditional roles.

Economic and Political Status: Women in India participate in voting, run for public offices and political parties at lower levels more than men. Political activism and voting are the strongest areas of women's political participation. Women turnout during India's parliamentary general elections was 65.63%, compared to 67.09% turnout for men.

The status of women cannot be elevated by the sheer number of legal enactments and constitutional sanctions in their favour. These legislative policies need to be translated into reality to improve the status of women. The general public ought to be made aware of these rights.

The social, economic and political position held by women in society serve as general indicators of their status. They are determined by the responsibilities, rights, roles, and opportunities for participation of women in economic and political activities. It is generally accepted that the economic status of women is an indicator of a society's stage of development. Besides, patterns of women's activity are shaped by social attitudes and institutions, which in turn differ according to the stage of economic development. The extent of women's empowerment determines their political status. Though equal franchise and right to participate in elections are granted on paper, few efforts have been made to reserve electoral seats for women, primarily in the Panchayats, Zilla Parishads, Municipalities and Municipal Corporations. In 1974, the Committee on the Status of Women in India, in its report titled "Towards Equality", highlighted the lack of opportunities for rural women in decision-making. One of their findings was that posts reserved for women in the village Panchayats were either not filled at all or were occupied by women belonging to upper caste and well-to do families. There were few women representatives from the weaker sections of rural society. The Committee strongly recommended the creation of statutory women's Panchayats to enable women to share power at the grass roots level.

Reservations for women are part of the larger effort by the government to ensure fair if not equal representation of all sections of the society in mainstream activities.

Q3. How women have been portrayed in Indian Media?

Or

Explain the portrayal of women in media.

Or

Critically analyse the projection of women in a television serial of your choice. [Dec-2019, Q.No.-2]

Ans. Women are shown as playing a secondary and passive role in various programmes, episodes and films. They are depicted as mothers, housewives, sisters, sister-in-law, etc., always serving and caring for the other members of the family or community.

The reality reconstructed by the media, does not match the one encountered by women in their daily life. There is a great difference between the reality of day to day life and the so-called reality recreated by the media. In media, most realities have happy endings and desired reconciliations, which unfortunately do not occur often enough in our lives.

Portrayal of Women on Television: Women in the world of television are presented in the role of domestic help, a wife, a mother and being portrayed as submissive and engrossed in common family affection and duties. Men are depicted as employed, spirited and combative. The truth is that television programming does not include the image of the working class woman or peasant woman. What is required, is the wholesome depiction of various categories of women. Those who belong to different backgrounds, perform different types of work and play multiple roles in their day-to-day life, all ought to be shown. Viewers have to be provided with these images lest they believe that only limited roles exist for women in society.

Ideal women and men were rewarded differently, just as deviant women and men were punished differently. The ideal women won everybody's approval, whereas the deviant women became outcasts. They were reformed by being taught proper lessons by the husbands who beat them into shape, or even sometimes by children. Men, whether ideal or deviant, were rewarded or punished by the outside world. Thus, fiction programmes very clearly demarcate the spheres for women and men, constantly propagating that a woman's world is restricted to her home.

If we talk about 'rural women', the image that is most likely to come to mind is of women working in the fields. However, radio and television programmes on agriculture are more often than not male dominated. Most of the experts, interviewers, and model farmers are men. Although rural women form a considerable section of the agricultural work-force, they do not find a place in agricultural programmes.

Even rural development programmes on radio and television, on topics like training, credit or agricultural extension work, are addressed invariably to male farmers, that too upper class and upper caste men. The programmes never address women of marginal and small farmer sections and female agricultural labourers.

Programmes that do address women, boil down to those urging them to adopt birth control measures. It is apparent from the general theme of these programmes that women are considered illiterate and ignorant, and the singular cause for the explosion in population.

Portrayal of Women in Advertisements: Commercials often depict women using products such as soap and shampoo to enhance their personal appeal so as to be rewarded with male approval. The male concept of an ideal woman as one who is young, fair, slim and beautiful, is propagated through commercials. There is a possibility that these idealised norms, make a woman with ordinary looks, feel insecure and inferior. A market for these products is cultivated by encashing on the anxieties and insecurities of young women.

Print Media and Women's Issues: As a majority of the Indian population is non-literate, print media does not enjoy a widespread reach as compared to electronic media. Most issues of special concern to women, do not fit into the traditional concepts of what constitutes news. While atrocities perpetrated against women like dowry deaths, rape and sati receive considerable media attention, subtle forms of harassment of women at their place of work and even home, receive scarce mention. Perhaps the vociferous and visible campaigns of women's groups, against atrocities of women force the press to report these incidents. The advent of women reporters and the presence of some senior women journalists in positions of responsibility may have made a difference to the coverage of women's issues in the print media. This aspect needs to be probed.

Newspapers and magazines do not overtly pursue an anti-women line. But women are asked to model themselves after male figures and not other women who have made a name for themselves. Men are not asked to aspire after the achievements of women, in the same coin, though.

Looking at the example, the inherent bias against women is also manifest in the page make-up of newspapers. A serious articles on dowry death with as unjustifiable a caption is "burn baby burn", is seen published alongside a cartoon. "It doesn't pay to kill wife" was the frivolous headline of a newspaper item reporting the award of life sentence to a businessman for murdering his pregnant wife.

Q4. "Media as a crusade for women's education". Explain.

Or

Define how media can be used as a crusade for women's education?

Ans. Media can teach a large number of women as it is a non- formal way to teaching in the matters of nutrition, health, family welfare, etc. The health of women refers to their mental and social well-being, which is shaped as much by societal norms and attitudes as by their biological construction.

Women's Literacy and Print Media: Illiteracy is often considered a cause of poverty, the prime reason for the inhuman conditions in which the poor live. This needs to be strongly challenged just as much as the assumption that the poor are poor because they bear too many children. Such assumptions arise when we look at the problems, divorced of their socio-economic context. In developed countries, literacy and universal primary education came after the process of development and industrialisation.

A perusal of the literacy primers, brought out by government and non-government organisations, shows that they completely ignore the conditions in which people live.

An exception is the programme launched two years ago by a voluntary organisation in Andhra Pradesh. Named 'Jana Vignana Vedika', it published primers for literacy which contained stories of women's resistance to evils like the problem of drinking.

These stories created a stir among women who then led a major movement against arrack in several villages of Andhra Pradesh. It is quite pertinent to mention here that these primers, dismissed summarily as anti-governmental, were to be banned by the government. The campaign swept the entire state of Andhra Pradesh for over a year, posing a threat to the state's exchequer because the state government gets a revenue of over rupees 800 crores on country liquor. Yet it did not figure in any programmes of Doordarshan except a brief mention on the national network.

Role of Television: Health programmes telecast on Indian television, focus on social problems with a Specialist doctor to answer queries in an interview format. Most of these problems relate to women and children. These programmes provide information on common diseases and their treatment. More married, young, educated women watch these health programms than unmarried ones, and that their frequency of viewing is independent of their parents' education and occupation. It has also been found that family income, family size and type of family do not have any impact on the frequency of viewing health programmes.

Role of Radio: All India Radio, broadcasts special women's programmes from all its stations, at least twice a week, meant for rural women. 'Nutrition' is a topic of special interest to them and UNICEF has distributed 5,000 transistor sets to Mahila Mandals so their members may listen to programmes about nutrition.

The Family Planning Units of AIR, produce programmes on-the small family norms for rural audiences, industrial workers, women and youth. Information on family welfare, maternity, child health and nutrition is provided through these programmes.

Q5. Explain the employment of women in India.

Ans. Women workers in India encounter very different conditions from those found in most Western countries. There is no system of universal state welfare benefits for periods of unemployment or for old age. Women without the financial support of a man must rely on the wider family structure if they are unemployed or underemployed, and this reliance is exacerbated when they have dependants. At the same time, there are strong cultural prohibitions in some parts of India against women undertaking paid work outside the home, both for the purpose of demonstrating men's status as providers, and to protect women's sexuality (and thereby men's honour) from other men.

Employment of women in the media is low, particularly in decision-making levels. Men not only lead women in absolute numbers but also constitute the bulk of the management and top editorial ranks in the media. This is so, irrespective of whether it is a developed country or a developing one. The UNESCO sponsored study of the new world information order, popularly called the MacBride Commission, has pointed out that "Journalists dealing with serious issues and political events are seldom women, and few women because editors or hold directing positions". Employment figures of individual media institutions in the United States show that the common employment pattern is one in which proportionately more men are hired, especially at the top levels. Sexist bias is a conspicuous feature of the British media which are accused of biased presentation of women and sex discrimination when hiring personnel. The dominance of males in some sections of media is defended by arguing that the major carrier ladders to top positions usually involve professional and educational skills which are more common with men than women. A survey of Indian films found that, out of 46 women who appeared as characters, only twelve were in employment and nine of these were in traditionally female jobs. A study of fiction in Soviet magazines found that no information about their employment was given in the case of 48 per cent of the female characters while the job status of only nine per cent of the men depicted, went unidentified.

However, the number of women hired in the media cannot be

considered in absolute terms, since the number of women looking for such jobs is still small as compared to men. Media are not the fundamental cause of the subordinate status of women. But they can and should work together with the rest of the society to help reduce the suffering of women kind.

Q6. What do you mean by contradictory media policy and practice?

Ans. A number of television programmes revolve round middle class ideologies that limit a women's roles to wives and mothers. While 36 per cent of the agricultural work-force is female, women continue to be considered non-producers with absent or restricted roles beyond home. Only domestic duties are deemed their 'work'. The plurality of Indian culture and the diverse roles that women play are neither acknowledged nor communicated. Such a unidimensional projection of reality reinforces stereotype images and role specifications of women. Urging that Doordarshan should formulate clear-cut guidelines and policies at the earliest, regarding the positive portrayal of women, the Joshi Committee Report recommended that this portrayal take note of all facets of women's lives, as workers and contributors to family survival and the national economy. It pointed out that the need of the hour was to integrate women in terms of equality in all sectors of national life and the development process. An attentive observation of television programmes reveals that the majority of images of women are urban, middle class, upper caste Hindu and North Indian. Also, they are housewives or single, independent, self-assured, "eligible", youthful women. Doordarshan should not ignore the contemporary Indian women's movement which has established itself as a vocal and visible lobby, acquiring validity and public space. The ban of country liquor in Andhra Pradesh is a case in point.

Q7. What are the environment issues? Explain.

Ans. Environmental issues are harmful effects of human activity on the biophysical environment. Environmental protection is a practice of protecting the natural environment on the individual, organisational or governmental levels, for the benefit of both the environment and humans. Environmentalism, a social and environmental movement, addresses environmental issues through advocacy, education and activism.

Oil spills on the oceans; smog over cities; holes in the ozone layer; noxious fumes in the air; muddied drinking water; denudation of forests;

extinction of wildlife species; and heavy silting of fresh-water rivers: desertification of vast tracts of fertile land: topsoil erosion; rising global temperatures, acid rain.

These are some of the many facets of environmental pollution. Every phenomenon listed here has long term implications and effects. None is a natural disaster. Each is wrought by human interference with the precarious balance in Nature. Untreated and non- decomposable wastes are wreaking havoc on the environment. From nuclear wastes, chemical effluents and harmful refrigerants to countless polythene covers. plastic material rind suspended particulate matter in water and air, we humans have 'disposed' of man- made wastes without a thought for the consequences. We have quite willfully unbalanced the carefully poised equilibrium in the ecosystem. The result is a series of regressive effects on our environs. These in turn create problems for our very survival. They constitute 'environment issues' which require immediate attention.

Several governments and groups of citizens have expressed the need to reduce the ill- Environment and Media effects of our lifestyles on our environment. However, it is not possible for a few, isolated groups to achieve their aim of cleaning the environment. The entire population has to be made aware of this danger to their very survival. The media comes into the picture here. They can help by shouldering the responsibility of informing and educating the people, making them environmentally conscious. The media enjoy the confidence of their audiences. Therefore, they are the best agencies to contact the masses and convince them of the urgency of these matters. They can involve everyone in the community to participate and contribute to a successful environment movement. Environment friendly experiments can be popularised through the media.

Q8. How the Media Promotes Environment Issues?

Ans. Unless man leans lo control his greed, his actions will destroy the earth itself. Clean environment is no longer just a matter of good health, it is the key to our very survival on earth. The mass media have played an important role in spreading this awareness. Till the late 1960s, little thought was given to the need to protect our environment. Even the word 'Ecology' was absent from many dictionaries. Today we are familiar with such words due to the actions of men and women who have used the mass media to spread this awareness about the environment.

One of the finest examples of how the mass media have shaped society's responses to the environment is Rachel Carson's book 'Silent Spring' published in 1962. 'Silent Spring' is a mass medium, a book that reached millions not only in the U.S. but all over the globe. Thus, it was able to influence many fields such as law, government, agriculture, economics and education. The publication or 'Silent Spring' galvanised people into action. Works such as 'Silent Spring, help shape the environment movement through their influence on society. They highlight the various environmental issues and help generate a public debate over them. In this way the media focus our attention on issues which may otherwise escape our attention.

Such articles generate debates and force us to think on all aspects of a particular problem. In the process, the truth is laid bare before the public. Another vital function which the mass media perform is to draw our attention to men and women who have made important contributions to the cause of the environment. It is in this way that the society comes to know, who the heroes of the environmental movements are and thus supports them. In our own country, the media have done well in reporting on issues and persons. It is through the media that we come to know about the contribution of environmentalists. We thus know of Dr. R. H. Richharia, our leading rice expert, who had the courage to resist the international conspiracy to spread objectionable and susceptible rice material all over India. Through investigative journalism the mass media help reveal matters of vital public interest, that are at many times concealed by relevant departments or institutions.

A study of the American Environment Movement reveals how the mass media has contributed to the growth of the movement by highlighting its activity. In 1969 the tragic Santa Barbara oil spills created an alarm in the US. Almost 3.25 million gallons of oil were dumped over eight hundred square miles of water and shoreline. The mass media responded to the tragedy by talking about it. People in California could see with their own eyes the suffocating oil spills along a one hundred mile stretch of coastline. This led to the first wave of grassroots activity on the West Coast. But the mass media took the event to the doorsteps of the entire American nation and even beyond. People reacted to pictures such as those published in "Life" magazine showing thousands of birds, animals and fish smothered by oil. The mass media focussed on the health of the American people and the planet earth. It brought reports to the people showing babies in Manhatten and Chicago breathing air so dirty that the particles showed up on their white clothes. Then in 1970 the Lake Eire caught fire due to another environmental accident. The coverage of all these events by the mass media no doubt led to the crystallisation of the American Environment Movement.

Q9. "Environmentalists take Advantage of the Media". Explain.

Ans. To reach large number of people, mass media are a powerful means for environmentalists.

TV affects its audience most profoundly because it has the capacity to show people events and things, which otherwise they may not be in a position to see. Thus, any action of the environmentalists which is caught by the camera is viewed by millions over the TV screen. Therefore, the environmentalists indulge in activities that can attract the attention of the mass media. The more dramatic the activity and the more controversial it is, more are the chances of it bang covered by the mass media and thus one can get more publicity out of the exposure. Keeping this basic law in mind the environmentalists have learnt to use the media as a strong weapon in their hand .In their fight for environment protection. Such activists indulge in dramatic activity in order to attract attention. 'The friends of the wolf' a group of environmental activists in Canada tried the following strategy to save wolves from being killed in a government sponsored hunt. Three of their members two young women and a man dropped Into the middle of the sponsored hunt in British Columbia by floating down In parachutes in cold weather. The media immediately took up the event and thereafter the government had to suspend the hunt to avoid a confrontation.

Q10. What are the drawbacks of media?

Ans. The media can play a very important and helpful role. The disadvantages of the media include a risk of inaccurate reporting and a loss of privacy. Sometimes, in a rush to be the first to break a story, the media puts out incorrect or inaccurate information.

It is a drawback of the mass media that they select only those events which are likely to evoke interest and captivate audiences. On the other hand, they ignore events which may be very beneficial to the society though they are not perceived attractive enough. Thus, constructive work of a serious nature is many times ignored, while activities of a destructive nature, which attract immediate attention, get coverage on the mass media more often. Another drawback of the mass media is what is called the corruptive influence of the mass media. Consider an advertisement of cigarettes. These depict themes related to conservation of wildlife. Some of these may depict situations such as the rescue of a helpless fawn. But what does rescuing a fawn have to do with smoking. In order to promote their product the producers of the ad want to link in their viewers minds, qualities such as gallantry, courage and kindness to animals, with the manly puffing of a cigarette. Further, you can guess why the cigarette company pays for such ads. Because it knows that a large number of people watch these advertisements. They also know that themes such as wildlife are popular. On the other hand, authorities permit such ads because they know the people will like them and thus will remain tuned in to their programmes. Therefore, you can note that popularity is the main concern and the fact that cigarette smoking is injurious to health, is ignored by all.

Q11. How various interest-groups approach the same environment issue?

Or

While reporting environment, do you think media is sometimes biased towards the interest groups of the society? Explain.

[June-2019, Q.No.-6]

Ans. Experts have pointed out that environmentalists must equate their message about the environmental crises to one of human need. A crisis is felt by each one of us because it affects our daily lives is no other single factor does. To help develop such a realisation, the various myths being cultivated by the powerful elites, through the media, need to be exposed. Thus, there has to come into existence a mass medium which is different. One which is an alternative to the various types of propaganda being dished out. This should be a mass medium which exhibits a sense of responsibility towards the general well-being of the society, aid the environment in particular.

In this direction, the most important step is to understand how the powerful elites are using the mass media to exploit the environment. To achieve this they have adopted the following strategies:

- to spread the notion that the fears of the environmental crises are an exaggeration,
- to lay the blame on the public for not-supporting measures which would have reduced environmental destruction,

- to propagate the notion that every human action involves some kind of environmental degradation thus, it is natural for environmental degradation to occur due to development, and
- science and technology will provide a solution to all the environmental problems and thus, there is no need to worry on this account.

A good example of how this strategy has been applied in India, is the much talked about Green Revolution. The powerful international interests that wanted to maintain their technological superiority and provide a market for their chemical fertilisers and pesticides, worked through their contacts in our country to build up the myth, of a green revolution. Indians fell prey to the myth because of the wide media coverage given to chemical applications on crops. But now the ill effects are becoming clear. The 'green revolution' has led to vast areas of land becoming unsuitable for cultivation due to the heavy use of chemical fertilisers. The green revolution has also become a threat to the native gene pool of crops. Thus, the various varieties of crops that were found in nature have been replaced by a single type.

Q12. What do you mean by consumerism? Explain the rights of buyers and sellers.

Ans. Consumerism is the idea that increasing consumption of goods and services purchased in the market is always a desirable goal and that a person's wellbeing and happiness depends fundamentally on obtaining consumer goods and material possessions.

The protection of the purchaser's interests is termed 'consumerism'. This is practiced by the government through legislation. Committed persons in society may form consumer organisations for this purpose. Suppose you buy a matchbox in which every other matchstick fails to light on striking. Then, your right to expect the matches to conform to standards is not met. Though it may appear an insignificant matter, it is not in the purchaser's interests. The government and voluntary agencies have to involve the general public in the consumer movement. This they do by informing the people about the quality that they can expect, when they buy any item. These agencies also keep a close watch on the market for sub-standard goods and services.

The Rights of Buyers and Sellers are empowered with rights that govern their transactions. Traditionally, the balance was tilted in the seller's favour. Now, due to greater consumer awareness, equal if not more power and rights exist within the buyer's reach. A few of the traditional rights of both sellers and buyers are enumerated here.

The traditional sellers' rights include:

- The right to introduce any product in any size and style, provided it is not hazardous to personal health or safety or, if it is, to introduce or with proper warnings and controls.
- The right to price the product at any level, provided there is no discrimination among similar classes of buyers.
- The right to spend any amount to promote the product, provided it is not defined as unfair competition.
- The right to formulate any product message, provided it is not misleading or dishonest in content or execution.
- The right to introduce any buying incentive schemes they wish.

The traditional buyers' rights include:

- The right not to buy a product that is offered for sale.
- The right to expect the product lo be safe.
- The right to expect the product 10 be what it claims to be.

Comparing these rights, many believe that the balance of power lies on the sellers, side. It is true that the buyer can refuse to buy any product. But it is generally felt that the buyer is really without sufficient information, education, and protection to make wise decisions in the face of hard sell strategies. Consumer activists therefore suggest the following additional consumer rights.

- the right to be adequately informed about the more important aspects of the product.
- thc right to bc protcctcd against questionable producers and marketing practices. The right to influence products and marketing practices in directions that will enhance the 'quality of life'.

The proposals related to additional consumer protection include:

- the strengthening of the position of consumers in cases of business.
- the demand for more safety to be designed into products.

- the issuing of greater powers to existing governmental agencies.

The proposals relating to quality of life consideration include:

- regulating the ingredients that go Into certain products and packaging.
- reducing the level of advertising and promotional "noise".
- creating consumer representation on company boards to introduce consumer welfare considerations in business decision making.

Q13. Explain the origin of consumerism.

Ans. In the West: In western countries, consumer emerged after they reached a level of affluence which is characteristic of post-industrial society. There was adequate production and distribution of essential as well as luxury products. In these circumstances, the objectives of consumer were:

- to seek more information about the merits of competing products and services, and
- to represent the collective views of consumers in order to influence producers.

As a result of the consumer movement in the West, greater awareness prevailed regarding the claims made by producers about their products. Besides, consumers closely examined alternative goods and services. They sought accurate information and assurances about new and sophisticated products. Ralph Nadar was a pioneering consumer activist. In the United States of America He disciplined many American companies into obeying government regulations.

In India: The reasons for the origin of consumerism in India are quite different. They are :

- the shortage of essential commodities and inflation during early 1973-74, which gave a fillip to the consumer movement. The consumers were confronted with shortages, adulteration and black market prices.
- the lack of high standards in technology and advertising which prevents a range of alternative products and claims from flooding the market. It is largely been a seller's market of shortages and high prices, although there are exceptions.

- possession of lesser disposable finances and time when compared to consumers in the West.

Q14. Explain consumer protection laws.

Ans. Consumer protection is the practice of safeguarding buyers of goods and services, and the public, against unfair practices in the marketplace. Consumer protection measures are often established by law. Such laws are intended to prevent businesses from engaging in fraud or specified unfair practices in order to gain an advantage over competitors or to mislead consumers. They may also provide additional protection for the general public which may be impacted by a product (or its production) even when they are not the direct purchaser or consumer of that product.

The following are some of the laws that deal with consumer protection and consumer rights:

(1) Different Laws for Consumer Protection

(i) Protection of Consumers under the Code of Civil Procedures, 1908.

(ii) The Sale of Goods Act, 1930.

(iii) The Agricultural Produce (Grading and Marketing) Act. 1937.

(iv) The drugs and magic remedies (Objectionable Advertisements) Act, 1954.

(v) The Prevention of Food Adulteration Act,1954.

(vi) The Essential Commodities Act, 1955.

(vii) The Protect1011 of Civil Rights Act, 1955

(viii)The Trade and Merchandise Marks Act, 1958.

(ix) The Export (Quality Control & Inspection) Act, 1963.

(x) Protection of Consumers under the Code of Criminal Procedure, 1973.

(xi) The Water (Prevention& Control of Pollution) Act, 1974.

(xii) The Standards of Weights and Measures Act, 1976.

(xiii)The Prevention of Black marketing & Maintenance of Supplies of Essential Commodities Act, 1980.

(xiv)The Air (Prevention and control of Pollution) Act, 1981.

(xv) The Bureau of Indian Standards Act, 1986.

(xvi)The Environment (Protection) Act, 1986.

(xvii)Consumer Protection Act. 1980.

(2) Consumer Protection Act, 1986: The act confers the following rights on the consumer:

(i) right to be protected against the marketing of goods hazardous to life and property.

(ii) right to be informed about the quality, quantity, potency, purity, standard, and price of goods in order to be protected against unfair trade practices

(iii) the right to be heard and to be assured that the consumers interests will receive due consideration at appropriate forums

(iv) the right to be assured, wherever possible, access to a variety or goods at competitive prices.

(v) the right to seek redressal against unfair trade practices or unscrupulous exploitation or consumers.

(vi) the right to consumer education.

Unfair Trade Practices: The term "unfair trade practice" broadly refers to :

(i) any misleading advertisement or false representation

(ii) bargain sales.

(iii) bait and switch sales

(iv) offer of gifts or prizes without eventually honouring the promises.

(v) conduct of promotional contests which are subject to certain exceptions.

(vi) unfair practices such as supplying goods that do not conform to prescribed standards.

(vii) hoarding or even the destruction of goods

(viii)refusal to sell goods or make them available for sale.

Q15. Explain the code of self- regulation in advertising.

Or

"Self-regulation by, media is the best regulation." Comment.

[June-2019, Q.No.-9]

Or

"Advertising is a powerful means to influence brand choice". Do you agree with the statement? Substantiate your answer.

[Dec-2019, Q.No.-6]

Ans. A code of Self-Regulation in Advertising, formulated by the

Advertising Standards Council of India (a body of advertisers and advertising agencies) in December 1983, lays down that advertisements should be honest, truthful, fair, responsible and not offensive.

According to the council, the objective of the code is:

- to ensure the truthfulness and honesty of representations and claims by advertisements and to safeguard against misleading advertisements;
- to ensure that advertisers observe fairness in competition so that the consumer's right to be informed on choices available in the market place and the canons of generally accepted competitive behaviour in business, are both observed;
- to safeguard against indiscriminate use of advertising for the promotion of products which are hazardous to society, and
- to ensure that advertisements do not offend generally accepted standards of public decency.

Q16. Explain the role of consumer organisations.

Ans. The consumers' organisations play a significant role in eliminating the evils of adulteration, hoarding, black- marketing, and under-weight selling. Whenever there is an unnecessary rise in the prices of certain things, the consumers' organisation raise a voice of protest against it.

(1) Accelerating Consumer Awareness/Educating Consumers: The first priority of a consumer organisation is to accelerate consumer awareness towards their rights. To accomplish this task following efforts are made:

(i) To publish brochures, journals and monographs.

(ii) To arrange conferences, seminars and workshops.

(iii) To educate consumers to help themselves.

(iv) To provide special education to women about consumerism.

(v) To encourage to follow desirable consumption standards.

(2) Product Rating: To help consumers choose from a range of products, some of these agencies even carry out tests on the products and report their findings. In the United Kingdom, magazines like 'Handyman Which' and 'Money Which' publish these findings exclusively. The Consumer Guidance Society of India too brings out a journal on similar lines.

(3) Liaison with the Government and Producers: The task of consumer organisations is cut out for them. They need to present the consumer's case to the government and to producers. The government looks after the process of smooth distribution of essential commodities. Therefore, consumer right activists approach the government to sort out problems of consumers in these matters. When industry makes a reasonable profit and grows, the process turns out to be favourable to the consumer too. It is only a growing and profitable business that can undertake steps necessary to meet the aspirations of its consumers, Factors like quality production, distribution, and investment in R & D, become secondary to survival for any unprofitable business. This cannot benefit the customer in any way.

Q17. Explain the concept of human rights.

Ans. Human rights are rights inherent to all human beings, regardless of gender, nationality, place of residency, sex, ethnicity, religion, color or and other categorisation. Thus, human rights are non-discriminatory, meaning that all human beings are entitled to them and cannot be excluded from them. Of course, while all human beings are entitled to human rights, not all human beings experience them equally throughout the world. Many governments and individuals ignore human rights and grossly exploit other human beings.

The present concept of human rights took shape in the late 18th century. The American Declaration of Independence in the Virginia Bill of Rights of 1776, the French Declaration of the Rights of Man and the Citizen and the American Bill of Rights were among the first quarters of nations to include human rights.

U.N. Declaration of Human Rights: The United Nations, Universal Declaration of Human Rights was adopted on 10th December 1948. It is the only official document of its kind, worldwide, till date. It proclaims economic, social and cultural rights in addition to political and civil rights and freedoms for the people of this world. These rights are considered the foundation of freedom, justice and peace in the world.

The preamble to the Declaration quite rightly points out that contempt for human rights has resulted in barbarous acts. These have outraged the conscience of mankind. It further proclaims that the freedom of speech and belief and freedom from fear and want are the highest aspirations of the common people. The United Nations reaffirmed their faith in the worth of human beings and the equal rights for men and women, through this declaration. They expressed a determination to promote social progress and better standards of living. for the large majority of the people. The Declaration states that all are equal before the law and are entitled to equal protection from it. The right to work, to free choice of employment. to just and favourable conditions of work and to protection against unemployment are personal rights granted by this declaration. The right of employees to form and join trade unions for the protection of their interests is the freedom they possess; IS a group. There is a special emphasis on the basic provision of the right to a standard of living adequate for the health and well being of individuals and their families. It includes access to food, clothing, housing, medical care and necessary social service. It is important to note that these rights are universally accepted. However, a successful mechanism to enforce them is yet to be developed. This is the reason for the large scale inequalities along with peoples of the world. Even within a country, inequalities based on caste, class; wealth, creed and gender exist. This is quite apparent in India where the structure of the society is based on a rigid cast system.

Q18. Explain human rights in Indian context.

Ans. Human rights in India is an issue complicated by the country's large size and population, widespread poverty, lack of proper education, as well as its diverse culture, despite its status as the world's largest sovereign, secular, democratic republic. The Constitution of India provides for Fundamental rights, which include freedom of religion. Clauses also provide for freedom of speech, as well as separation of executive and judiciary and freedom of movement within the country and abroad. The country also has an independent judiciary as well as bodies to look into issues of human rights.

The 2016 report of Human Rights Watch accepts the above-mentioned facilities but goes to state that India has "serious human rights concerns. Civil society groups face harassment and government critics face intimidation and lawsuits. Free speech has come under attack both from the state and by interest groups. Muslim and Christian minorities accuse authorities of not doing enough to protect their rights. The government is yet to repeal laws that grant public officials and security forces immunity from prosecution for abuses.

There are various agencies to monitor the human rights situation in different ways. The government is answerable to the state legislatures and the Parliament The presence of opposition parties is crucial to any healthy democracy. The opposition remains watchful and, when necessary, pulls up the government for its misdeeds or for the lack of initiative. Human rights organisations arid institutions working in this area, ensure that all sections of society gel their due rights. None is first among equals before the law. The mass media, coupled with these agencies and organisations can ensure the implementation of the Human rights enshrined In our constitution. The mass media can generate a strong public opinion about human rights issues. They can support the people and institutions working in this area. They can very well provide a strong network of communication to help propagate an informed opinion about human rights. The media can at once be mediator and leader, of the people by championing the cause of human rights. However, they must take precautionary steps in order not to be misled by some vested interests.

Q19. Explain the role of mass media.

Ans. The role of media in human rights is very important. A person should be well informed of the human rights issue before taking the topic to the people.

It is never possible to bring about favourable changes with just one stroke of the pen, or an infrequent programme or two. The poor would continue to live conditions of insufficient food, clothing and shelter and the rich would maintain a luxurious life style, even after this information were conveyed to them. Instead, what could be hoped for, is to make every citizen aware and conscious of their rights and to enable them to recognize a violation of human rights, when they come across such events in daily life. The news media can then bring about and maintain a healthy Human Rights Movement.

Traditional folk media like Tamasha and Burakatha, which communicate with their audiences at a more personal level can inform and influence them. For this, the communicators themselves must be knowledgeable about human rights issues. They can narrate instances of violation of human rights and relate them to the daily lives of the masses.

The Electronic Media: The electronic media transcend the barriers of literacy and enjoy a widespread reach. However, these plus points are not taken advantage of, to the full extent possible. Government ownership and lopsided programming are their major drawbacks. Firstly, informative programmes need to be based on healthy debates and discussions and not on propaganda and image-building exercises of leaders, & is usually the case. Secondly, only sensitive personnel can put across a point clearly and in a wholesome perspective. Such sensitivity cannot be found in people who equate a career in communication to a mere 'job'. It needs more than a mechanical approach to sensitise the public to the egalitarian goals of equality, freedom and justice. It is not in the fitness of things to project an image that "all is well with the world", when there are serious violations of human rights in different walks of life. The electronic media have the potential to act as information disseminators. To fulfil this role, they have to provide complete information to the audience. The piecemeal treatment of issues causes both confusion and harm. Neither is an informed public opinion generated by taking this approach.

The Print Media: Quite naturally, the print media have literate audiences. Big industrial houses have a monopoly over ownership of the press. This fact determines the nature of relations between the press and the government. Newspapers openly take sides for or against the policies of the government. For instance, the 'Indian Express' has 21 penchant for writing against the government in power. The nexus between the print media and the government is strengthened by a sort of 'give and take' policy. The press receives government patronage in terms of supply of newsprint and advertisements in return for favourable write-ups about the government. In such a situation, violations of human rights by the state are unlikely to surface. The same is the case if the rights of workers in the press Industry itself were to be violated.

The regional language press obtains scarce attention in competition with major national dailies. Few individuals attempt to start a newspaper or magazine at a local level, because of the large amounts of investment and technology involved. Consequently, the first casualties are the freedom of the press and the standard of journalism.

Feedback is the breakfast of Champions.

Ken Blanchard

You can Help other students.
"Inform any error or mistake in this book."

We and Universe
will reward you for Your Kind act.

Email at : feedback@gullybaba.com
or
WhatsApp on 9350849407

4 INTERNATIONAL COMMUNICATION

INTRODUCTION

Production and distribution of information has become a very complicated and competitive business. There are hundreds of agencies, which are in the business of supplying information to the mass media. These agencies are referred to as news agencies, feature services, and syndicates. The news agencies supply material to suit the print as well as the audio-visual media. In India we have the Press Trust of India and United News of India. BBC and VOA are good examples of international broadcasting. Information is linked with trade, economy, aid and relations among nations. Information flows freely to the underdeveloped countries from developed countries. There is a tremendous amount of imbalance in the information flow from and to the Third World countries. Given this scenario in the international information flows, the non-developed countries demanded that these imbalances in the information flow be corrected, and measures be taken to redress their grievances. The need now is to consolidate the achievements, and step up efforts so that, at least, in the coming decades, there is equality and balance among nations in all aspects of communication. So, any alternative information distribution system should call for a radical redefinition of several concepts, like "freedom of information", "access to information", etc. Given the decreasing bargaining power of the poorer nations, there is a greater possibility in the near future, of information and news flows turning more favorable to the rich and developed nations. Hence, it is essential for the developing countries to evolve their own response to the unfolding global changes.

Q1. Describe in detail the nature and functions of news agencies.

Ans. A news agency is an organisation that gathers news reports and sells them to subscribing news organisations, such as newspapers, magazines and radio and television broadcasters. A news agency may also be referred to as a wire service, newswire, or news service.

The media depend on material supplied by the news agencies mainly out of economic necessity. To have wide coverage, which the readers of any standard publication expect the newspaper has to maintain a costly network of staff reporters, correspondents, offices, bureaus and telecommunication equipment on a world-wide scale. But we are aware that many newspapers of our country, and for that matter, most of the newspapers of the Third World countries cannot even maintain a proper network of correspondents within their own country of operation. Only a few newspapers can afford this investment and recurring expenditure. For a majority of the news media, the news agencies are a major source of news supply. The subscribers to the news agencies include the daily newspapers, the radio and TV stations, the local newspapers, magazines, offices and institutions, particularly government agencies, large corporations in the private and public sector, banks, and commercial establishments.

The proliferation of the news agencies began with World War II, especially after many countries gained their independence. When you compare the contents of the newspapers, you will notice, especially in international news that there is a high degree of similarity. The reason is that almost all the newspapers subscribe to common sources for their foreign material. Any one of the several global or, as they are better known, transnational news agencies can be regarded as a common source. In our country, the two leading news agencies, the United Neb of India (UNI) and the Press Trust of India (PTI), have a contractual agreement with these global news agencies. Certain studies reveal that about 1200 news agencies are operating in the world, However, the five large transnational agencies, Renters, Agence France Presse (AFP) Sovetskavo Soyusa (TASS) put out around 35 million words per day, and claim to provide nine-tenths of the total foreign news output of the world media. Also, there are other major agencies, like the Deutsche Press Agenteur (DPA) of Germany, Kyodo of Japan, and Xinhua of China.

One reason for us to focus on a few agencies (AP, UPI, Reuters, AFP, and TASS), in this unit, is that, as described earlier, their output is quantitatively very high. Further, they have been able to maintain their dominance with their vast scale of operations. Consequently, other agencies are effectively blocked from setting up rival services. Another reason is that the history of these news agencies is closely linked to the consolidation of colonial empires in the nineteenth century. For a very long time, the communication of information depended on the physical movement of people. You must be knowing that in the good old days the kings and emperors would have messengers, who would move from one place to another carrying messages on hone back. Eventually, submarine cables along sea routes and cables across land outpaced the physical movement of information through people. The news agencies utilised this system, and thereby established a wide network. It was in this context that the first news agency was founded by a Frenchman, Charles Havas, in 1835. Havas is historically very significant because he laid the foundation for the French (AFP), UK (Reuters) and German (DPA) news agencies. We shall now briefly look into the background of the five global news agencies.

Q2. Describe global news agencies.

Ans. Thomson Reuters, originally Reuters, Canadian information services company. Founded as the Reuters news agency in Great Britain in 1851, it became one of the leading newswire services in the world. Its headquarters are in Toronto.

The agency was established by Paul Julius Reuter, a former bank clerk who in 1847 became a partner in Reuter and Stargardt, a Berlin book-publishing firm. The firm distributed radical pamphlets at the beginning of the Revolutions of 1848, which may have brought official scrutiny on Reuter. Later that year he left for Paris, where he worked for a short time as a translator. In 1849 he initiated a prototype news service, using electric telegraphy as well as carrier pigeons in his network. Upon moving to England, he launched Reuter's Telegram Company two years later. The company was concerned with commercial news service at its inception and had headquarters in London serving banks, brokerage houses, and leading business firms.

Reuters supplies news to its media clients such as other news agencies, newspapers, the radio and television stations under various categories. These include general and economic news, news pictures and

TV news. Information is collected from around 160 exchanges and markets. It has a network of about 1200 journalists, photographers and cameramen, who operate through 100 bureaus in different parts of the world. Under its present form of ownership, a public company, Reuters claims that it can ensure that no particular interest group or faction can have control. Consequently, it hopes to preserve its integrity and freedom from bias. These claims are questioned by many Third World countries.

The Associated Press (AP) is an American non-profit news agency headquartered in New York City. Founded in 1846, it operates as a cooperative, unincorporated association. Its members are U.S. newspapers and broadcasters. AP news reports, distributed to its members and customers, are produced in English, Spanish and Arabic. The AP has earned 54 Pulitzer Prizes, including 32 for photography, since the award was established in 1917.

The AP has been tracking vote counts in U.S. elections since 1848, including national, state and local races down to the legislative level in all 50 states, along with key ballot measures. The AP collects and verifies returns in every county, parish, city and town across the U.S., and declares winners in over 5,000 contests.

By 2016, news collected by the AP was published and republished by more than 1,300 newspapers and broadcasters. The AP operates 248 news bureaus in 99 countries. It also operates the AP Radio Network, which provides newscasts twice hourly for broadcast and satellite radio and television stations. Many newspapers and broadcasters outside the United States are AP subscribers, paying a fee to use AP material without being contributing members of the cooperative. As part of their cooperative agreement with the AP, most member news organisations grant automatic permission for the AP to distribute their local news reports. The AP traditionally employed the "inverted pyramid" formula for writing, a method that enables news outlets to edit a story to fit its available publication area without losing the story's essentials, although in 2007, then-AP President Tom Curley called the practice "dead."

AP with its wide communications network using advanced technology has bureaus in more than 100 countries. Its 5000 plus correspondents and a host of stringers cater to about 1300 newspapers, 3400 broadcasters in the US and 1000 private subscribers.

United Press International (UPI) is an international news agency whose newswires, photo, news film, and audio services provided news material to thousands of newspapers, magazines, radio and television stations for most of the 20th century. At its peak, it had more than 6,000 media subscribers. Since the first of several sales and staff cutbacks in 1982, and the 1999 sale of its broadcast client list to its main US rival, the Associated Press, UPI has concentrated on smaller information-market niches. United Press International (UPI), American-based news agency, one of the largest proprietary wire services in the world. It was created in 1958 upon the merger of the United Press (UP; 1907) with the International News Service (INS). UPI and its precursor agencies pioneered in some key areas of news coverage, including the wired transmission of news photographs in 1925.

A major set back occurred in 1918. It sent a report that the war had ended, and later it turned out to be false. Its credibility suffered. Slowly, it recovered, and it is said that the UPA news reports "were dynamic and, like the Scripps papers, conformed to the needs and interests of the mass of readers". On the contrary, AP was looking down upon human interest stories and was still concerned with straight reporting. The backgrounds and personal accounts enabled UPA to score over AP. Parallel to these developments emerged a third press association, the International News Service (INS). INS was founded to use the existing leased wire facilities of the Hearst newspapers. It faced severe competition from AP. To offset this pressure, INS began to concentrate in a few centres only, and focus on good writers who could do extensive and well researched pieces. The newspapers never looked towards INS as a major source, but subscribed to the service for well written stories and major news beats. Although it was emerging as a major service, by 1956, it decided to merge with AP, in 1958, to form the second major global news agency in the US, the United Press International. UP1 claims to have an overseas electronic strength of about 200 journalists overseas distributed in Europe, Latin America, Asia and Australia. Unlike the AP and Reuters, LPI has not diversified much into specialised economic services. However, its broadcast related services are considered to be a specialisation.

Agence France Presse: AFP is a post-war successor to the Agence Havas, founded in 1835. The French newspapers come the agency by having the maximum representation on its board of directors. Although AFP is described as an unsubsidised autonomous organisation, in effect, the French government and various agencies under its control subscribed to AFP, and provided good support Through a wide network of bureaus within the country and abroad, AFP is regarded as one of the major global news agencies. AFP is important in another sense, and that is its history. As already mentioned, it was a successor to Havas. It grew out of a translation agency, which sold the translations to various newspapers. Two of its employees, Paul Julius Reuter and Bernard Wolff, started news agencies in the UK and Germany. All the three countries, France, the UK and Germany were leading European empires. Accordingly, the news agencies, Havas, Reuters and Wolff took control of large segments of the world for news coverage. Many writers argue that this laid the foundation for a close relationship between communication and empire-building. AFP has more than 10,000 newspapers and 70 agencies as to its subscribers. Its operations are in more than 150 countries with a network of 110 foreign bureaus. Its daily output is about 3,350,000 words contributed by 170 full-time correspondents and more than 500 stringers. om AP. To offset this pressure, INS began to concentrate in a few centres only, and focus on good writers who could do extensive and well-researched pieces. The newspapers never looked towards INS as a major source but subscribed to the service for well-written stories and major news beats. Although it was emerging as a major service, by 1956, it decided to merge with AP, in 1958, to form the second major global news agency in the US, the United Press International. UP1 claims to have an overseas electronic strength of about 200 journalists overseas distributed in Europe, Latin America, Asia and Australia. Unlike the AP and Reuters, LPI has not diversified much into specialised economic services. However, its broadcast related services are considered to be a specialisation.

Telegrafnoi Agentsvo Sovetskavo Soyusa (TASS): Often it was customary to exclude TASS from the "globals" as the transnational news agencies are called. However, in terms of influence, impact and coverage, TASS was in no way different from the other agencies. With the changes in the erstwhile USSR, the relevance of understanding TASS as one of the globals may have minimised, but recent changes and the formation of ITAR and Russia was given it a new outlook and depth of penetration, in terms of coverage. However, from a historical perspective, it is necessary to understand TASS. This global news agency began on the foundation of what was known as the Petrograd Telegraph Agency, in 1917. When it stuffed functioning under the new regime after the socialist revolution, it was considered as a major publicity organ dealing with the country's economic life. The domestic news operations were coordinated under the Chief Department of Home Information. It supplied news through a network of correspondents in all regional and territorial centres. Officially, its role was to supply balanced information, objectively reflecting the economic life of all republics, territories and regions by taking into account their economic potential and peculiarities. According to one source, TASS has approximately 20,000 subscribe to both domestic and foreign. The work of TASS was complemented by another information agency, Novosti Press Agency (APN). This was established in 1961 by the Union of Soviet Journalists, the Union of Soviet writers and a few other organisations. The objective was to promote information for peace and friendship among nations. TASS, in comparison to APN, claimed to be the single state system of information, while APN became the organ for public organisations.

Q3. What do you mean by International Broadcasting.

Ans. International broadcasting is broadcasting that is deliberately aimed at a foreign, rather than a domestic, audience. It usually is broadcast by means of long wave, medium wave, or (more usually) shortwave radio, but in recent years has also used direct satellite broadcasting and the internet as means of reaching audiences.

Although radio and television programs do travel outside national borders, in many cases reception by foreigners is accidental. However, for purposes of propaganda, transmitting religious beliefs, keeping in touch with colonies or expatriates, education, improving trade, increasing national prestige, or promoting tourism and goodwill, broadcasting services have operated external services since the 1920s.

Broadcasting beyond national boundaries has been a parallel activity for many countries along with the development of their domestic systems. The external services or international broadcasting by different countries are aimed at serving their people settled in other countries, and also to propagate the policies of the respective countries. Since broadcasting developed in the colonial era, the colonial powers sought through the Radio to build stronger ties between themselves and the peoples they ruled around the world. England and Holland were the first to think along these lines. However, it was Adolf Hitler of Germany who saw the potential use of the domestic and international radio for purposes of propaganda. During World War 1, the international short wave radio as a weapon to conquer people's minds.

British Broadcasting Corporation (BBC): Authors interested in broadcasting suggest that the British were adept in using, international radio. Broadcasting in the United Kingdom has undergone phenomenal changes since then. Yet, the British Broadcasting Corporation (BBC) occupies a central place in terms of its international reach and influence. We in India, have always been fascinated by the "BBC World Service". Now through satellites, a few million homes have the benefit of watching the BBC-TV. BBC is a central institution in the broadcasting system of the United Kingdom. In 1922, several radio manufacturers established the British Broadcasting Company. In 1926, it became a public corporation. It currently operates two national colour television networks (BBC-1 and BBC-2) and four national radio networks, 1,2,3 and 4, and several local radio stations. BBC draws international news from its correspondents. BBC's international character is based on the fact that it is at the forefront of the United Kingdom's international broadcasting operations. The operations are not commercial, and finance is provided in the form of a special grant approved by the British-Parliament. Consequently, the government is directly involved in the international broadcasting system. The External Services Department has responsibility for international broadcasting. Within this department, there are subunits which oversee the operation of programs covering different parts of the world. Thus, there is the European Service, the Overseas Service comprising the African, Arabic, Eastern, Far Eastern and Latin American Services. The World Service provides a range of entertainment and informational programming in English 24 hours a day around the world. According to BBC, the objectives of the External Services are to give unbiased news, to reflect the British opinion and to project the British life and culture and developments in science and industry. Available statistics indicate that the external services broadcast each week about 700 hours of programmes in 17 European languages and 21 non-European languages plus English. It claims that about 75 million adult listeners tune into it at least once a week. This audience size does not reflect the full impact of the BBC, as it is an important source of information for the influential community in different countries. For example, in India, it is very common to hear people say that they had heard the news first on the BBC. Further, during the internal emergency (1975-77), the BBC was criticised heavily by the

Government for its "biased" coverage.

Voice of America (VOA): Another country which has systematically used and realised the potential of the radio and television in international affairs is the United States of America. This realisation is traced to the year 1941 when the USA entered World War II. Given the private nature of broadcasting within the country, the Government did not have any broadcasting outlet of its own. However, the private companies had short wave transmitters, which the Government procured on a lease basis. Two government organisations, the Office of War Information and the Council of Inter- American Affairs were responsible for international broadcasts during the period. The programming titled Voice of America was done on a contractual basis by the private US broadcast corporations. After the war ended, VOA would have closed down, had it not been for the dawn of a cold war between the USA and the erstwhile USSR. Therefore, when the United States Information Agency (USIA) was established, in 1953, VOA became one of' its divisions. At a time when many countries did not have their local stations, VOA and BBC could command huge audience bases. When local stations developed, VOA directed its programmes to the politically curious.

Although VOA has grown and expanded considerably, its influence is debatable. Critics argue that the disapproval of the US* politics in many lands had its impact on VOA's operation and its influence. On many fronts, the Vietnam War, and the Gulf Conflict, VOA has been criticised. Apart from VOA, there is a separate television service of the USIA. Here, the emphasis is on promoting the programmes to be telecast on the local stations. Through satellite networking, it also arranges for direct telecasts. VOA broadcasts in 35 languages and puts out about 800 hours of programmes per week. It may be necessary for the US in India to know that the location of the VOA transmitter in Sri Lanka is a rallying point in our foreign policy pronouncements. In the future, these operations may change. For example, through satellite dishes, it is possible to receive direct telecasts. The popularity of CNN news during the gulf conflict is a good example. VOA and BBC are not the only international broadcasting organisations. Every other country in varying degrees does a certain amount of international broadcasting.

VISNEWS: It is related to the international broadcasting service in the supply of audio-visual material similar to the news agency services that have been discussed earlier. One of the major suppliers of visuals for TV networks around the world is VISNEWS.

VISNEWS is a London based international TV news film agency owned by a consortium of the BBC, Reuters, Canadian Broadcasting Corporation, Australian Broadcasting Corporation, and New Zealand TV. The service has over 170 subscribers in 95 countries and is the largest contributor to the daily Eurovision exchange programme.

Q4. Explain in brief UNESCO and ITU.

Ans. The role of international organisations is helping to set the international agenda, mediating political bargaining, providing a place for political initiatives and acting as catalysts for the coalition- formation. They facilitate cooperation and coordination among member nations.

United Nations Educational Scientific and Cultural Organisation (UNESCO): UNESCO is a specialised agency of the United Nations (UN) aimed at promoting world peace and security through international cooperation in education, the sciences, and culture. It has 193 member states and 11 associate members, as well as partners in the nongovernmental, intergovernmental, and private sector. Headquartered in Paris, France, UNESCO has 53 regional field offices and 199 national commissions that facilitate its global mandate.

In November 1945, representatives of forty-four nations met in "war-scarred" London in a quest for peace. The then Prime Minister of UK, Clement Atlee, and the American Poet, Archibald Macleish together coined the striking message: "Since wars begin in the minds of men, it is in the minds of men that the defences of peace must be constructed" This is in the forefront of UNESCO's constitution, and is also the key to UNESCO's activities, from its early days. UNESCO has been concerned both with the development of the media and also the problems such development brings with it. UNESCO is always alert to find how the media and development work in the Third World countries. For UNESCO, it is necessary to understand that the purpose of the organisation is to contribute to peace and security by promoting collaboration among the nations through education, science and culture. To realise this purpose, UNESCO has sought to "collaborate in the work of advancing mutual knowledge and understanding of peoples, through all means of mass communications, and to that end recommend such international agreements as may be necessary to promote the free flow of ideas by word and image". Realising that, qualified personnel were needed to man the media in the 'decolonised' parts of the world, which try constitute the bulk of the so-called Third World countries, it published its first study on the professional training of journalists. Based on this study, it set up training institutions in different parts of the world. UNESCO also realised that only a few of the developing countries had any newspapers and more so, news agencies, which could provide the media with the news. Early efforts in this direction are the Union of African News Agencies and the organisations of Asian News Agencies, in 1963. It has established training centres to give training to the news agency journalists. In India, the Indian Institute of Mass Communication (IIMC), New Delhi, offers a specialised course in news agency journalism. UNESCO has played a key role in the introduction and expansion of mass media, especially television, in many developing countries. Over the years, UNESCO's activities in communication have changed from what has been described as an "Adhoc" attempt to develop mass communication media to integrated programmes m which the communication package is regarded as a whole approach. Efforts in this direction are the preparation of national models and establishing documentation infrastructures. The role of UNESCO became more significant i n the context of the demand by many developing countries for a better deal from the developed countries. The first step in this direction was a call for the establishment The first step in this direction was a call for the establishment of a New International Economic Order (NIEO). It was realised that the NIEO cannot be independent of socio-cultural factors, apart from political and economic factors. The Fifth Conference of the Heads of State or Government of the non-aligned Countries (1976) and the 19th General Conference of UNESCO crystalised the idea of a New International Information and Communication Order (NIICO). The report of the International Commission for the study of communication problems, "Many Voices One World", better known as the Macbride report is a landmark document in this direction.

ITU: The International Telecommunication Union (ITU; French: Union Internationale des Télécommunications or UIT), is a specialised agency of the United Nations responsible for all matters related to information and communication technologies. Established in 1865 as the International Telegraph Union (French: Union Télégraphique Internationale), it is one of the oldest international organisations in operation. The ITU was initially aimed at helping connect telegraphic networks between countries, with its mandate consistently broadening with the advent of new communications technologies; it adopted its current name in 1934 to reflect its expanded responsibilities over radio and the telephone. On 15 November 1947, the ITU entered into an agreement with the newly created United Nations to become a specialised agency within the UN system, which formally entered into force on 1 January 1949.

The main functions of ITU are to: allocate frequencies to avoid interference; co-ordinate efforts to eliminate interference; foster the creation of telecommunication in newly independent or developing countries; promote safety measures, and undertake studies in the area of telecommunications. In the context of NWICO, ITU has assumed a different role and perception. On the one hand, it has to promote telecommunications development taking into account a host of factors - political, technological and economical. On the other hand, it has to manage a vital resource, the electromagnetic spectrum. It is in these two areas that* there is an increased dialogue and conflict between the developed and the developing countries. For example, the use of satellites is related to the availability of parking slots in the orbit. While many developed ' countries are ready to park their satellites, the developing countries argue that certain slots should be reserved for them to use it at a time when they can either develop or afford a satellite. The debate is a continuous one. Although ITU performs a very technical function, it is an important agency that is central to communication development.

Q5. What do you mean by Inter- Governmental Agencies?

Ans. The term intergovernmental organisation (IGO) refers to an entity created by treaty, involving two or more nations, to work in good faith, on issues of common interest. In the absence of a treaty an IGO does not exist in the legal sense.

IPDC: The IPDC is the only multilateral forum in the UN system designed to mobilise the international community to discuss and promote media development in developing countries. The Programme not only provides support for media projects but also seeks an accord to secure a healthy environment for the growth of free and pluralistic media in developing countries.

Over the last 40 years, following the decisions and guidelines of the

Intergovernmental Council and its Bureau, the IPDC has focused its projects on the most urgent priorities in communication development all around the world.

The efforts of the IPDC have had an important impact on a broad range of fields covering, among others, the promotion of media independence and pluralism, development of community media, radio and television organisations, modernisation of national and regional news agencies, and training of media professionals. IPDC has mobilised some US$ 120 million for over 2000 projects in more than 140 developing countries and countries in transition.

IPDC is co-ordinated by an intergovernmental council, composed of 35 member states, elected by and responsible to the General Conference of UNESCO on the basis of equitable geographical distribution and applying the principle of rotation. The task of this council is to implement the objectives of IPDC. IPDC council seeks to avoid conflict and work on consensus. Funds received through contributions shall also be administered by the council. The basis of allocation of funds by the council to various projects is determined through criteria that is defined by the council from time to time. Over the years. IPDC has played a significant role. An analysis of its funding for various projects in one year indicates that the IPDC assistance is provided under various heads; audio-visual media, printed press, training and research, news agencies, media education, computerisation and data banks, and book production.

Q6. What do you mean by information as wealth and power?

Ans. Information is associated with data, as data represent values attributed to parameters, and information is data in context and with meaning attached. Information also relates to knowledge, as knowledge signifies understanding of an abstract or concrete concept.

In terms of communication, information is expressed either as the content of a message or through direct or indirect observation. That which is perceived can be construed as a message in its own right, and in that sense, information is always conveyed as the content of a message.

Information can be encoded into various forms for transmission and interpretation (for example, information may be encoded into a sequence of signs, or transmitted via a signal). It can also be encrypted for safe storage and communication.

Information-rich West: The countries of Western Europe and North

America, since the 15th century, undertook various expeditions to know the world beyond the seas. The traders undertook long voyages to expand their business. Kings conquered other countries to enlarge their kingdoms and bring new nations under their rule. All these activities helped the European countries to gather information, constantly, to create knowledge for their own economical and political benefits. Take the example of Great Britain. There was a time when it was said, "The sun never sets on the British Empire". It was information alone that helped the British to exploit its colonies for centuries. As science progressed, the instruments to gather information became more sophisticated. As a result, the West always remained years ahead of the underdeveloped countries in information technology.

The Renters of Britain, Agence France Presse (AFP) of France, the United Press International (UPI), Associated Press (AP) of the USA, and ITAR-TASS of Russia, have complex networks to gather information and feed the world with hundreds of stories every day. These global agencies make money through subscriptions and are sustained by multinational corporations of newspapers, the governments and the corporate sector, with perhaps the sole exception of ITAR-TASS. Apart from the news agencies, the western countries have information agencies to gather facts or data and disseminate the same after proper packaging.

Information Poverty in the Underdeveloped Countries: An opposite state of information network is in existence in the underdeveloped countries. The flow of information within some of the developing or underdeveloped nations, particularly in Africa, is so weak that it takes days for the information to travel from the place of origin to other comers of the country. Even the telephone systems are old and dilapidated. The existing news agencies in most of the countries of the Third World have a very weak network and work with the old technology leftover from colonial times. Only a few countries like India, Bangladesh, Malaysia, Indonesia, Brazil, Nigeria and Kenya can afford news agencies and are slowly getting into the information business. Above all, qualified and competent people shun away from this business of information. Thus, both in terms of hardware and software, the situation is deplorable. Most of the underdeveloped countries are in utter poverty. One important point has to be made here. Some of the underdeveloped countries have made some progress m the field of information, but this progress, when compared to the existing situation in the developed countries, looks so small and inadequate. Thus, unlike the developed world, the underdeveloped countries have failed to use the information to create knowledge, which, as and when applied would produce wealth and power. Hence, as far as information is concerned, the West has information in abundance, while the underdeveloped countries, caught in the vicious cycle of poverty and illiteracy, have not capitalised on information technology.

Q7. Explain historical dimension of international information.

Ans. Advantageous Position of the First World Countries: Most of the European countries started expanding beyond their shores from the 15th century, for various reasons, political, economic and religious. They reached Africa, Asia and Latin America, the raw materials of which attracted more and more traders from the West. But once these countries were politically subjugated, their control over economic affairs was absolute. Thus, western countries maximised their economic gains through the control of political machinery.

The nations - Britain, France, Spain, Portugal, Netherlands - which built empires in Asia, Africa and Latin America invested all their profit, extracted from these colonies in their own countries. Therefore, the capital formation was at a tremendous pace and in unimaginable quantity. Whereas in these colonies, there was no investment, the capital formation was absolutely nil. This continued for centuries. In The meantime, because of unprecedented capital formation, at the centre, the colonial powers ventured into new areas for economic gains. Education, health, research, technology, and other areas got improved in these countries because of the economical advantages that these countries acquired by colonisation. Such influence could come about due to the strong economic base of the West, built from the wealth of the colonies. Information played a crucial role for them to hold on to their advantageous position. They used a huge amount of capital to set up a complex and efficient information network. Today's major communication instruments, such as the telephone, telefax, and satellite, etc., exist because of the efforts put in for centuries. These efforts were largely undisturbed and without any resistance. As a result, these countries have radio stations with high-powered transmission facilities, like the Voice of America, British Broadcasting Corporation, DeutchWelle and Radio Japan. The television networks are hooked up with a satellite to cater to the whole world, like

CNN, NBC, BBC and Star TV. The five giant news agencies of the United Press International, Associated Press, Agence France Presse, ITAR-TASS and Reuters have totally wired the world. These historical developments of the infrastructure have given the West a position of dominance and pre-eminence.

The Closed Situation in Socialist Countries: The fall of the Czar and the Bolshevik Revolution in Russia, in 1917, has radically changed the equations among nations. Armed with the Communist Manifesto of Karl Marx, I the revolutionaries, led by Lenin, ushered in a new era for h working class - the proletariat in Russia The state-owned everything, private property was abolished and I everything belonged to the commune to be used for the common good. However, the communist regimes established in Eastern Europe before and after World War I1 converted their secluded world. China followed Russia, and under the leadership of Mao-ze-Dong, I captured power and ushered in communism. The communist countries centralised all their activities, especially information, which was put under heavy censorship. The secret service agencies, such as KGB, were created to neutralise any noncommunist effort to sabotage the effort of the communist regimes. This was largely on the lines of the CIA and the McCarthyist forces, which launched an anti-communist drive in the USA during the early '50s. The communication and information networks in socialist countries were all-pervading. The news agencies like TASS, the radio networks like Radio Moscow and Radio Beijing were there to gather information for the decision-makers, and used by them to disseminate any information which they thought would promote communism. These communication networks were also used to propagate communist ideologies and counter the propaganda of the Western capitalist countries. Thus, during the 'cold war' period, 'information' and 'disinformation' had become synonymous in the light of the activities of these two giant polarised camps. The communist countries used their information campaigns to have an effective hold on their population as well as to influence the newly independent countries of the Third World. The whole period of the cold war could be tanned as the era of 'information war'. To win this war, both the West as well as the socialist countries invested a lot of money to develop their information propagating instruments. The latest developments in satellite technology were a result of this race to win the information war. The dramatic collapse of the East European countries, and the disintegration of the 'Soviet Union' in 1989-91, brought an end to this ever-increasing Won of the undeclared information war. But, then, one can only look back and say that it helped communication technology and the process of the dissemination of information leap-frogged decades as never before.

The Third World: After World War II, there was a dramatic change in the political composition of nations. Most of the colonised countries became independent, some through violent means, the rest peacefully. The First and Second Worlds were waging an undeclared war, and the newly independent countries were caught in between. The Third World had no proper infrastructure, no industry, no food, no medicine and, above all, no capital but a huge population to feed, clothe and provide shelter for. Disease, hunger, and death were their only companions. The leaders of these newly independent countries had very bitter experiences of exploitation by the colonial powers. They were aware of the danger of going back to these imperialist powers for aid to feed their people, to build infrastructure, to set up industries, etc. On the other hand, they were suspicious about the communist countries. Thus, the newly independent countries were in a precarious situation. They had to ask for aid from their former colonial masters, on their terms and conditions, or play into the hands of socialists and communist countries. Faced with this choice a few countries succumbed to the temptation and joined one or the other group. Regional and international alliances, like SEATO, NATO, WARSAW PACT, and COMECON, came into being. However, a few of the Third World countries decided to form their group called the Non-aligned Movement (NAM). India, dong with Egypt, Yugoslavia (formerly) and Ghana, played a very important role in this movement. The NAM countries, while remaining neutral between the two camps, could gain from both for their economic development. Sincere efforts were made by many NAM countries to develop their information networks. India stands out in this endeavour. It had the Press Trust of India (PTI) and United News of India - two major national news agencies. Not many countries were as fortunate. Their political instability, corruption, economic backwardness, ethnic conflicts, religious wars, foreign debt servicing, etc., hindered growth in the field of information and communication.

Q8. What is the concept of free flow of information?

Ans. The "Free Flow of Information" is a concept linked to the basic human right of freedom of speech and opinion. Everyone has the right to freedom of opinion and expression. This right includes freedom to hold opinion without interference and to see, receive and impart information and ideas through any medium regardless of any frontiers. The term means that any person or persons and/or any organisation or organisations can own and operate any media or information agency, gather any information, and disseminate the same, if they so desire, to any target audience, wherever and whenever they want. Further, the ownership of the media or information agencies should be restricted to a certain category, the gathering of the news, facts and information, and their dissemination should be unhindered. The concept is basic to the history, culture and life of the liberal capitalist Western society. Any challenge to this concept is rejected on grounds that it is undemocratic, inhuman, and even uncivilised. The philosophy of free flow resulted in the consolidation of the centres of information gathering and dissemination in the Western countries. The Socialist and the Third World countries could see that they were not being represented objectively in the Western media. Significant happenings in their countries were paid scant attention, and whenever done, those were only half-truths coloured by Western perceptions. Thus, a very awkward situation developed in the world due to the concept of the 'free flow' and operations of the international networks in the Third World countries.

Concept of Imbalance: The Third World countries, knowing fully well that the information disseminated from these agencies docs not represent all the truths about them, consume them, as they do not have any other sources. This imbalance is, in terms of volume of information, flowing into the Third World countries, when compared to the volume of information flowing out from them. There is imbalance also in terms of ownership and control, in terms of areas and items covered by these agencies. The Third World countries argue that their struggle to make the living conditions better for the teeming millions go unnoticed by these transnational news agencies. They are mostly misreported, and never appreciated, whereas the shortcomings, weaknesses; and failures get prominence in the Western media. They argue, that volumes of information about the merit, comfort, and goodness of their lifestyle, their produce and irrelevant items are fed to them through the Western media channels. Therefore, an information imbalance, biased against the Third World, and tilted towards the West, exists today.

Origin of the Concept of Imbalance: The communication specialists thought that when the socio-economic development projects were aided by communication inputs, such as the radio and television programmes, the undeveloped and traditional societies could be speedily transformed into the developed, dynamic, and modem societies. They thought that what the West achieved in centuries, the Third World could achieve the same in a matter of decades if aided by the mass media. Two eminent Western scholars were at the forefront to suggest this theory. Daniel Lenier in his famous book The Passing of Traditional Society: Modernising the Middle East, described that a small isolated village called Balgat in Turkey was changing as it came in contact with Ankara. And, he elaborated on how this small village could be transformed through the help of the mass media, particularly the radio. It could increase the rate of literacy, promote good health, and create new aspirations for the people too) work for higher earnings. So also Wilbur Schramm, in 1964, wrote Mass Media and National Development for the UNESCO, in which he described two families, one in Central Atria, the Ife Family and another in South Asia, the Bvani family. He described the development and growth of the Bvani family and how their aspirations could be raised through the mass media, especially the radio.

Development during this time meant the creation of a stable and sustainable democratic nation, and replacing the authoritarian regimes with democratic governments, and implementing projects and programmes to uplift the living conditions of the common man in society. It was assumed that the mass media, used for these purposes, would transform the developing societies into modern, vibrant, and stable societies. However, a decade later, it was found that despite all these efforts, most of the social problems remained unsolved. Instead, more problems were created as a result of the rising aspirations and expectations of the millions. Thus, political instability, poverty, illiteracy, unemployment and corruption became the salient features of a developing society. These negative developments were heavily focused by the Western media organisations. Some other experts and scholars pointed out that the focus of the development communication was very limited. It focused on persons without taking the social, political and economic situations into consideration. And thus, development communication did not bring about the expected results. On the contrary, it created more problems than solutions.

The Imbalance Debate: Together with Herbert Schiller, there were quite a few who took up the issue of the international news flow in various international fora. Schiller's early work spoke about the Dependency Model, .a Marxist approach to analyse the international information flow and the state of imbalance emanating from it. His dependency theories stated that the imperial powers of the West would like to have economic centres in their own country, and control all the economic activities in the periphery through the modem instruments of mass communication. Mustapha Masmoudi, Secret. of Information of Tunisia, and later on its ambassador to the United Nations, attacked the West with such venom and strength that his counterparts of the West were baffled and puzzled. He argued in various international fora on the following lines:

- The Western countries had monopolised the flow of international information. They decided on what news items/information must be consumed by the people of the developing countries.
- Through these international information networks, the West had retained their hedonic power over the Third World Even after decades of independence, they still dominate and rule over (indirectly) the Third World countries.
- The information set up in the international arena reflects a very strong political, economic and cultural colonialism opposed to the aspirations of the people of the developing countries.
- The mass media have replaced the armies of the colonial powers in this era.

The outcome of these arguments was to have a New World Economic and Information Order (NWEIO). This shall be dealt with elaborately in the next unit. Now, the points of the NWEIO, voiced by its representatives, were the following:

- The West must transfer wealth to the Third World to set up suitable information centres.
- There should be a balance in the flow of information from the Thud World to the First World.

- The advanced technology should be transferred to the developing states from the west.
- Development News should be promoted, and it should include everything from literacy and health to agriculture practices, from family planning to the environment.
- Political News, such as Protocol News, should be given prominence. These news items would depict pictures of good harmonious relations among nations.
- The communication networks among the Third World countries should be developed.

Q9. Explain the contemporary trends in media and international relations.

Ans. After the end of the cold war, Developments in the US, on the domestic front, and their balance of payment position, and, in Russia, on the political and economic front, have dampened the dominant outlook presented at the beginning of the current decade. The fight to influence the developing countries has ended. Most of the communist countries are now desperately trying to get aid and cooperation possible far restructuring their own countries. In India, the new economic policy has been formulated and is being implemented now. The economy is opening up for the participation of foreign companies. But this is not shaping up as planned, and already there are misgivings, internally, and fears expressed about the stability of the country by the foreign investors. Ironically, in such a fluid situation, the experts from both the West and Third World countries, like India, are discussing such issues -like environment protection, AIDS, NPT, etc., to salvage mankind from being wiped off from the face of the earth. This contradiction needs to be resolved before any meaningful effort could be made to reverse the trend in the Third World.

In the Third World, there is a sharp decline in autocratic and dictatorial rules. The military-led regimes in South American, African and Asian countries have gone back to the barracks. The popular governments are taking over be rams of running their countries. There is marked visibility of people at the grassroots level participating in government. What we are witnessing is a phase of maturity in the former colonies of the imperialist powers. The media of the Third World does realise this change in the national and international political and economical spheres.

Exchanges of TV programmes, special educational programmes, are quite frequent, though the flow is still imbalanced because more western programmes are seen on the TV screens of the Third World countries. In the recently concluded International Film Festival in New Delhi, the quality of the movies from the West left much to be desired. This revealed the status the West still gives to such an important country like India. Thus, despite the large-scale changes brought about by technology, imbalance persists in the media and coverage of the developed West vis-a-vis the developing countries of the Third World.

Q10. What were the debates and developments?

Ans. A major consequence of the monopoly of news and information flow was the 'one-way flow' of news and information, generally from the developed to the developing world. The nature of the flow, as the eminent journalist, D. R. Mankekar, describes, was "imbalanced, iniquitous, sometimes even biased and West-oriented, impervious" to the needs of the developing world. As this was detrimental to their interests in more than one way, the developing nations attacked the free flow concept and its concomitant - the transnational media empires. For they believed that the monopolistic media empires of the west created and sustained distorted pictures of the world that were far away from reality. These developing nations campaigned a 'new order' in the field of international information and communication, which would facilitate a 'free and balanced flow' of information capable of breaking through the stereotypes created and nurtured for over 50 years by the Western media empires. The new order, they maintained, would create a new international information climate that would foster a closer and better understanding among nations and individuals.

The ensuing debates in the international forum lasted for nearly a decade, beginning from the early 1970s. This period is reckoned as a watershed in the history of international communication. Indeed, it was a period of many significant developments. First, the developing nations, under the Non-aligned umbrella resolved to address themselves to the international communication issues. Second, to offset the ill effects of One-way flow. alternative means of exchange for meaningful and relevant news and information among the non-aligned nations took roots. The most important step in this direction was the hunching of the Non-aligned News Agencies Pool, in 1975, followed by the establishment of many other news distribution systems at national, regional and international levels. 'Third, notable revisions also occurred in the concepts and thoughts governing international Communication. The 'free-flow' concept was amended to 'free- and balanced flow', when a declaration on the role of the media in the promotion of international understanding and peace (generally referred to as the mass media development) was approved by the UNESCO, in 1978. Commensurately, the corollary doctrine, the 'the right to know' was transformed into 'the right to communicate'. Fourth the new order debates led to the setting up of an International Commission for the study of communication problems better known as the "MacBride Commission", whose report was accepted by UNESCO, in 1980. Fifth, resolution 4.19 of the 21 UNESCO General Assembly, held in 1981, outlined the basic character and content of the 'new order'. Sixth, in the same year, the International Programme for the Development of Communication (IPDC) was set up to assist the development of the communication infrastructure in the developing countries.

Nomenclature: Nomenclatureis a system of names or terms, or the rules for forming these terms in a particular field of arts or sciences. The principles of naming vary from the relatively informal conventions of everyday speech to the internationally agreed principles, rules and recommendations that govern the formation and use of the specialist terms used in scientific and any other disciplines.

The non-aligned nations coined the phrase, New International Information Order (NIIO), The MacBride Commission broadened the schism by substituting the term 'world' for 'international' and incorporating 'communication' along with 'information'. Since then the phrase the 'New World Information and Communication Order (NWICO), or its shortened form the NWICO, has been widely used. The nomenclature NWICO is used. Also note that the terminologies of the Third World and Developing World, and the First World and Developed World are used interchangeably.

News Flow Controversies: Most of the scholars me the origin of the demand for new international information and communication order to the cold war era, and the emergence of the Third World consciousness in the 1950s. Some of the contentions and problems aired now by the mind World that a handful of media-rich countries determined the nature and kind of news and information flow between nations, that the international news and information business operations benefitted only the media-rich nations, and that such operations are detrimental to the interest of media poor countries, were as fundamental to the media controversies of the early decades of the 20th century as to the 1970s new order debates. Ever since the birth of the international news agencies, the monopolistic practices in the international news business have been in evidence. Fit, their home regions came under their monopoly. Subsequently, through the cartel agreements of the 1870s the European agencies extended their monopoly in regions under the influence of their home countries. But, in several aspects, the relations among the cartel members was unequal. In terms of territory, Britain's Reuters had an area as vast as the British empire, spread across Africa, Asia, America, Australia and Europe, covering almost one-month of the globe. In teams of influence too, it was the Reuters that mattered. Its extensive network supported by Britain's control of the world's transoceanic cables, helped it to become the most powerful agency in The monopoly of the international news business by the Evan triumvirate was not to continue unchallenged in the fast-changing political climate of the 20th century. Much of the resistance to the European agencies came from the US, which, by the end of World War I, was switching its role from an international debtor to that of a major creditor. Its increasing control over transoceanic cables and an expanding media at home provided the much-needed muscle power to its agencies to challenge the European cartel. Many in the US had come to realise the advantage that would accrue out of the international news business. At this juncture, the AP synthesised its commercial interest with the diplomatic interest of the US by stressing how the Reuters, through European news cartels, controlled all foreign news sent into the US, and all American news to the rest of the world, and how such practices promoted Britain's interests while affecting the interests of both the US and the AP. Finally, the AP ceded in the cartel, in 1934, and independently went to the business of news collection and distribution around the world, heralding the impending domination of the US in the coming years.

Free Flow Ideas: A major factor that helped the growth of US agencies was the wireless transmission technology, perfected at home, which reversed the world communication imbalance to the overall advantage of the American interest. Yet another factor responsible for the growth of the US communication network abroad was a general reduction in the US of the advantages that world communication control bestowed on foreign trade and commerce. , Following such realisations, ideas on the unrestricted flow of communication between nations began to crystallise m the US. Fit, the American Society of Newspaper Editors adopted a resolution urging the political parties to support freedom of information and unrestricted flow of communication throughout the world. Subsequently, with the Democrats and Republicans adopting these aims, the free flow doctrine became an integral part of the US political ideology and foreign policy. The UN too came under its influence. Its declaration on Freedom of Information (United Nations General Assembly Resolution 59.1), issued m 1946, made the first reference to the free flow of information: "All states should proclaim policies under which the free flow of information, within countries and across frontiers, will be protected. The right to sell and transmit information should be insured in order to enable the public to ascertain facts and appraise events."

Q11. What was the demand for NWICO?

Ans. The following overlapping and mutually complementing factors are at the base of the demand for a new order in the field of information:

- The emergence of new nations following the dissolution of the colonial empires after World War II.
- The asymmetrical economic relationship between the new nations and the Western industrialised nations which, while strengthening the latters' wealth and power, perpetuated the new nations' dependency, not merely economic but political and cultural as well.
- The coming together of the new nations under the umbrella of non-alignment in the wake of aggressive bloc-building by the US and the USSR.
- The new nations' realisation that their under-development was related to their dependence on rich nations followed by a firm resolve to assertive actions to correct imbalances in world trade and commerce and cultural exchanges.
- Their gaining in strength in international organisations, such as the UN and the UNESCO.

Four stages can easily be identified in the history of the NWICO. The first stage, from 1973-76, marked the evolution of a new order. The second stage, from 1976-79, saw the accumulation of data and empirical evidence to give credence to the new order demand. The third stage followed the publication of the MacBride report in 1980. The fourth stage is the period following the adoption of the NWICO Resolution in the UNESCO, and the setting up of IPDC.

Generally, the evolution of the new order concept is credited to the Non-aligned Movement WAM). However, the attribution of the UNESCO cannot be ignored But in the early years the UNESCO also played the willing tool role to the hilt It propagated the doctrine of F the free flow of information because of its domination by the West. But, with the continual t addition of newly-freed status to the UN in the '60s and '70s, the UNESCO underwent changes not only in its structural makeup, but also in its concerns, policies, and programmes v in several areas including communication.

The Algiers Summit: From the viewpoint of the NWICO history, the Algiers Summit of the non-aligned countries, held in 1973, is a major landmark, for it was here that communication concerns were addressed directly in more than one paper in the context of their economic development programmes. Around this time, the UNESCO was in the midst of a crisis, which had arisen out of a resolution moved by the Soviet Union, with the support of the Third World, at the 17th General Conference of the UNESCO, held in the 1970s, calling upon the UNESCO Director-General to prepare a declaration on the Fundamental Principles Governing the Use of the Mass Media, with a view to strengthening of peace and understanding, and combating War, Propaganda, Racialism and Apartheid, hereafter referred to as the Mass Media Declaration (MMD). This resolution was to influence significantly the tone and tenor of the information flow debates. While it provided an opportunity for the Third World to bring forth its views on the free-flow concept and its consequences of inadequacies and imbalances in international news and information flow, it opened a new chapter in the East-West struggle, which was to last until 1978. To avoid the further deepening of the crisis, the 19th UNESCO General Conference postponed the consideration of the draft on the MMD to its next session to be held in 1978 and adopted a resolution inviting the Director-General to undertake a review of the problems of communication in modem society. In response to this, the Director-General constituted a 16-member Commission for the study of Communication Problems under the chairmanship of Sean MacBride, a distinguished diplomat and winner of both Nobel Peace Prize and Lenin Peace Prize. The Commission's work, a major landmark in international communication history, is one of the major outcomes of the NWICO debates. The 20th UNESCO general conference, held in 1978, was marked by a spirit of compromise. The behind the scene negotiations for reconciliation bore fruit: the new MMD text now retitled as 'Declaration on Fundamental Principles Governing the Contribution of the Mass Media in Strengthening Peace and International Understanding and in Combating war Propaganda, Racialism and Apartheid' was approved. The six-year-long controversy finally ended. The new text satisfied all.

Q12. Elaborate the MacBride report.

Ans. Many Voices One World, also known as the MacBride report, was a written in 1980 by United Nations Educational Scientific and Cultural Organisation UNESCO which reports to its International Commission for the Study of Communication Problems. Based in Paris, France, the main goal of UNESCO is to end the world's poverty through collaboration and the exchange of scientific, cultural objects and education between nations. The book MacBride report was named after peace and human rights activist, Irish, Nobel laureate Seán MacBride. As of January 2019, The Organisation has 193 members and 11 Associate Members. Task include analyse communication problems in modern societies, particularly relating to mass media and news, consider the emergence of new technologies, and to suggest a kind of communication order (New World Information and Communication Order) to diminish these problems to further peace and human development.

Among the problems the report identified were concentration of the media, commercialisation of the media, and unequal access to information and communication. The commission called for democratisation of communication and strengthening of national media to avoid dependence on external sources, among others. Subsequently, Internet-based technologies considered in the work of the Commission, served as a means for furthering MacBride's visions. In the 1970's and 80's, major changes in media and communication were happening thanks to the MacBride report. They promoted policies directed at the liberalisation of the Telecommunication market, monopoly powers as well as the comparative advantage, or dominance, of broadcasting and newspaper companies.

While the report had strong international support, it was condemned by the United States and the United Kingdom as an attack on the freedom of the press, and both countries withdrew from UNESCO in protest in 1984 and 1985, respectively (and later rejoined in 2003 and 1997, respectively).

The Commission viewed communication as a basic social need of individuals, communities and nations with an inseparable relationship with politics, as an economic force, with a decisive influence on development, as an educational tool, and as an integral part of the culture. Thus, any change in any aspect of communication within and among nations would call for changes in all these aspects of communications. The issues of imbalances and inequalities were fully recognised by the Commission. Attributing the imbalance to a historical process of unequal growth of nations and complex political, economic and socio-cultural realities, the Commission supported the view that 'free flow' was nothing more than 'one way free flow', and also that the principle, on which it was based, should be restated to guarantee 'free and balanced flow'. It identified imbalances in flow between the developed and developing countries. The Commission took note of imbalances in the flow of news through the instruments of technology. The developed world, which has access to modern technology, has had both positive and negative influence on the Political, economic, socio-cultural fabric of their home regions and other nations, which have come to depend on them for their news and information needs. A positive influence was that they extended facilities for cultural development. Their negative effect was the promotion of alien values across cultural frontiers. Thus, they were practising cultural imperialism through their control of communication infrastructure, news circulation, cultural products, educational software, books, films, equipment, and training. The Commission concluded that the primary factor in imbalance and inequalities was an economic one. It said that the one way-flow in communication is a reflection of the world's dominant political and economic structures, which tend to maintain or reinforce the dependence of the poor countries on the rich nations.

The MacBride Commission's recommendations and the resolution given above are normative only; nothing in these is binding on the member countries. In brief, the establishment of the NWICO depended upon five major factors: (1) the will of the developed and developing countries to bring about changes in all areas of communication within their respective regions; (2) cooperation between the developed and developing nations for removing all obstacles to a two-way and balanced flow of news and information among nations; (3) sharing of communication resources, including technologies, for countering monopoly of the international news flow by a few; (4) cooperation among the developing countries to correct imbalances with their regions by increasing horizontal flows and (5) cooperation between the media-rich and media-poor for mobilisation of resources to strengthen communication infrastructure in the latter's region.

Q13. Describe the character and content of NWICO.

Ans. The New World Information and Communication Order (NWICO) was a political proposal concerning media and communication issues emerging from international debates in the late 1970s. The term originated in discussions within the Non-Aligned Movement (NAM), following the proposal for a "new international economic order," and became the expression of the aspirations of many countries in the global south to democratise the international communication system and rebalance information flows worldwide. UNESCO played a major role in fostering the debate until the early 1980s, especially through the work of an independent commission chaired by Irish diplomat Sean MacBride (→ UNESCO).

The exhaustive MacBride report, though not a definitive work, received bouquets and brickbats in good measures from scholars around the world. Notwithstanding several shortcomings and deficiencies, the 21st General Conference of the UNESCO, held in 1981, accepted it, aid unanimously adopted Resolution 4.19, outlining the basic character and content of the NWICO. Paragraph 14 of the Resolution is reproduced here in its entirety as it contains the essence of the resolution:

The General conference considers that:

(1) this new world information and communication order could be based among other consideration,

- (i) on the elimination of the imbalance and inequalities which characterise the present situation).
- (ii) elimination of the negative effect of certain monopolies, public or private; and excessive concentrations;

(iii) removal of the Internal and external obstacles to a free flow and wider and better-balanced dissemination of information and ideas;

(iv) the plurality of sources and channels of information;

(v) the freedom of the press and information;

(vi) the freedom of journalism and all professionals in the communication media, a freedom inseparable from responsibility;

(vii) the capabilities of the developing countries to achieve the improvement of their situations, notably by providing their equipment, training their personnel, improving their infrastructures and making their information and communication media suitable to their needs and aspiration;

(viii) the sincere will of the developed countries to help them attain these objectives;

(ix) respect for each people's cultural identity, and for each nation to inform the world public about its interests, its aspirations and its social and cultural values;

(x) respect for the right of all peoples to participate in international exchanges of information based on equality, justice and mutual benefits;

(xi) respect for the right of the public, of ethnic and social groups, and individuals to have access to information sources, and to participate actively in the communication process;

(2) the new world information communication order could be based on the fundamental principles of the international law, as laid down in the character of the united nations;

(3) diverse solution to information and communication problems are required, because social, political, cultural and economic problems differ from one country to another, and within a given county, from one group to another.

Q14.What are the problems and prospects of the NWICO?

Ans. Today the evolving goals of the NWICO rest with not just the UNESCO, but a large number of international organisations such as the Organisation for Economic Cooperation and Development (OECD), the International Telecommunications Union (ITU), the IPDC, and the Third World and its organisations for moving the aims of the NWICO to a higher plain. The prospects are not bleak. Some work has already been done. The Third World has demonstrated through Pool that it is serious about increasing news-flow within its region. The IPDC, which commenced work in 1982 has done its best to help develop communication capabilities of the media-poor regions. It needs more resources than are being made available to it. As of January 1986, some 42 member states together pledged a little over the US $10 million to the IPDC special account, and nearly US $4.5 million for funds-in-trust financing by eight member countries. Such monies are not enough to match the growing requirements. Between the second session, in 1982, and the seventh session, held in January 1986, it had allocated the US $9.74 million for some 120 communication projects in the developing countries those included three regional news agency projects - Pan Africa News Agency (PANA), the Agencia Latino Americana De Servicios Especiales do Information (ALASEI), and the Asia-Pacific News Network (ANN)- 14 national news agency projects in Angola, Bangladesh, Cameroon, Madagascar, Malaysia, Maldives, Mongolia, Mozambique, Nicaragua, Senegal, Sierra Leone, Togo, Tunisia and Zanzibar.

These agencies and news exchange arrangements operating within the developing countries, no matter how inadequate they are, indicate that the NWICO has set itself on its evolutionary path. But there is more to be achieved. Imbalances in the flow of news and information at the international level have not ceased to exist. The one-way flow is still very much in evidence. Most of the news flowing through the transnational agencies into the developing regions concerns the developing world. The agencies continue to view the developing world's events and issues from their perspectives. As a result, news everywhere is seen through the prisms of the West, the developed world. Western media giants continue to set the world's news agenda. This was amply demonstrated during the Gulf War. The Western-centric bias in international news flow becomes apparent even for a casual observer - the developments in the West, both in the US and Europe, including the erstwhile 'Soviet Union, dominate news everywhere, but the problems of the poor regions of Africa, Asia, and Latin America receive only a token coverage. The problems arising out of a unipolar world (if it exists), particularly in the context of the Developing World economies, are being treated as matters of less significance.

Viewed against these realities, the need for the establishment of the

NWICO cannot be undermined. In fact, in the unipolar world of today, the relevance of the NWICO stands enhanced. The geopolitical and economic uncertainties arising out of the developments in Europe and the erstwhile Soviet Union, and the strife between the new republics are bound to affect progress in realising the goals of the NIEO as well as the NWICO. Therefore, a renewed effort has to be made by both the developing and the developed world.

Q15. What measures should be adopted by the developed and developing countries?

Ans. The developed countries should be more open to redress the ever-increasing asymmetrical economic relations between them and the poor countries. This calls for hastening the pace for the establishment of the NIEO as it is linked with the WCO. As funds for the media development in the developing world are scarce, the developed world could, either through bilateral agreements or through organisation such as IPDC, make available more resources for communication specific projects in the poor regions of the world.

In the area of technology transfer and sharing, more action is needed. New technologies need to be viewed as resources for the benefit of mankind, and not as a new tool for exploitation of the disadvantaged. The media in the developed world needs to take steps in establishing a balance in the information flow by devoting more space and time to news and issues concerning the developing countries.

The developed countries should join hands with the devel6ping countries in making the telecommunications tariffs more suitable for better use of the existing systems and, thereby, enhance the flow of communication material from the developing to the developed regions. The developing world, on the other hand, needs to formulate communication policies, keeping in view the sweeping changes marking the external as well as their regions. Without clear-cut policies, the media development would get hampered, and this would make the media restrictive in its reach and out of step with the needs and interests of a vast majority of people. In the Third World countries, in particular, the press must make conscious efforts to free itself from the attitudes fostered by the Western news criteria. In this direction, professional organisations and institutions, such as the Asian Mass Communication Research and Information Centre (AMIC), Singapore, the Press Institute of In New

Delhi, the Indian Institute of Mass Communication, New Delhi, and the International Press Institute, just to name a few, can play a significant role by conducting refresher orientation courses for the working journalists. The IPDC can contribute substantially by providing the necessary inputs.

Q16. Explain the advancement of communication technology and the growth of the information systems.

Ans. There was a revolutionary change in technological advancement after the second World War.

The information explosion provided the impetus for this technology to disseminate news and information across national boundaries. The electronic and computer systems have vast potential for information storage, retrieval, and delivery. Naturally, it revolutionised the media in the developed world in Europe, North America, and Japan. With the introduction of the communication satellites in outer space, the TV, and the transistor, the impact of information revolution could be felt in the remotest villages in the Himalayas and the Sahara. The scientific and technological revolution led to the borderless outflow of information to the Third World countries, and the advanced industrialised nations, grasping the scope of this technological advancement, have set up controls over information flows.

The Dominance Syndrome: The countries of North and South are separated by an enormous gap in their respective communication capacities. The developed countries continue to exercise considerable political, economic, and technological control on information flows.

Nearly 80 per cent of the information disseminated in the world originates from five largest transnational news agencies i.e., the AP, UPI, Reuters, AFP and ITAR-TASS. You have already learnt about the extent and significance of the operations of these news agencies, in the earlier units. About 15 great media corporations dominate the production of the radio sets television sets and printing equipment including printing devices, radio, and television communication satellites, paper, inks, and other elements of mass media technological infrastructure, ten of these corporations belong to the United States of America.

The statistical details cited above might have changed to some extent, but one should try to see the truth beyond the facts. These figures are noted to provide you with a feeling of the extent of the disparities that exist, and the dominance of the North in the field of information, thus making the countries in the South dependent on them.

Due to our dependence on the media delivery systems of the West, we also become dependent on the west. To understand this, we shall now discuss the various forms of dominance in the information flow with a couple of concrete examples. You may study, on your own, several such instances in your daily exposure to foreign news.

Example 1: During the British war with Argentina over their claim on the Falklands Islands, several developing countries supported the Argentinian claim, but 'their newspapers were receiving the stories put out by the transnational news agencies, which were biased in favour of Britain. The newspapers in these developing countries could not afford to send their correspondents to cover the Falklands war.

Example 2: The Gulf War provides a classic example of how dependence on the West for news and information can distort the news content of the Third World media.

During the Gulf War, India's language dailies could not cover the war events through their correspondents. Almost all the newspapers depended upon the news originating from the Western news agencies. Interestingly, the usage of words in the news dispatches became a form of psychological warfare during the so-called "Gulf War". To build up the image of the US-led multinational forces, the label 'Allied Forces' was used, a reminder of the Second World War. The Indian dailies published all these news items. The control over news flow in the Indian print media could be shown by citing the example of the news of 600 Iraqi soldiers, buried under the sand by the tanks of the Allied Forces, which was suppressed by the Western media. No Indian newspaper carried the news item.

Q17. Why there's a need for self reliance?

Or

Discuss the need of self reliance in communication flow in developing countries. **[June-2019, Q.No.-7]**

Ans. It's essential for the following reasons:

- To provide the media with a national identity and personality,
- To facilitate the analyses of the world events not from the perspective of the West but the national perspective,

- To foster better understanding among the developing countries, which is far more essential now than ever before,
- To prevent the unwarranted entry of foreign and alien ideas, cultures, and life-styles, that always tend to contribute to shaping public opinion in favour of foreign countries, particularly of the West, and
- To provide an objective account of the news and developments that were considered newsworthy by the indigenous media.

The Role of NAM: The first important step towards achieving some self-reliance in news collection and dissemination was the effort made by some of the non-aligned nations. First, the call for New World Economic Order was articulated from the non-aligned centres as a reflection of the movement's general antipathy to the former colonials. This was evident from the first statement on information endorsed by the fourth summit of the Movement in Algiers, in 1973, and there could be no doubt about such an orientation in the documents on information endorsed by the fifth summit in Colombo, in 1976. Ultimately, it was the New Delhi declaration of NAM which said:

- "The present global information flows are marked with inadequacy and imbalance. The means of communicatory information are concentrated in a few centres. The majority of countries are reduced to be passive recipients of information, which is disseminated from a few centres.
- This situation perpetuates the colonial era of dependence and domination. It confines judgments and decisions on what should be known, and how it should be made known to a few.
- Just as political and economic dependence are legacies of the era of colonialism, so is the case of dependence in the field of information, which, in turn, retards the achievements of political and economic growth.
- In a situation where the means of information are dominated and monopolised by a few, the freedom of information comes to mean the freedom of these few to propagate information in the manner of their choosing and the virtual denial to the rest, and the right to info- and being informed objectively and accurately. The enunciation of the Non-aligned Movement's New Delhi Declaration is perhaps the running thread that it

continues in all the NAM documents on the information. These statements are precisely the t philosophy of the Non-aligned Movement regarding information flows. Its efforts to combat the existing information imbalances emerge from this understanding.

Formation of Non-aligned: News Pool As per the directives of the UNESCO to establish a news pool or consortium of news agencies, the "Pool" of news agencies of the non-aligned countries was formally launched in July 1976, at the New Delhi Conference of Information Ministers and Representatives of the news agencies of the non-aligned countries. According to a statement of the Conference, the objective of the Pool is to expand the mutual exchange of information among the non-aligned countries in a spirit of collective self-reliance. The former Prime Minister of India, the late Mrs. Indira Gandhi, in her address to the Conference, called upon the non-aligned countries to know one another directly, not through the eyes and ears of the Western media.

Besides the creation of optimum possibilities for the exchange of information, the tasks of the Pool, as formulated at its General Conference in Belgrade, in 1979, were mainly a programme for training the journalists working in this service, and also the creation of bilateral regional and multi-national communications systems and their link-up to the overall communication systems of the non-aligned countries. The Conference stressed that the creation of a communication network of the non-aligned countries is one of the main long term aims of the Pool.

Restraints on Growth of the Pool The biggest obstacle to the broad development of information and news exchanges among the non-aligned countries through the Pool have been:

- **Communication Restraints:** Many of the developing countries do not have an extensive and elaborate telecommunication network. For some other countries, high tariffs are major barriers. Hence, it is clear that the development of communication. Systems in the non-aligned countries are imperative to their overall development. It should also be understood that the optimum information exchange also depends on the level of development of communication systems in the individual non-aligned countries. It is worth noting here the statement of the former Director-General of the

UNESCO, Arthur M'Bow, who said: "The creation of the widespread communication system of the non-aligned countries is intrinsically linked to the overall development of these states.

- **News Flow:** According to a study by J. S. Yadava, a few years ago, about 85 per cent of the news items received by PTI from the Pool partners were spiked. The reasons for this were given as delay in news reception, poor quality, low news value, or propaganda material.
- **Lack of Training:** The lack of proper training among the non-aligned journalists and their inability to match the professional standards of the journalists of the transnational news-agencies, are the reasons for the poor quality of material put out by the Non-aligned News Agencies Pool.
- **Political Constraints:** Due to the totalitarian and despotic governments in many non-aligned counties, the news agencies are under the strict control of the governments in these countries. The first casualty of such a solution is the objectivity of the news and information put out by their agencies. For instance, the news agencies in Pakistan or Sri Lanka, which are the partners of the Pool, hardly provide any objective news, either about their news events, issues, and problems, or those of other countries. Even the coverage of the movement for democracy in their own countries lack objectivity and are highly lopsided and biased. Should the Indian news media publish or use these materials, just because they have to foster cooperation and exchange among the non-aligned countries?
- **The Media's Lukewarm Attitude:** The editors of private-owned newspapers in the democratic countries like India, either is not convinced of the need for such inter-regional cooperation or they do not respect the news coverage of several agencies, which are participants of the Pool.

Q18. Explain inter-regional cooperation.

Ans. The essence of any inter-regional cooperation in the field of information is to bring about a new sense of common destiny and unite news agencies operating under different levels of development. The UNESCO played the role of more than a catalyst in fostering inter-regional cooperation in the field of information. The fundamental problem in the inter-regional news networks and cooperation is that the participating news agencies in the networks being, essentially, domestic agencies are geared to serve purely national needs in their news coverage. This has often been quoted as the reason for the non-descript coverage of the Pool News. Another area is about the issue of relevance. Most of them are editorially ill-equipped to produce copy for the consumption of the other agencies in the region. They are mostly irrelevant to each other's needs. Further, in most of the networks, almost all agencies are, in principle, committed to producing a regional file containing news reports and features, specially prepared for the consumption of the readers outside their national frontiers. However, the tendency that persists is to move copy originally written for domestic readership for the network transmission without necessary rewriting. A great deal of information may be missing in such reports for the readers abroad, or much more than necessary is included. For instance, proper designation of a politician in the story, the conversion of local currency into internationally known monetary units, are essential when the story is disseminated abroad. But, criticism of several agencies, which are part of such networks, is that they do not make amendments and changes in the news reports, keeping in view the requirements of the readers abroad.

When we look at the small degree, of success of the Pool and similar such efforts, we see that inadequate facilities and improper planning continue to impede strengthening inter-regional cooperation. Several countries, though involved in such regional bodies articulate their resolve to strengthen cooperation, but hardly take any steps to achieve their goals. Mutual distrust continues to remain a major obstruction, in addition to the allurements dangled before these poor countries by the advanced and developed countries in the shape of aid and help.

For instance, can any meaningful exchange of news or other information be possible between the media of Pakistan and India, when there is a tension between the two countries with both being tempted by the rich Western powers to tilt towards them? Under such conditions and relations that exist among different countries in the same region, any inter-regional cooperation will, at best, prove to be a mechanical exchange of information rather than a media of one country enjoying the confidence and credibility of the media of another. Suppose, the Pakistani news agency, the Associated Press of Pakistan (APP), sends a report on the situation in Sindh, and the Press Trust of India (PTI), as a nodal agency in the inter-regional cooperation among the SAARC nations, disseminates that news report fed by the APP to all Indian newspapers.

Q19. What do you mean by south- south cooperation?

Ans. In this cooperation, a suggestion was made to remedy the situation to develop infrastructures. Elaborate infrastructural facilities, like telecommunication network with reduced tariff structure, proper news-gathering facilities, sharing satellite time, etc., should be developed. The editors have to be convinced of the importance of expanding the news network abroad. For instance, it is ironic that most of the major Indian newspapers are able to afford to have correspondents in Western capitals, but do not have their own men in the neighbouring countries. As a result, the two neighbouring countries have to know each other through the eyes of a biased Western press. This was amply proved between India and Pakistan on the issues of Ayodhya and Kashmir. It has also been suggested that inter-regional cooperation should not confine to just the governmental level, but, such an exchange and cooperation should be encouraged at the media-to-media level, between newspapers, journalists, editors, etc. Efforts are to be intensified to foster mutual confidence by providing easy access at the people-to-people level. All artificial barriers existing in the way of the free movement of the journalists should be bridged. A recent interaction among the SAARC journalists, held at Hyderabad, recommended doing away with visa regulations among the seven South Asian countries. Proper training should be imparted to the journalists in these countries. Finally, while these efforts are going on, what we need to see is that the editors and decision-makers in the different media are "educated" on the need for such a cooperation at the South-South level by removing their firm belief that the "West is the best".

These steps would lead to the establishment of an alternative news and information system suited to the needs of the developing countries and relevant to the conditions existing in these countries.

Q20. Explain alternative news distribution systems.

Ans. Alternative media are media sources that differ from established or dominant types of media (such as mainstream media or mass media) in terms of their content, production, or distribution. Sometimes the term independent media is used as a synonym, referencing independence from large media corporations, but this term is also used to indicate media enjoying freedom of the press and independence from government control. Alternative media does not refer to a specific format and may be inclusive of print, audio, film/video, online/digital and street art, among others. Some examples include the counter-culture zines of the 1960s, ethnic and indigenous media such as the First People's television network in Canada (later rebranded Aboriginal Peoples Television Network), and more recently online open publishing journalism sites such as Indymedia.

In the matter of broadcasting, the Western powers insist upon the "open skies" policy, which they claim to be consistent with the principle of freedom of information. On the face of things, this seems a plausible argument. The metaphor of open skies seems to connote a situation of unfettered information exchange of knowledge flowing freely across the national boundaries. On the contrary, the same Western countries, in a different forum - the multilateral trade negotiations, popularly called GATT (Gend Agreement on Tariff and Trade) - show a complete disinclination towards free trade by imposing heavy tariffs to protect their products. However, they link their intellectual property rights, by using Super 301 against countries like India and China. These developments call for greater unity among the Third World countries to come out of the dependence and dominance in the field of information and promote self-reliance. So, any emergence of alternative information systems should be understood in this changing world scenario and current concept of a "unipolar" world dominated by the West, particularly the USA. The existing world information order provides an opportunity to the richer nations to use the scarce global natural resources, such as the radio and satellite frequency range, and exclude the poor nations from using the same. For instance, the radio frequency range and the geosynchronous orbital slots for parking communication satellites are both natural Western monopolies today. Added to this, an attempt is made through the ongoing GATT talks to impose stronger forms of monopoly control over the content of information flows. Let us also examine what the Third World countries are doing at the global level on the question of providing access to the communications media. The allocations of the radio ' frequency spectrum and geosynchronous orbital slots are done through the instrumentality of the World Administrative Radio Conference (WARC), convened every ten years, by the International Telecommunications Union (ITU). A sub-session of the WARC, held in February 1992, marked a new low m the ability of the Third World to influence the international negotiating agenda in matters relating to the utilisation of me global resources. The Third World underwent a volte-face in the WARC. More than a decade ago, in the WARC 1979 Conference, the Third World made a united bid and could make the West accept the principle of equity in the allocation of the radio frequency spectrum. However, to date, this has not been translated into reality.

Q21. Explain satellite television.

Ans. The satellite television became very popular during the gulf war. The concept of the Cable TV and the availability of the foreign television channels via satellite in India are a recent phenomenon. The CNN's Gulf War coverage revealed the potential of such antennae for receiving foreign broadcasts. With the start of the satellite television for Asian Region (STAR TV) by a hongkong-based conglomerate of companies, the Satellite television has made a decisive entry into India. The foreign programmes received through satellite used by the STAR TV include an entertainment channel (STAR plus), a sports channel (Prime Sports), and a music channel (MTV). The STAR TV added yet another channel, the BBC World Service, from October, 1991. The Asian Television Network (ATN), an international Hindi satellite television service was started from January 1992. The sixth channel on the STAR TV, ZEE TV meant for entertainment programmes in Hindi, was launched on October 1,1992. Concomitant with the penetration of foreign TV services, the Asian region saw a steady rise in the popularity of the TV as a news medium.

Social and Cultural Implications: Satellite TV faces the wrath of many on the ground that it encourages an alien world view, culture, lifestyle, etc. Though the reach of the satellite TV is largely confined to the upper-middle class, there is a possible danger to these classes of people, due to the unhibited exposure to an alien transnational socio-cultural environment. Further, there has been severe criticism that the foreign satellite broadcasts do not respect national boundaries and national sovereignty, that calamities and scandals were given more importance than the development programmes in countries to which they are beaming their news telecasts. For example, the BBC's live telecast of the demolition of Babri Masjid on December 6 by the Kar Sevakas certainly heightened communal passions and shook the confidence of the minorities.

The satellite TV programmes have a serious impact on the audience, especially on the children and youth. Studies indicate that these foreign telecasts provide a clear role-model for the Westernisation of the youth. The teachers and parents complain of excessive TV viewing in the households having satellite and cable connections. In a study, done in a Delhi Public School, the students revealed that the introduction of the satellite TV coincided with a marked decline of school grades. Studies also indicate that children were experiencing steep disturbances, and learning and teaching were taking a backseat. A study done in Sardar Patel School in New Delhi revealed that the cable TV programmes hamper the children's studies. Reading for pleasure has been curtailed. Many children in the survey revealed that at times strong will power is needed to leave the cable TV programmes and get back to studies.

5 MEDIA ETHICS AND LAWS

INTRODUCTION

The Media are indispensable for a democracy. Their right to free expression has won constitutional recognition in India. But there is an understanding that the freedom of the press should be used to further the interests of the society and the nation. A press council may be voluntary or statutory. In India we have a statutory press council. The present system of employing a press ombudsman is a voluntary arrangement by the press. For all the media persons an understanding of the basic tenets of the Constitution is necessary, because they come into contact with it regularly in the performance of their duties and functions. Our Constitution has certain prominent features which distinguish it from other constitutions. Freedom of expression has been given the pride of place among the six fundamental freedoms guaranteed by our constitution. The freedom of the Press has a constitutional right to function freely and without fetters. But, at the same time, it must exercise this right within the framework of certain reasonable restrictions laid down in various laws. There is partly a constitutional law, partly a special law and mostly the ordinary law which together constitute the press law. Defamation or taking away the fame from someone, is an offence punishable with imprisonment from the earliest times of civil government. Defamation is treated as a criminal offence under the section 499. Defamation gives rise to both civil and criminal action. Defamation is punishable under the same section of IPC. The press, being a written and printed medium, is likely to commit an offence of libel only. Defamatory publication is for the public good. Once an imputation is proved to be defamatory, it **is** for the accused to show that he is protected by any of the exceptions to section 499 IPC. The Proprietor, Editor, Author, Publisher and Printer of a newspaper or journal would be jointly and separately, liable for any defamatory matter published in the newspaper or journal and may be sued as such. However, we also stated the precautions one should take before publishing reports and articles containing allegations against individuals or public organizations.

Q1. What do you mean by freedom of speech and expression? Explain the historical development.

Or

Write a detailed note on freedom of speech and expression.

[June-2019, Q.No.-8 (b)]

Or

Critically analyse the importance of the Right to Freedom of Speech and Expression in today's times with suitable examples.

[Dec-2019, Q.No.-8]

Ans. Article 19 of the Universal Declaration of Human Rights, adopted in 1948, states that:

Everyone has the right to freedom of opinion and expression; this right includes freedom to hold opinions without interference and to seek, receive and impart information and ideas through any media and regardless of frontiers.

Today, freedom of speech, or the freedom of expression, is recognised in international and regional human rights law. The right is enshrined in Article 19 of the International Covenant on Civil and Political Rights, Article 10 of the European Convention on Human Rights, Article 13 of the American Convention on Human Rights and Article 9 of the African Charter on Human and Peoples' Rights.

Freedom of speech and expression is an issue, which, for various socio-political and economic reasons, has not yet taken the shape it should have acquired. Nonetheless, it is an issue. The more, we are aware of it, the better it is for our society to pursue its democratic principles. Through the ages, man has expressed his ideas through several media like symbols, signals, speech, script and print, and now computer language. Man's greatest invention is language. The invention of the script has helped mankind to preserve human thought and learning. It has helped society to conquer both space and time.

Enemies of Freedom: An important product of the script was the book; though, in the early stages, its circulation was restricted to only a few literate persons. The books helped older civilisations like the Chinese and the Indian civilisations to preserve heritage. Books spread ideas which set people thinking, as a prelude to individual and group action. For this reason, they met opposition from guardians of political and religious doctrines. The report of a United Nations commission, popularly known as Sean Macbride commission:

"Debates on the possible boundaries of freedom, in the India of Ashoka, are known to have taken place; dissident Hebrew sects took refuge in caves and bid their scrolls; in Athens, Socrates paid with his life for "corrupting the young" Throughout history, we see kings, tribal chiefs, dictators, the State and the Church intervening, sometimes in the name of God, to choke voices of articulate people and to prevent ideas and information from reaching intended audiences. These groups had to justify the restrictions they placed on the freedom of speech and expression. They found in the ideas of learned men like Plato, Machiavelli, Thomas Hobbes and George Hegel a justification for State intervention to regulate the freedom of expression. Plato argued that wise men alone could rule and this right could not be distributed equally among the people. In his book titled The Republic, Plato wrote that in a collectivist society, the State would control education, in all its aspects-literature, art, music and even gymnastics, because citizens themselves belonged to the State.

Champions of Freedom: But these attempts to suppress freedom of expression never went unchallenged. They gave birth to champions of freedom of expression and speech. John Milton' (1608- 1674) in Areopagitica (1644) gave a solid reason for the freedom of the Press. According to him, in a free and open encounter in public view between truth and falsehood, the truth shall prevail. In his essay On Liberty (1859), John Stuart Mill (1806-1873), proclaimed that liberty was the right of the individual. "All action should aim at creating, maintaining and increasing the greatest happiness of the greatest number". He said, "If all mankind minus one, were of one opinion and only one person were to be of the contrary opinion, mankind would be no more justified in silencing that one person than he, if he had the power, would be justified in silencing mankind".

Recognition: Before India gained independence, there were laws in the country to restrict freedom of speech and expression. These laws were a response to the birth and growth of the Indian Press, beginning with the publication of the well-known Hickey's Bengal Gazette. The first press law required that every newspaper should publish the names of the editor, printer and publisher. It also reminded that all material to be published be submitted to pre-censorship. Then came the Indian Penal Code making defamation, obscenity, sedition, etc. equal to Offences. Among other important laws restricting press freedom were the Official Secrets Act and Press and Registration of Books Act. The latter required that a copy of every book and newspaper published in the country be supplied to the government. All these laws were intended to stifle individual and collective expression, especially in the context of our independence struggle. They were also a reaction not only to the mainstream Indian newspapers in English and Indian Languages but also to such journals whose exclusive focus was to overthrow the colonial government, as Annie Besant's Young India, Gandhi's Harijan, Tilak's Kesari and so on. The laws made by the British in India mostly aimed at protecting the State from legitimate criticism of its oppressive rule.

Article 19(1) (a): With the gaining of independence, freedom of speech and expression were recognised as fundamental rights and were included in the Indian Constitution. In the Article ' 19(1) (a) of our Constitution, it is stated: "All citizens shall have the right to freedom of speech and expression". Article 19(2) provides reasonable restrictions on freedom of expression. Article 19(2) says that the State can impose reasonable restrictions on the exercise of the freedom of expression and speech in the interests of (1) sovereignty and integrity of India; (2) the security of the State; (3) friendly relations with foreign states; (4) public order; decency or morality; (5) contempt of court; (6) defamation and (7) incitement to an offence. It means that the law has to limit itself to the eight areas mentioned above. The restrictions imposed on the freedom of speech and expression must be reasonable. Article 361A of our Constitution says: No person shall be liable to any proceedings, civil or criminal in any court in respect of the publication in a newspaper of a substantially true report of any proceedings of either House of the Legislature of a State unless the publication is proved to have been made with malice. The Supreme Court delivered judgements in a few cases proclaiming that freedom of speech and expression included freedom of the press also. An important case was that of the Sakal decided by the Supreme Court in 1962. In that case, the Supreme Court held that the right to propagate one's ideas was inherent in the concept of freedom of speech and expression and that to propagate his ideas, every citizen had a right to publish, disseminate and circulate them.

First Amendment: In the USA, freedom of the press was very clearly recognised for the first time in Virginia.Bil1 of Rights in 1776 which said: "freedom of the press is one of the great bulwarks of liberty, and can never be restrained but by despotic governments." In 1791, the First Amendment to the American Constitution clearly stated that "Congress shall make no law respecting an establishment of religion, or prohibiting the free exercise thereof or abridging the freedom of speech, or the press; or the right of the people peaceably to assemble and to petition the Government for a redress of -grievances. Later, several court judgements supplied substance to this bare American declaration and delivered judgements which have covered every inch of the territory of press freedom from prior restraint to disclosure of the source of information.

New Written Law: Unlike the USA, Britain has no written Constitution. But it has hen the fountain of all philosophy concerning freedom of speech, expression and the press, as John Milton did most of his work in Britain. A myriad of laws made by the British Parliament and rulings of its courts provide the basic framework for restricting freedom of expression in Britain. The rights of free speech, expression and the press are in a constant process of evolution.

Press Freedom: Absolute Vs. Limited: When the media began to address wider audiences, sociologists and other researchers began studying the influence of these media on individuals and society. As governments became more complicated and power-conscious, these developments led to debates everywhere, including Britain, the United States and India, on whether these freedoms are absolute or limited by variables such as the citizen's right to privacy, or the need to preserve public peace or protect national culture from invasion, etc.

Q2. What do you mean by freedom of press?

Ans. Freedom of the press or freedom of the media is the principle that communication and expression through various media, including printed and electronic media, especially published materials, should be considered a right to be exercised freely. Such freedom implies the absence of interference from an overreaching state; its preservation may be sought through constitution or other legal protection and security.

With respect to governmental information, any government may distinguish which materials are public or protected from disclosure to the public. State materials are protected due to either of two reasons: the classification of information as sensitive, classified or secret, or the relevance of the information to protecting the national interest. Many governments are also subject to "sunshine laws" or freedom of information legislation that are used to define the ambit of national interest and enable citizens to request access to government-held information.

Meaning of Freedom In our country :the concept of freedom of the press evolved over the years as a result of the struggle, first under the British rule against restrictive press laws and after independence against such laws as the Press Objectionable Matter Act, 1951. Both in the United States and India, constitutional provisions do not define freedom of the press.

In general press freedom means freedom, unless specifically prohibited by law, to gather, print and publish information and to set up technologies in pursuit of such objectives, to claim and gain access to information. This freedom extends to press photographers too. In practice, freedom of the press means freedom of the owner of a newspaper. Journalists enjoy only that much freedom as is given to them by the owner of their newspaper/magazine. Generally, freedom always means freedom from government. But, it is recognised that there are other agencies too that threaten this freedom, for example, militants, language chauvinists and regional pressure groups. Freedom of the press sometimes is also threatened by big advertisers, as they are an important source of newspaper income. The freedom is also threatened by the newspaper proprietor's other businesses.

Basis of Democracy: From the beginning, freedom of the press was sought and obtained on the ground that it was a prerequisite to democracy. Without the medium of the press, people had no means of judging the performance or credentials of aspirants to power in a democracy. Even otherwise, people depend on the press daily for a variety of needs. It does without saying that all other freedoms become irrelevant without freedom of the press because a denial of this freedom means the strangling of democracy. The press, including individual journalists and media organisations, demand freedom because of the functions they discharge for the benefit of society. Both society and the State need information on a day-to-day basis. Though governments have their machinery to gather information, they rely on the media as barometers of public opinion. The public or the citizenry depends on the media for fair and impartial information regarding the government's activities. As watchdogs and neutral observers, the media are in an advantageous position to monitor and disseminate information relating to government activities. In today's context, freedom of the press is only an extension of the citizen's right to freedom of speech and expression. It is the press alone which can thwart the attempts of any government to deny this right to the citizen. Daily hundreds of decisions are taken by the government which affect the citizens directly. It is the press alone which analyses and interpret the consequences of these decisions for the citizens. In every country, its population is dependent on the press and other mass media for information, advice and guidance daily. Without freedom, they cannot discharge the functions that society expects from them.

Reasonable Restrictions: In connection with the limitations on the freedom of the press, the very first thing we must remember is that the right of the freedom of the press is only an extension of the citizen's right to freedom of speech and expression. Therefore, all those laws imposing restrictions on this right of the citizen apply to the press too. It has no special privilege that the citizens do not enjoy in this area. Since a newspaper is generally brought out by a company, one may ask if the rights of the citizen could be extended to the company also. There is some fuzziness about judicial pronouncements on this matter and, therefore, the Second Press Commission recommended that all Indian companies engaged in the business of communication and whose shareholders are citizens of India should be deemed to be Indian citizens for the Purpose of the relevant clauses of Article 19.

In all western societies and m India, the institutions as well as the general laws of the countries set the limits for the exercise of freedom of the press. Therefore, about freedom, the press is not on any higher footing than the ordinary citizen, because it is an extension of the individual's right. Since the press is also a business and an industry, all those laws which apply to business and industry, also apply to newspaper organisations.

Q3. What are the responsibilities and social obligations of the press?

Ans. Pt. Jawaharlal Nehru once said, "There is no such thing as absolute freedom. Freedom is always accompanied by responsibility. Freedom always entails an obligation, whether it is a nation's freedom or individual's freedom or group freedom or the freedom of the Press".

Responsibility and its Rationale: Here, there is a need to distinguish between responsibility and accountability. When we say that somebody is responsible, we mean that he has to do something; when we say someone is accountable, we mean that if he fails to do what is his duty, he is accountable to some person or an institution or the State. Thus, the right to freedom of speech and expression carries with it, among other things, a duty not to disturb public peace. If he so disturbs it he is accountable to the State for such breach of responsibility. The press and other media derive their rights to free speech and expression because they do a service to society. The rights arising from the role and functions the media are entrusted with, in society and responsibility and accountability co-exist with these rights. Since the media circulates information for the obvious consumption of individual members of the society, it is natural that they should be responsible (judicious) in the dissemination of the information. With every increase in the power of the media, this responsibility towards the society also increases.

Unwritten Understanding: We often hear editors and others saying that they have a right to inform the public. These arise from an unwritten understanding between the media and society. The public has several information needs, the most important being the need to know how the government is functioning. This knowledge helps them to take correct decisions in relation to the government. From the early days, the media assumed this responsibility to inform the public. On that basis the media have fought for and gained the right to free speech and expression. Just as the press has assumed certain responsibilities, the State too assumes responsibilities to benefit the society. As a result, the State imposes certain responsibilities on the press. For example, it is the duty of the States to maintain public order. Therefore, the State imposes an obligation (responsibility) on the media not to publish anything that leads to, or has a tendency to lead to, a breakdown of public order. These are responsibilities imposed in addition to, and sometimes in contrast to, self-imposed responsibilities. Thus, the State imposes on the media such responsibilities which are in the end intended to protect individuals and institutions from libel, defamation or invasion of privacy.

Press Commissions of India: The First Press Commission appointed in 1952 was asked to look into factors which influence the establishment and maintenance of high standards of journalism in India. The Commission was appointed because after independence the role of the press was changing. It was fast turning from a mission to business. The Commission found that there was a great deal of scurrilous writing often directed against communities or groups, of indecency and vulgarity and personal attacks on individuals. The Commission also noted that yellow journalism was on the increase in the country and was not particularly confined to any area or language. The Commission, however, found that the well-established, newspapers, on the whole, had maintained a high standard of journalism. It remarked that whatever the law relating to the press maybe, there would still be a large quantity of objectionable journalism, which, though not falling within the purview of the law, would still require some checking. It felt that the best way of maintaining professional standards of journalism would be to bring into existence a body of people principally connected with the industry whose responsibility it would be to arbitrate on doubtful points and to ensure the punishment of anyone guilty of an infraction of good journalistic behaviour. An important recommendation of the Commission was the setting up of a Statutory Press Commission at the national level, consisting of press people and lay members. It did not say though that the council should have.

The Government of India appointed a Second Press Commission in 1978 after the internal emergency in the country ended. During the emergency the press had to face heavy curbs on its freedom. The Second Press Commission wanted the press to be neither a mindless adversary nor an unquestioning ally. The Commission wanted the press to play a responsible role in the development process. The press should be widely accessible to the people if it is to reflect their aspirations and problems. The question of urban bias too has received the attention of the Commission. The Commission said that for development to take place, internal stability was as important as safeguarding national security. The Commission also highlighted the role (and, therefore, responsibility) of the press in preventing and deflating communal conflict. The positive role of the press in bringing together diverse elements in the nation's life was as important as the avoidance of objectionable or communal writing. The Commission, by majority, recommended that the Press Council of India should be given statutory power to recommend actions against the newspapers, which consistently violated the Council's rulings. Both Press

Commissions of India included several respectable members from the press. The recommendations of the First Press Commission for the first time provided an idea of what a responsible press should be. The Second Press Commission formulated in a clear manner that development should be the central focus of the press in a country which is building itself to become a self-reliant and prosperous society.

The Commission declared that a responsible press can also be a free press and vice versa. Freedom and responsibility are complimentary but not contradictory terms. From the role that the two Commissions recommended for the press, we can summarise the responsibilities of the press thus:

- Help the country in its development process both by making constructive suggestions as well as criticism of delays and distortions in the development process;
- Give the widest possible access to people, reflecting the pluralistic composition of Indian society;
- Maintain internal stability and safeguard external security;
- Prevent and deflate social conflict.

Press and Social Responsibility in the USA: The United States, where the press and other media have been free for long, also witnessed intermittent debates on the performance of the press. The Pultizer Hearst circulation war which ended in the Spanish-American war, the New York Sun's hoax about a new form of life on the moon (1835) and the press tirade against President Roosevelt in the 1930s led to some introspection. On the initiative of Time Magazine, Robert Hutchins, Chancellor of the University of Chicago at that time, and several others studied the performance of the US Press and came out with a report in 1946. The report shocked the American public and angered many editors. The Hutchins report was the first scientific study of the press in the USA and first scientific formulation about its responsibilities. This report became the basis for the social responsibility theory formulated by Theodore Paterson, Fred S. Siebert and Wilbur Schramm in their book Four Theories of the Press. The Hutchins Commission Report said that the freedom of the press was in danger in the United States, "because in the hands of a few gigantic business units, the media of mass communication vital to the life of our democracy, have failed to accept the full responsibility to the public". The Commission observed that freedom of the press in America was in danger because "those who controlled" the press did not facilitate the communication of a wide spectrum of ideas.

Press and Social Responsibility in Britain: In India the concept of Press Council came from Britain. Therefore, it is necessary for us to have a brief discussion about the British Press. ! In Britain, as early as in the 1930s it was felt that there must be a voluntary organisation of press persons to self-regulate the press. A report of an organisation I called Political and Economic Planning, gave its recommendations in this regard. After the Second World War, the First Royal Commission on the Press recommended the setting up of a voluntary press council in Britain. At first, the press resisted but later submitted due to great parliamentary pressure. Thus, a voluntary Press Council was established in 1953. The Council has now been replaced by a voluntary Press Complaints Commission. One of the major difference between the Council and the Commission is that the Commission does not venture into the areas of protecting press freedom. The Council used to venture into these areas.

Q4. What was the code of conduct for journalists?

Ans. There was a time when press was working regardless of their responsibilities throughout the whole world.

Media ethics apply mostly to cases not specifically covered by the law. For instance, there is no law laying down principles of objectivity. Since a picture of public affairs, not informed by objectivity, is likely to mislead the audience, media organisations have voluntarily accepted objectivity as a sacred media tradition.

The birth of journalism schools and departments and the sudden surge in communication research together imparted a great boost to the ideal of objectivity. Of course, one can always trace the birth of objectivity to the birth of news agencies whose primary obligation was reporting only facts. However, facts themselves sometimes could lead to social conflict. In such cases, objectivity alone does not save a situation. This is where responsibility too should be an important element of journalism.

New Conditions: The advances in communication and information technologies have imparted greater power to communicate and, therefore, a sharper edge to its consequences. A moving and. talking picture of an event is a hundred times more impactful than a printed word or a still picture. This has imparted a new urgency to the entire debate of responsibility and the need to draft and re-draft existing codes of ethics.

Today, the magnitude and the economics of mass media operations have resulted in primacy being acceded to market objectives. Consequently, there has been a reshuffle in media priorities. The editor's role is governed by the advertisement and circulation department needs.

Some of the recent findings of the Press Council call for a return to objective journalism. The Council mildly chided the Times of India for its reporting of Indira Gandhi's assassination. The Council advised that in reporting on or writing about communal or other sensitive matters, newspapers should exercise proper restraint and caution. In recent times, The Illustrated Weekly of India was sued by former Orissa Chief Minister, J.B. Patnaik for damages worth rupees one crore. The Sunday Observer was in trouble for linking the sister of a famous film actor with the Prime Minister of Pakistan in a romantic manner. Performance by such leading newspapers was what compelled the Press Institute of India to make those remarks about investigative journalism. The United States was rocked in the 1980s, by a woman (Janet Cooke) who wrote a piece of fiction in the Washington Post and managed to win the Pulitzer Prize for the story. It was the Post which later found that the piece was a fiction.

Code of Ethics: This Code of Ethics guides and mandates public, online, professional and personal conduct expected of every employee of The Print. The reputation of The Print rests on the conduct of each of its employees.

This document is a binding commitment for all employees of The Print and is signed by them in acknowledgement. All non-editorial employees also acknowledge and understand this code and commit to avoid doing anything that violates its principles.

All the content that is produced under The Print banner (by employees, guests and contributors) must be put through the highest standards of professional due diligence, rigour, accuracy, fairness and integrity that this code demands.

VirSinghvi, Editor of Sunday, wrote in The Illustrated Weekly of India 14 September 1986: "Never before has the Indian press been as much in the news as it is today. Few people have addressed themselves to the central question of a code of ethics. At present journalists operate without any guidelines at all". Writing in the issue of 14 February 1987 issue of The Illustrated Weekly of India, the late D.R. Mankekar wrote: "A poll taken in the USA some years ago, though on a limited scale, confined to 28 editors and 25 public officials and civic leaders, showed that 65 per cent of public representatives concluded that newspapers are not to be trusted because they carry half-told or misleading stories resulting from lax standards of reportorial research and back grounding of news stories". That charge could be equally levelled against much of Indian reporting. Suggesting a Code of Ethics for Indian newspapers, Mankekar said, "A Code of Ethics for journalists will not, however, be worth the paper on which it is written unless we can graft teeth onto such a code to make it enforceable by an appropriate, recognised authority. The obvious and appropriate authority for that purpose is the Press Council of India, as recommended by the First Press Commission.

The Second Press Commission lists a number of codes drafted in India, the USA and Britain through the years. The All-India Newspaper Editors' Conference formulated a Code of Ethics and a Charter for Editors in 1953. During the emergency, 17 editors drafted a similar code. The National Union of Journalists, the A, India Small and Medium Newspapers Association (1975) had all drafted similar codes. But the Editors Guild of India refused to draft any code arguing that responsible people do not need such a formal code. The Second Press Commission said that it would not be desirable to draw up a code of ethics for newspapers. Some senior editors who regard journalism as a public service have suggested some guidelines. Vir Singhvi has suggested that any Code of Ethics must cover five basic areas: defamation and privacy; the acceptance of gifts and hospitality; conflict of interest; the willingness of the investigative reporter to accept 'leaks'; and the role of the proprietor. According to him, all five areas are grey areas at the moment. Whatever codes exist are on paper only and are known to very few journalists. Mankekar says: The universally accepted tenets are (1) the story must be of public interest, i.e., it conforms to the universally accepted human rights; the right to know or the right of information; (2) the story should not violate a person's right to privacy (even a criminal condemned to be hanged is entitled to his right to privacy); (3) the story should not infringe on the country's security; and (4) the story is not subjudice and is privileged for publication. To these may, be added: The story shall not incite communal discord and violence.

Ombudsman: There is no effort by professional bodies or other agencies to monitor whether the existing codes are being observed. Meanwhile, the Times of India set a new trend by appointing Justice P.N.

Bhagwati, former Chief Justice of the Supreme Court of India, as its internal ombudsman, but the paper does not regularly publicise this fact in the paper. The Nav Bharat Times, a Hindi daily of the Times of India group, also appointed, Mr. T.N. Chaturvedi, former Comptroller and Auditor General of India, as its ombudsman.

The idea of an ombudsman is of Swedish origin. In Sweden, the Press ombudsman at the national level is not appointed by any newspaper organisation, but by all the newspaper organisations together. Ombudsman generally means an intermediary, investigating complaints by private citizens against government officials or agencies. However, at present private or voluntary organisations are also having ombudsmen to decide public complaints made against themselves or their members. In India the Lok Ayuktas ill some states are ombudsmen. Though both the word and concept of 'ombudsman' originated in Sweden, it was first adopted by the press in the USA. In 1967 an ombudsman was appointed for Counter-journal and its sister publication, Louisville Times, and thus for the first time in the world, newspaper ombudsmanship came into existence.

Q5. Write about the press council.

Ans. The Press Council of India is a statutory, adjudicating organisation in India formed in 1966 by its parliament. It is the self-regulatory watchdog of the press, for the press and by the press, that operates under the Press Council Act of 1978.

In 1970, news agencies were also put under its jurisdiction. The Council was abolished during the internal emergency. However, after the emergency, it was restored in 1978. The present Council has powers to levy a graded fee on newspapers and news agencies to meet its expenditure and to reduce its dependence on government's financial support.

The Council has a chairman – traditionally, a retired Supreme Court judge, and 28 additional members of which 20 are members of media, nominated by the newspapers, television channels and other media outlets operating in India. In the 28 member council, 5 are members of the lower house (Lok Sabha) and upper house (Rajya Sabha) of the Indian parliament and three represent culture literary and legal field as nominees of Sahitya Academy, University Grant Commission and Bar Council of India .

Justice Chandramauli Kumar Prasad is Chairman of the Council as of 2015. He has been appointed for a second term. The predecessor was Justice MarkandeyKatju (2011 – 2014).

Complaints Procedure: The complaints to the Press Council of India can be from the press or against the press. The complainant should first write to the editor of the newspaper by drawing attention to what the complainant considers to be a breach of journalistic ethics or an offence against public taste. If he fails to evoke a reply from the editor, he should mention this fact in his complaint to the Council. Otherwise, if the complainant is not satisfied with the reply or rejoinder or explanation of the newspaper, he should send to the Council all the correspondence between him and the editor and show to the satisfaction of the Council that the matter published had been objectionable. If it is a complaint by the press against a State agency, the newspaper or journalist should state whether the action of the agency had interfered with press freedom. Trivial complaints-and sub-judice matters are not taken up by the Council.

A complaint to the Council is considered by an inquiry committee, which is a body of the members of the Council. The committee gives a hearing to the parties, considers the materials on record and arrives at a conclusion. The committee's conclusions are forwarded to the full Council in the form of a recommendation. The Council takes a decision and the complaint is finally disposed of. The Council has no power to take legally enforceable punitive action. The Council enjoys complete autonomy and independence in the performance of its functions. It does not charge any fee from the complainants.

Q6. Explain Copyright Act, 1957.

Or

Write a detailed note on Copyright Act. [June-2019, Q.No.-8 (a)]

Ans. A work of literature, drama, music or art is an intellectual property. It must be protected from illegal copying or reproducing it. The copyright Act, 1957 accords this protection.

This law is based on two competing considerations. One, the creator's property, that is, the original works need to be protected. Two, for advancement of knowledge in the interest of the society, there should be some amount of freedom to produce parts ,of other people's copyrighted works. Copyright has been held to be a right which a person acquires in a work which is the result of his intellectual labour. The primary function of the copyright law is to protect from annexation by other people the fruits of a man's work, labour or skill.

In respect of the Press, copyright means, under Section 14 of the Copyright Act, 1957, the exclusive right in the case of a literary, dramatic or musical work, to do and authorise the doing in substantive form of any of the following acts, namely:

- to reproduce the work in any material form;
- to publish the work;
- to make any adoption of a work; and
- to reproduce or publish translation of the work.

Punishment for knowingly infringing or abetting the infringement of a copy right is imprisonment which may exceed upto one year or fine or both.

Q7. Explain national integration council code.

Ans. The National Integration Council (NIC) is a group of senior politicians and public figures in India that looks for ways to address the problems of communalism, casteism and regionalism.[1] Council members include cabinet ministers, entrepreneurs, celebrities, media heads, chief ministers, and opposition leaders.

In June 1962 the National Integration Council (NIC) drafted a Code of Conduct for the media which goes beyond the traditional responsibilities of the press. Accordingly, the press should:

- take all active steps to develop a feeling of unity, solidarity and cohesion in the hearts of the people and should create a sense of common citizenship and a feeling of loyalty to the nation;
- subordinate group loyalties based on caste, community, religion', region or language to the national interest;
- condone no move of any person, party or group to divide the country or to create tension between its peoples;
- condemn unreserved incitement to violence or advocacy of violence as a means of settling conflicts;
- with hold publication of unverified news, which would tend to create discord, and refrain from giving prominent display to such news;

- contradict or rectify all inaccurate reports or comments relating to such news.

The logic behind the NIC guidelines is clear. That is, there are certain national tasks which are the responsibility not only of the government and the society in general but also of the press. The press, as a part of the society, has as much duty to foster a sense of national unity and integration as the government. The country continues to tackle communalism, regionalism, secessionism, etc. The press can play voluntarily a role in highlighting and fighting these tendencies. Any glorification of violence. whether for political or commercial reasons, is to be abjured. Bhindranwale and Velu Prabhakaran owe their "stature" to media charity.

The fifth guideline stated here directly relates to the new trend of investigative journalism which seems to flourish on the assurance that people in general or even politicians have little time or inclination to go on repudiating every word of media fiction. The Press Council came down heavily on the performance of a section of the Freedom of Speech and press about the Ayodhya-Babri Masjid coverage.

Q8. Explain the preamble and federal system.

Ans. Premble System: The Constitution of India begins with a preamble which embodies its basic objectives or main purposes. According to K. Subba Rao, former Chief Justice of India, the preamble contains, in a nutshell, the Constitution's ideals and aspirations. The preamble of the Constitution reads as follows: WE, THE PEOPLE OF INDIA, having solemnly resolved to constitute India into a SOVEREIGN, SOCIALIST, SECULAR AND DEMOCRATIC REPUBLIC, and to secure to all its citizens:

JUSTICE, social, economic and political;

LIBERTY of thought, expression, faith, belief and worship;

EQUALITY of status and opportunity; and to promote among them all:

FRATERNITY, assuring the dignity of the individual and the unity and integrity of the nation;

IN OUR CONSTITUENT ASSEMBLY, this twenty-sixth day of November 1949, do HEREBY ADOPT, ENACT AND GIVE TO OURSELVES THIS CONSTITUTION. The words "Socialist, Secular" were not in the original preamble. The Forty Second Amendment to the

Constitution added these words after the word "sovereign".

The Preamble embodies the spirit of the Constitution, the determination of the Indian people to unite themselves in a common adventure of building up a new socialist, secular nation which will ensure the triumph of justice, liberty, equality and fraternity.

Federal System: Federalism is a system of division of political power between the central and the regional (state) governments so that each government within its sphere, is independent of any other. There are various forms of federalism. Federalism in India. Canada, Australia and America are not the same. Each reflects a variation of federalism. Federalism in each country has its characteristics depending upon its historical evolution. The general trend until 1947 in India was to work out a federal system with a measure of autonomy for the provinces. This trend had to be modified by the time the Constituent Assembly met to draft a constitution for independent India, because of the major challenges in the form of large scale outbreak of communal violence, regional pulls and the collapsing economy. The partition of the country finally made the constitution-makers go for a federal setup with dominant unitary features. Although Article 1 of the Constitution speaks of a dual polity, due to the provision of single citizenship, single integrated judiciary, uniform civil and criminal law for all the federating States and a unified All-India Civil Service, India remains a unified polity. The Constitution gives general supremacy to the Union Parliament and Executive in all matters vis-a-vis the States (vide: Article 365) especially in the making of laws on items included in the State List, in the appointment and dismissal of governors, in the dismissal of State Ministry, in the appointment of Judges to the States High Courts. Further, it gives the residual powers to the Union (vide: Articles 24546, 249-54, 356) and assigns a larger share of the revenue and a greater fiscal authority to the Centre (vide: Part XII). There is inequality of status of the federating States (vide: Article 2, 370-373: and Parts VI-X). But more than this, it has given a legitimate handle in the form of Emergency powers (vide: Articles 352- 360) to enable the Centre to transform a federal system into virtually a unitary system under three conditions: a) foreign aggression; b) threat of aggression of armed rebellion; c) breakdown of law and order. There is no right of succession for the States, on the principle that "union is indestructible".

Since the late 1960s, when for the first time non-Congress parties formed governments in several States, the demand for more autonomy and freedom for States has been gaining momentum. Among the measures suggested were the changing of the present centralised federation into a co-operative and constructive federal polity by (i) territorial reorganisation of States on the criterion of providing to the States maximum homogeneity within and maximum identity without, (ii) amendment to the constitution for increasing the autonomy of the States, (iii) implementation of Panchayati Raj and Nagar Palika system, and (iv) building of a new federal-national consensus between parties, social activist groups and citizens.

Q9. Explain the fundamental rights.

Ans. Fundamental rights are those rights which are essential for intellectual, moral and spiritual development of citizens of India. As these rights are fundamental or essential for existence and all-round development of individuals, they are called 'Fundamental rights'. These are enshrined in Part III (Articles 12 to 35) of the Constitution of India.

These include individual rights common to most, such as equality before the law, freedom of speech and freedom of expression, religious and cultural freedom, Freedom of assembly (peaceful assembly), freedom of religion (freedom to practice religion), right to constitutional remedies for the protection of civil rights by means of writs such as Habeas Corpus, Mandamus, Writ of Prohibition, Certiorari and Quo Warranto.

Fundamental rights apply universally to all citizens, irrespective of race, birthplace, religion, caste, sexual orientation, gender or gender identity. The Indian Penal Code, Code of Criminal Procedure and other laws prescribe punishments for the violation of these rights, subject to the discretion of the judiciary. Though the rights conferred by the constitution other than fundamental rights are also valid rights protected by the judiciary, in case of fundamental rights violations, the Supreme Court of India can be approached directly for ultimate justice as per Article 32. The Rights have their origins in many sources, including England's Bill of Rights, the United States Bill of Rights and France's Declaration of the Rights of Man. There are six fundamental rights recognised by the Indian constitution:

- Right to equality (Articles. 14-18)
- Right to Freedom (Articles. 19-22)

- Right Against Exploitation (Articles. 23-24)
- Right to Freedom of Religion (Articles. 25-28)
- Cultural and Educational Rights (Articles. 29-30), and
- Right to Constitutional remedies (Articles. 32)

As a result of' the 44th Amendment; Article 31 entitled "The Right to Property" was omitted from the Chapter on Fundamental Rights. At the same time 31A, BC, which are related to the Right to Property continue to find the place. A new Article 300 A relating to Property Rights was added by the 44th Amendment under a separate Chapter in Part XII. The Fundamental Rights place limitations not only on the Union Government but also on the States and on every authority that has got the power to make laws or has discretion vested in it. However, the rights are not abso1ute: The Constitution itself enumerates in each case the restrictions, exceptions, limitations and qualifications. One important feature of Fundamental Rights is the "right to constitutional remedies" which has been made to guarantee all the other rights. Under Article 32 the Supreme Court and High Courts are empowered to issue appropriate writs or orders as the occasion demands for the restoration of the enjoyment of a Fundamental Right that is violated. Article 226 deals with the writ jurisdiction of High Courts.

Q10. Explain directive principles of state policy and fundamental duties.

Ans. The Directive Principles of State Policy of India are the guidelines or 15 principles given to the federal institutes governing the State of India, to be kept in citation while framing laws and policies. These provisions, contained in Part IV of the Constitution of India, are not enforceable by any court, but the principles laid down there in are considered in the governance of the country, making it the duty of the State[1] to apply these principles in making laws to establish a just society in the country. The principles have been inspired by the Directive Principles given in the Constitution of Ireland which are related to social justice, economic welfare, foreign policy, and legal and administrative matters.

Directive Principles are classified under the following categories: economic and socialistic, political and administrative, justice and legal, environmental, protection of monuments, peace and security.

The Articles dealing with Directive Principles cover a wide range of

State activity embracing economic, social, legal, educational, administrative, cultural and international problems. Some of the important Directives are the following:

(1) To secure and protect a social order which stands for the welfare of the people. (Art. 38)

(2) In particular, the State shall direct) its policy towards securing: (i) adequate means of livelihood to all citizens; (ii) a proper distribution of the material resources of the community for the common good; (iii) the prevention of concentration of wealth to the common detriment; (iv) equal pay for equal work for both men and women; (v) the protection of the strength and health of workers and avoiding circumstances which force citizens to enter vocations unsuited to their age or strength; (vi) the protection of childhood and youth against exploitation of moral and material abandonment.

(3) To provide free legal aid to ensure that opportunities for securing justice are not denied to any citizen because of economic or other disabilities. (Art. 39A).

(4) To organise village panchayats as units of self-government. (Art.40).

(5) To secure the right to work, education (Art. 40) and public assistance in cases of old age, sickness, etc., (Art. 41).

(6) To ensure just and humane conditions of work and maternity relief. (Art. 42)

(7) To secure work, a living wage, a decent standard of life, leisure and social and cultural opportunities for people, and in particular to promote cottage industries. (Art. 43).

(8) To secure the participation of workers in the management of undertakings engaged in any industry. (Art. 43A).

(9) To bring about the separation of the Judiciary from the Executive. (Art. 50).

(10) To endeavour to secure: (i) the promotion of international peace and security; (ii) the maintenance of just and honourable relations between nations; (iii) respect for international law and treaty obligations in the dealings of organised people with one another, and (iv) the settlement of international disputes by arbitration. (Art. 5 1)

Though the State must apply the Directive Principles in making laws, they are not justiciable under Article 37. It means that the courts have no power to enforce them. This is in contrast with the Fundamental rights which are justiciable and therefore enforceable by the courts of law. Despite their non-justiciable character, Directive Principles are given due recognition in the making of laws and their observance. The Constitution has been amended at times to give effect to the spirit and content of the Directive Principles.

Fundamental Duties: The Constitution prescribes the following Fundamental Duties for the citizens:

(1) to abide by the Constitution and respect its ideals and institutions, the National, Flag and the National Anthem;

(2) to cherish and follow the noble ideals which inspired our national struggle for freedom;

(3) to uphold and protect the sovereignty, unity and integrity of India;

(4) to defend the country and render national service when called upon to do so;

(5) to promote harmony and the spirit of common brotherhood amongst all the people of India transcending religious, linguistic and regional or sectional diversities; to renounce practices derogatory to the dignity of women;

(6) to value and preserve the rich heritage of our composite culture;

(7) to protect and improve the natural environment including forests, lakes, rivers and wildlife, and to have compassion for living creatures;

(8) to develop the scientific temper, humanism and the spirit of inquiry and reform;

(9) to safeguard public property and to abjure violence.

(10) to strive towards excellence in all spheres of individual and collective activity so that the nation constantly rises to high levels of endeavour and achievement.

Q11. What do you mean by union and state legislatures?

Ans. A state legislature is a legislative branch or body of a political subdivision in a federal system. ...The legislative branches of each of the fifty state governments of the United States are known as state legislatures.

The Parliament of India consists of the President and the two Houses- the Rajya Sabha (Council of States) and the Lok Sabha (Home of the People).

The Union of India as of today is composed of twenty-five States and seven Union Territories as specified in the First Schedule of the Constitution. The territory of the Union is divided amongst the States and the Union territories. A law made by a State Legislature can be applicable only in the territory of that State. The Union Parliament can make laws for the whole or any part of the territory of India. The Constitution provides for a three-fold distribution of legislative powers between the Union and the States. A list I of the Union List contains 97 subjects over which Parliament has exclusive power to make laws. List II or the State List includes 66 entries over which State Legislatures have got exclusive power of legislation. List III the Concurrent List contains 47 items on which both the Parliament and the State Legislatures can make laws. While in their respective spheres as allotted by the Constitution, the Parliament, as well as the State Legislatures, enjoy complete autonomy, the scheme of distribution of powers emphasises the general predominance of Parliament in the Legislative field.

Even in the spheres exclusively reserved for the States, the Parliament is authorised to legislate under certain circumstances, the Parliament also enjoys the power to legislate for implementing any treaty, agreement or convention with any country or any decision made at an international conference, association or other body on any subject, even if it falls in the State List.

The two Houses of Parliament enjoy co-equal powers and status in all spheres except in financial matters and regarding the responsibility of the Council of Ministers, which are exclusively in the domain of the Lok Sabha, Accordingly, the following limitations have been placed on the powers of the Rajya Sabha:

- A Money Bill cannot be introduced in the Rajya Sabha.
- The Rajya Sabha has no power either to reject or amend a Money Bill. It can only make recommendations on the Money Bill. If such a Bill is not returned to the Lok Sabha within fourteen days, the Bill shall be deemed to have been passed by both the Houses at the expiration of the said period in the formalin which it was passed by the Lok Sabha.
- Whether a particular Bill is a Money Bill or not is to be decided by the Speaker of the Lok Sabha.
- The Rajya Sabha may discuss the Annual Financial Statement. It has no power to vote on the Demands for Grants.

The Rajya Sabha has no power to pass a vote of no-confidence in the Council of Ministers. It should not, however, be taken to mean that the. Rajya Sabha is less important or has been given a secondary position about the Lok Sabha. The powers of the Rajya Sabha are at par with those of the Lok Sabha in case of non-money Bills. Every non-financial measure must be passed by both the Houses individually before it can become an Act. It has equal powers with the Lok Sabha in important matters. The Parliament at present is more than a law-making body. It has become more and more a multifunctional institution performing a variety of roles-many of these inter-related and often meshing into one another.

This, however, is often not appreciated and the disproportionate emphasis is laid only on one or two aspects of the working of the Parliament.

The main functions of the Parliament are:

- Political and financial control (or Executive Responsibility);
- Surveillance of administration (or Administrative Accountability);
- Informational (Right to Information);
- Representational, grievance-ventilation, educational and advisory;
- Conflict-resolution and national integration;
- Constituent (Amending the Constitution);
- Leadership (Recruitment and Training).

Q12. Explain union and state executives.

Ans. The Constitution prescribes that there shall be a Council of Ministers with the Prime Minister at the head to assist and advise the President. The President appoints the Prime Minister, and on the advice of the Prime Minister, the other Ministers are appointed. Generally, the President invites the leader of the majority party in Lok Sabha to form the government who chooses his other Council of Ministers. The President has to act following the advice of the Council of Ministers. The Prime Minister occupies a key position in the government as well in the party at the national level. He symbolises the ruling power structure in the country. The Executive in the States is organised on the same pattern as that of the union Government. Hence, as in the Union, the government in the States is also organised on the parliamentary model. The Head of the

State is called the Governor, who is the constitutional head of the State as the President is for the whole of India. The chief executive of the State Government is called the Chief Minister who is the counterpart of the Prime Minister of India in the State. There is a Council of Ministers for each of the States as in the Union. The State Government is a true replica of the Union Government within the jurisdiction of each State; this helps the states to draw examples and inspiration from the working of the Union Government in almost every field of activity. The executive power of the State is vested in the Governor who is appointed by the President and who holds office during the pleasure of the President. The vesting of the entire executive power of the State in the Governor shows that he occupies the same constitutional position within the State as the President does concerning the Government of India. The Supreme Court stands at the apex of India's judicial hierarchy with the effective power to supervise and control the working of the entire system. Below the Supreme Courts are the High Courts, located in each State. Besides High Courts, we have District Courts and Subordinate Courts. The Supreme Court's jurisdiction is of four kinds:

- Original jurisdiction
- Appellate jurisdiction
- Advisory jurisdiction
- Review jurisdiction

The Supreme Court has exclusive jurisdiction in a dispute between the Union and a State, or between one State and another, or between a group of states and other. It is also the guardian of the Fundamental Rights of the citizen.

Q13. Explain the judiciary system of India.

Ans. The judiciary is the system of courts that interprets, defends and applies the law in the name of the state. The judiciary can also be thought of as the mechanism for the resolution of disputes. Under the doctrine of the separation of powers, the judiciary generally does not make statutory law (which is the responsibility of the legislature) or enforce law (which is the responsibility of the executive), but rather interprets law, defends and applies it to the facts of each case. However, in some countries the judiciary does make common law.

In many jurisdictions the judicial branch has the power to change laws through the process of judicial review. Courts with judicial review power may annul the laws and rules of the state when it finds them incompatible with a higher norm, such as primary legislation, the provisions of the constitution, treaties or international law. Judges constitute a critical force for interpretation and implementation of a constitution, thus in common law countries creating the body of constitutional law.

India has a single judicial system. Explaining the nature of this system, Dr B.R. Ambedkar said in the Constituent Assembly: "the Indian federation, though a dual polity, has no dual judiciary at all". The High Courts and the Supreme Court form one single integrated Judiciary having jurisdiction and providing remarks in all cases under the Constitutional law, the Civil law of the Criminal law. This is to eliminate all diversities in a remedial procedure.

Q14. Describe the centre-state relations.

Ans. Though India is a Federal State, the word 'federal' does not occur in its Constitution. In the Constitution the term 'Union of States' has been used to indicate that:

- The Indian federation was not the result of an agreement by sovereign units to join it,
- The country and the people were divided into different States for administrative convenience and State boundaries are changeable, and
- The federation not being the result of an agreement, no state has a right to secede from it.

The Constitution prescribes separate areas of operation for the Union and the States. To reduce overlapping of their areas of operation and interaction, the Constitution enumerates the power of the Central and State governments, under three lists: the Union List; the State List and the Concurrent List. Besides, the residuary powers that are not mentioned in any of the lists belong to the central government. The distribution of powers, functions and areas of influence between the Centre and the States leads to a question of the relationship between them in different areas of their association and interaction. The relationships between the Centre and the States can be classified into Legislative Relations Administrative Relations Financial Relations Relations in Planning and Development Relations in Trade and Commerce Of late, in all the above-mentioned relations, different forms of conflict are arising. Several

Committees and commissions studied the relations between the Union and the States and suggested various measures to maintain harmonious relations between the two levels of the government. Administrations Reforms Commission, Rajamannar Committee, Sarkaria Commission are some examples of the bodies which examined the relations. The Central government on the recommendation of these bodies initiated several measures to maintain a harmonious balance between the Centre and the States within the framework of the Constitution.

Q15. What does amending the constitution mean?

Ans. Amending the Constitution of India is the process of making changes to the nation's fundamental law or supreme law. The procedure of amendment in the constitution is laid down in Part XX (Article 368) of the Constitution of India. This procedure ensures the sanctity of the Constitution of India and keeps a check on arbitrary power of the Parliament of India.

However, there is another limitation imposed on the amending power of the constitution of India, which developed during conflicts between the Supreme Court and Parliament, where Parliament wants to exercise discretionary use of power to amend the constitution while the Supreme Court wants to restrict that power. This has led to the laying down of various doctrines or rules in regard to checking the validity/legality of an amendment, the most famous among them is the Basic structure doctrine as laid down by the Supreme Court in the case of Kesavananda Bharati v. State of Kerala .

The major provisions for amendment of the Constitution are provided for in Article 368 of the Constitution itself. This Article has three components. First, it deals with the amending power, second, it designates the body or bodies which can exercise that power and third, it establishes the form and manner in which an amendment of the Constitution can be put in effect. Of the three ways of amending the Constitution two are laid in the amending article itself and the third is provided for at least in twenty-two other articles. The amending article (Article 368) provides that an amendment bill can be introduced in either House of Parliament. If it is passed by a clear majority in each House with two-thirds of the members present and voting and has the assent of the President, it becomes an amendment. The amendments to the Articles dealing with the election of the President, the extent of the Executive power of the Union and the State governments, the Judiciary, the distribution of powers (including the legislative Lists), and the representation of the States in Parliament must not only be passed by Parliament in the manner just described but need also to be ratified by the legislatures of one half of the States. Some provisions of the Constitution can be amended by a simple majority vote in Parliament, followed by Presidential assent. Significantly, no provision of the Constitution is 'unamendable', but the basic features of the Constitution cannot be amended. The basic features of the Constitution constitute a new constitutional concept which had its origin in the majority judgement of the Supreme Court in the case of Kesavananda Bharti Vs. The state of Kerala in 1973. What constitutes 'basic structure did not emerge from the majority judgement, but we can identify from it the following features as the important constituents of the basic structure of the constitution:

- Supremacy of the Constitution
- Sovereignty and Unity of India
- Democratic Character of Polity
- Republican Form of the Government
- Secular Character of the Constitution
- Separation of powers
- Federal Character of the Constitution
- Individual Freedom Equality of Status and Opportunity
- Rule of Law

Since the commencement of the Constitution in 1950, over 75 Constitutional Amendments have been effected to this date. All this has been done in exercise of the Parliament's constituent powers and often to meet unforeseen difficulties created and situations brought about as a result of the decisions of courts and their interpretations of constitutional provisions. Sometimes the amendments had become necessary to clarify the constitutional intent- the intention of the framers of the Constitution behind particular provisions- and to bring the text of the Constitution closer to the accepted national goals and objectives as understood by the Parliament.

Q16. Explain brief history of press legislation in India.

Ans. The oldest surviving Press Regulation, "Press and Registration of Books Act", was passed in 1867. It regulates printing presses and newspapers throughout India. ... In 1910, the Indian Press Act was passed. This was a more comprehensive law and was directed against both offences of violence and sedition.

The foundation of the Press law in India had been laid even before the first newspaper began publication in the country. William Bolts, a former employee of the East India Company was ordered to leave Calcutta, proceed to Madras and from there take his passage to Europe when in 1776, he had simply expressed his intention to start a newspaper. All he did was to paste a notice on the gates of the Council Hall telling people that he had in his possession "in manuscript" many things to communicate which were of intimate concern to every individual.

Amended Similarly, intolerance was shown to later publishers and editors although they all happened to be British or other Europeans. James Augustus Hicky who started the first newspaper, the 'Bengal Gazette or the Calcutta General Advertiser,' in 1780, was so harassed that he had to finally close down his paper. Law Enacted In 1795, censorship was introduced. The 'Madras Gazette' was asked to submit to the Military Secretary all the general orders of the government for censorship before publication. Pre-censorship was one of the three methods resorted to deal with non-conforming editors. The other two being the denial of postal privileges and deportation. Major Point. This continued until 1799 when the first Press regulations were promulgated by Marquess of Wellesley. The Wellesley regulations required the newspapers to print' the names of printers, publishers and editors. They were also required to submit all the material for pre-censorship by the Secretary to the Government of India. Warren Hastings abolished these regulations. But, in 1823, Governor-General John Adams introduced licensing of the Press. His Ordinance required a previous license for the printing of all matters, except commercial matter.

Similar regulations were introduced in Bombay in 1825 and 1827. Licensing was abolished in 1835 and replaced by Metcalfs Act which only required a newspaper to declare the address of the printer and the publication. Press Legislation In India In the wake of the first war of Independence of 1857, licensing was reintroduced by Lord Canning. The Act of 1857 applied even to books and all other kinds of publications.

In 1860 a comprehensive law, the Indian Penal Code (IPC) was enacted. It contained offences like defamation and obscenity which writers, editors, publishers and printers must avoid. Sedition (S. 124A) was added to it in 1870, promoting enmity between classes (S. 153A) in 1898, outraging religious feelings (S. 295A) in 1927 and assertions against national integration (S. 1 53B) in 1927. The oldest surviving Press Regulation, "Press and Registration of Books Act", was passed in 1867. It regulates printing presses and newspapers throughout India. The Act, specifically meant. to curb the Indian language newspapers, called the Vernacular Press Act, was passed in 1878. This evoked widespread opposition in India and to some extent in England too. It was, therefore, repealed in 1881. This Act empowered the Government for the first time to issue search warrants and enter newspaper premises even without court orders.

The beginning of the twentieth century saw the enactment of more stringent anti Press laws to curb the activities of the revolutionaries and the British put various restrictions on newspapers preventing the reporting of and comments upon their activities. In pursuance of this, the Newspapers (Incitement to Offences) Act was passed in 1908, empowering magistrates to seize a press where a newspaper containing matter which incited murder or any other act of violence or an offence under the Explosive Substances Act was printed. In 1910, the Indian Press Act was passed. This was a more comprehensive law and was directed against both offences of violence and sedition. It empowered the Government to ask for a deposit of security from the press and where it deemed fit to forfeit it. The Act was made more rigorous in 1913 and 1914. But, following the report of a committee, the Acts of 1908 and 1910 were repealed after incorporating some of their provisions in other laws. In 1923, the Official Secrets Act was prohibiting the publication of any classified official information. After Independence, the Press (Objectionable Matter) Act, 1951 was to be a temporary law for two years but was extended up to February 1956. This Act provided for a judicial inquiry before demanding security from a printing press or forfeiting it.

In 1961; the Criminal Law Amendment Act was passed imposing certain restrictions on the freedom of the Press on grounds of the security of the State and public order. Defence of India Acts were promulgated in the wake of the external aggression in 1962 and 1971. These placed sweeping restrictions on the Press. An Act to establish the Press Council was passed in 1965 with the dual objective of protecting the freedom of the Press and raising standards of journalism including self-monitoring.

This Act was repealed in 1976 during the internal emergency clamped on the country by Mrs. Indira Gandhi's government, but was re-enacted with some changes by the Janata Party government in 1978. In 1969, Criminal and Election Laws Amendment Act was passed to amend certain sections of the IPC and the Cr P.C. as also to introduce certain new provisions. All these affected the Press. The Press was brought under strict censorship on the promulgation of internal Emergency in 1975. This was done by issuing the Central Censorship Order on June 26, 1975, under the Defence of India Act. The Order was revoked on March 22, 1977.

Q17.What is the constitutional law of press and freedom?

Ans. Freedom of the press in India is legally protected by the Amendment to the constitution of India, while the sovereignty, national integrity, and moral principles are generally protected by the law of India to maintain a hybrid legal system for independent journalism. In India, media bias or misleading information is restricted under the certain constitutional amendments as described by the country's constitution. The media crime is covered by the Indian Penal Code (IPC) which is applicable to all substantive aspects of criminal law.

Nevertheless, freedom of the press in India is subject to certain restrictions, such as defamation law, a lack of protection for whistleblowers, barriers to information access and constraints caused by public and government hostility to journalists. The press, including print, television, radio, and internet are nominally amended to express their concerns under the selected provisions such as Article-19 (which became effective from 1950), though it states freedom of "occupation, trade or business" and "freedom of speech and expression" without naming "press" in clause "a" and "g". The article allows a journalist or media industries to cover any story and bring it to the audiences without impacting the national security of the country.

To protect the intellectual, moral, and fundamental rights of the citizens, the government has taken several countermeasures to combat circulating fake news and restricting objectionable contents across the multiple platforms. The law of India prohibits spreading or publishing fake news through social or mass media, and could lead to imprisonment of a journalist or newspaper ban.

India is one of those countries which guarantee their citizens the right to freely express themselves. The Indian Constitution guarantees six fundamental freedoms, and the 'freedom of speech and expression' is the first among them. Article 19 (1) of the Constitution reads: All citizens shall have the right to:

- freedom of speech and expression;
- assemble peacefully and without arms;
- form associations and unions;
- move freely throughout the territory of India;
- reside and settle in any part of the territory of India;
- practice any profession, or to carry on any occupation, trade or business.

Thus, all Indian citizens enjoy a constitutional right to give free expression to their views, opinions and convictions. They have, for this purpose, the right to seek, receive and impart information and ideas. As the exercise of freedom of expression requires a medium through which information and ideas may be communicated, it naturally follows that the medium shall also be free. Our Constitution does not specifically mention the freedom of the Press as in the U.S. Constitution. However, the Supreme Court has, following the above logic, very explicitly ruled that freedom of the Press is included in the guarantee of the freedom of expression, which also includes the liberty to publish and circulate. The apex court has held that there was, therefore, no need to make a separate provision for the freedom of the Press. But, as this right has been guaranteed to all Indian citizens, the right of the Press is no more than that of a citizen. Therefore, the Press cannot claim any special privilege. Likewise, it cannot be subjected to any special restrictions which do not apply to the citizens. No right is absolute. In an orderly society, liberty cannot mean a license. Like other freedoms, the freedom of the Press is also not absolute. It is circumscribed by restrictions specified by the Constitution itself.

Clause (2) of Article 19 of the Constitution empowers the State to enact laws imposing reasonable restrictions on the exercise of this freedom. "In the interest of the sovereignty and integrity of India, the security of the State, friendly relations with foreign States, public order, decency and morality, or about contempt of court, defamation or incitement to an offence".

Thus, the Constitution permits certain restrictions to be placed on the Press to protect the greater interests of:

- the State, like the need to maintain its very existence,
- the society, in the form of public safety and tranquility, decency and morality, public confidence in the administration of justice, and
- the individual, in enjoying his reputation and fair name.

Q 18. Describe press and registration of books.

Ans. The earliest surviving enactment specifically directed towards the press was passed in 1867, the Press and Registration of Books Act (PRB Act) (XXV of 1867) (App, V). The objective was however not to establish governmental control over the freedom of the Press. It was a regulatory law which enabled Government to regulate printing presses and newspapers by a system of registration and to preserve copies of books and other matter printed in India. A number of minor amendments were made in the Act from time to time to make the Sections/Clauses compatible with the changing situation, more particularly after Independence. But major amendments were carried out in 1955 following the recommendations of the First Press Commission in 1953, consequent upon which the Office of the Registrar of Newspapers of India (RNI) was created and started functioning in 1956.

It also remained the fundamental law governing the rules for the regulation of the publication of newspapers and of having printing presses. Though no licence or permission is required for starting and running a newspaper, no paper can be published without complying with the provisions of this Act. A declaration made in the prescribed manner before the District, Presidency or Subdivisional Magistrate and authenticated by him is necessary before the newspaper is published. Similarly, no printing press can be set up without making a relevant declaration. The Ad requires that the name of the printer, the place of printing and the name of the publisher and place of publication must be legibly printed on every book or newspaper printed/published within India.

Every time a press is shifted to a new place a fresh declaration is necessary. But, if the change of the place is for a period less than 60 days, the new location also falls within the jurisdiction of the same Magistrate, and the keeper of the Press continues to be the same, no fresh declaration need be mad& In that case, and intimation regarding the change of place sent within 24 hours will suffice. Two conditions are necessary to be fulfilled for publishing a newspaper. One, the lame of the editor must be printed on every copy of the newspaper. Two, a declaration must be made before the District, Presidency or Sub-divisional Magistrate within whose jurisdiction the newspaper is to be published, stating the following facts :

- Name of the printer and publisher,
- Premises where printing and publishing is conducted,
- The title, language and periodicity of the newspaper. The declaration should be made by the printer and publisher either in person or through an authorised agent. If the printer or publisher is not the owner of the paper, the declaration should specify the name of the owner. But, making a declaration does not automatically pave the way for publishing a newspaper.

The publication can be started only after the said Magistrate authenticates the declaration. Every time the title, language or periodicity is changed, the declaration ceases to exist, and a fresh declaration must be made. Similarly, a new declaration is necessary as often as the ownership or the place of printing or publication of the newspaper is changed. However, only a statement furnished to the Magistrate will suffice if the change of place is for a period not exceeding 30 days. If the printer or publisher leaves India for a period exceeding 90 days or if he is by infirmity or otherwise incapable of carrying out his duties for more than 90 days, then a fresh declaration will have to be made.

No person who does not ordinarily reside in India or a minor can file a declaration or edit a newspaper. If the declaration is made following the provisions of the law and if no other paper bearing the same or similar title is already in existence in the same language or the same State, then the Magistrate cannot refuse to authenticate the declaration. However, before authentication, he must make an inquiry from the Registrar of Newspapers for India (RNI) about the existence of such other paper. The authentication is an administrative and not a judicial function, and the Magistrate must perform it without exercising his discretion. After authentication, the paper must be started within a specific period. The declaration in respect of a newspaper to be published once a week or more shall be void if it is not commenced within six weeks of the authentication. In case of all other newspapers, the time limit for commencing publication is three months. This means that a daily, a weekly or a bi-weekly newspaper must commence publication within six weeks and a fortnightly, a monthly or a quarterly can start publishing within three months after authentication.

The Magistrate can cancel the declaration and order closure of a newspaper for irregular publication. If in any period of three months, a daily, a triweekly, a biweekly or a fortnightly newspaper publishes less than half the number of issues which it should have published following the declaration, the newspaper shall cease to publish. A fresh declaration must be filed before it can be started again. In case of any other newspaper, the maximum period of non-publication must not exceed 12 months to keep the declaration alive. Two copies of each issue of a newspaper and up to three copies of each book must be delivered, in a prescribed manner to the Government free of expense. The declaration can be cancelled by the Magistrate after allowing showcasing to the person concerned if the Magistrate is satisfied on the following counts :

- the newspaper is being published in contravention of the provisions of this Act or rules made under it, or
- the newspaper bears a title which is the same as, or similar to that of any other newspaper published either in the same language or in the same State, or
- the printer or publisher has ceased to be so, or
- the declaration was made on false representation on concealment of any material fact.

The Magistrate's decision can be challenged in an appeal before the Press and Registration Appellate Board. The Board comprises a Chairman and another member nominated by the Press Council of India.

- **Parties:** If a newspaper (or a book) is printed or published without legibly printing the name of the printer and publisher as also the name of the place of printing/publishing, the printer or publisher can be fined up to two thousand rupees or imprisoned up to six months or punished by both. The same-punishment can be awarded for keeping a press without making the declaration or for making a false statement or for editing, printing or publishing a newspaper without conforming to the rules. In the last case the Magistrate, may in addition to this punishment also cancel the declaration in respect of the newspaper. Non-compliance with the requirement regarding the delivery of copies of newspaper will invite a penalty of up to Rs. 30 for each default. In case of publication of a book, the value of the copies of the book may be charged.

- **Registrar of Newspapers:** There is a provision for appointment of a Press Registrar by the Government of India for the whole of the country. The Press Registrar maintains a register containing the following particulars of each newspaper: Title, language, periodicity, name of the editor, printer and publisher; place of printing and publication; the average number of pages per week, number of days of publication in the year, the average number of copies printed, sold and distributed free; retail selling price per copy, and names and addresses of owners.

The Press Registrar also issues a certificate of registration to the publisher of the newspaper. He does this on receipt of a copy of the declaration from the Magistrate who has authenticated it.

Q19. Explain the official secretariat act,1923.

Ans. The Official Secrets Act 1923 is India's anti-espionage act held over from the British colonial period. It states clearly that actions which involve helping an enemy state against India are strongly condemned. It also states that one cannot approach, inspect, or even pass over a prohibited government site or area like an electrical substation. According to this Act, helping the enemy state can be in the form of communicating a sketch, plan, model of an official secret, or of official codes or passwords, to the enemy.

Prosecution and Penalties: Punishments under the Act range from three to life imprisonment (if intent is to declare war against India - section 5) imprisonment. A person prosecuted under this Act can be charged with the crime even if the action was unintentional and not intended to endanger the security of the state. The Act only empowers persons in positions of authority to handle official secrets, and others who handle it in prohibited areas or outside them are liable for punishment.

Journalists have to help members of the police forces above the rank of the sub-Inspector and members of the military with investigation regarding an offense, up to and including revealing his sources of information.

Under the Act, search warrants may be issued at any time if the magistrate determines that based on the evidence there is enough danger to the security of the state.

Uninterested members of the public may be excluded from court proceedings if the prosecution feels that any information which is going to be passed on during the proceedings is sensitive. This also includes media.

When a company is seen as the offender under this Act, everyone involved with the management of the company, including the board of directors, can be liable for punishment. In the case of a newspaper, everyone – including the editor, publisher and the proprietor — can be imprisoned for an offense. OSA is controversial to the modern RTI act 2005.

Criticism:

Conflict with right to information: In the OSA clause 6, information from any governmental office is considered official information, hence it can be used to override Right to Information Act 2005 requests. This has drawn harsh criticism. The Supreme Court of India has also held that the RTI overrides OSA.

Iftikhar Gilani Case: In June 2002, journalist Iftikhar Gilani was, arrested for violating the OSA 1923[3] . He was charged under the OSA, with a case under the Obscenity Act added to it. The first military report suggested that the information he was accused of holding was "secret" despite being publicly available. The second military intelligence report contradicted this, stating that there was no "official secret". Even after this, the government denied the opinion of the military and was on the verge of challenging it when the contradictions were exposed in the press.

The military reported that, "the information contained in the document is easily available" and "the documents carries no security classified information and the information seems to have been gathered from open sources". On 13 January 2004, the government withdrew its case against him to prevent having two of its ministries having to give contradictory opinions. Gilani was released the same month.

Reforms: After reviewing the provisions of the act, the Union Home Ministry in July 2017 submitted a report to the Cabinet secretariat. The goal was to amend the act to make it more transparent and in line with the Right to Information Act, 2005.

Recent News: Delhi court judgement in the case involving journalist Santanu Saikia

A Delhi court in a 2009 judgement, in a case involving the publication of excerpts of a cabinet note in the Financial Express ten years earlier by SantanuSaikia, greatly reduced the powers of the act by ruling publication of a document merely labelled "secret" shall not render the journalist liable under the law.

Saikia was arrested in February, 2015 in another case that the police said involved the writing of stories and analyses from documents allegedly stolen from the government. He was released on bail in May after spending 80 days in jail.

50 cases of violation of the Official Secrets Act were registered in the country since 2014. Of these 50 cases, 30 were registered in 2016, nine in 2015 and 11 in 2014 according to Union Minister of state for Home Hansraj Ahir. Of the 30 cases registered in 2016, eight were lodged in Tamil Nadu, followed by five each in Punjab and Uttar Pradesh.

Rafale fighter jets case details published by The Hindu newspaper 2019.

Attorney General KK Venugopal also told the three-judge bench that the government could invoke the Official Secrets Act 1923 ,against The Hindu newspaper, which had published the papers. He claims that the documents pertaining to the purchase of Rafale jets published by the media are genuine[9] Justice Joseph one of the three judges on bench asked government about Right to information act 2005, Section section 22 of RTI act have an overriding effect for official secret act and section 24 of RTI which mandates even security and intelligence organisations to disclose information on corruption and human right violations. Finally section 8(2) which compels government to disclose information "if public interest in disclosure outweighs the harm to protected interest".

- Right to Information Act
- Classified information
- Official Secrets Act

Q20. What are the contempt of court?

Or

What is contempt of court? In what cases is it applicable? Explain with examples. [Dec-2019, Q.No.-9]

Ans. Civil contempt means wilful disobedience to any judgement, decree, director., order, writ or another process of a court, or wilful breach of an undertaking given to a court (C1.2(b)). Criminal contempt means publication of any matter or doing of any other act whatsoever (Cl.2(c)), which (1) scandalises or tends to scandalise or lowers or tends to lower the authority of ally court or (ii) prejudices or interferes or tends to interfere with the due course of any judicial proceeding; or (iii) interferes or tends to interfere or obstructs or tends to obstruct the administration of justice in any other. manner. Scandalisation here means a scurrilous attack on the administration of justice or vilification of the entire judiciary, a particular judge or a particular court. Publication of anything which tends to create in the minds of the people an apprehension about the integrity, ability or fairness of a judge or which tends to deter litigants from complete reliance upon the court's administration of justice, amounts to contempt. Similarly, a publication which is likely to cause embarrassment in the judge's mind to the discharge of his official duty is a contempt of court. But, if it is proved that the concerned writing would undermine the prestige or authority of the court or public confidence in the administration of justice by it, then it is contempt even if the vilification criticism relates to the judge's non-judicial functions like the functions of an administrative judge. Imputation of improper motives in deciding a case is a contempt of court. However, the power to punish for scandalising the court is to be used sparingly and about the administration of justice only. It cannot be used for vindicating personal insult to the judge. Bonafide criticism that is a fair and reasonable criticism of a judicial act in the interest of the public good does not amount to contempt. But, if improper motives are attributed to the judges then it ceases to be bonafide. A judgement can be criticised as erroneous, but dishonesty on the part of the judge in delivering the judgement cannot be alleged. If a statement is likely to prejudice or interfere with the due course of justice, then the truthfulness of the facts on which it is based is no defence. 'Trial by newspapers' has been considered by courts as interference with the proper administration of justice in pending cases. These are but . a few examples of what amounts to the contempt of court. However, punishment can be awarded for interference with the due course of justice only if the interference is substantial. Similarly, a person will not be guilty of contempt of court for innocent publication of distribution, during the pendency of civil or criminal proceedings, of a matter which would otherwise deem to constitute contempt.

A fair and accurate report of judicial proceedings, a fair criticism of a judicial act, and a bonafide complaint concerning the presiding officer of a subordinate court do not constitute contempt of Court. supreme court and High Courts being the: courts of record can anybody for their contempt view High Court has also the power to punish contempt of courts like their own contempt punishments: A contempt can be punished with simple imprisonment only for a term extending up to six months or with a fine up to two thousand rupees or with both. If he makes a satisfactory analogue, the accused may be discharged or the punishment awarded may be remitted. In the case of civil contempt, the contempt cannot be sentenced even to simple imprisonment. He can be detained in civil prison for not more than six months; normally, a fine would be considered sufficient to meet the ends of justice. The time limit for action for contempt of Court is one year from the date on which the contempt is alleged to have been committed.

Q21. What are the privileges of parliament?

Ans. Parliamentary privileges are defined in Article 105 of the Indian Constitution. The members of Parliament are exempted from any civil or criminal liability for any statement made or act done in the course of their duties. The privileges are claimed only when the person is a member of the house.

Articles 105 (3) and 194 (3) of the Constitution empower Parliament and State Legislatures respectively to enact laws codifying their privileges. However, neither Parliament nor any of the legislatures of the States has so far done so. Therefore, according to the Constitution itself, the privileges enjoyed by them are the same as, and not more than, those of the British House of Commons. One has to wade through the rulings, customs and practices of the House of Commons and to seek guidance for the Rules of Business and Conduct of Proceedings of the House. Breach of privilege of either House of central or state legislature is usually known as 'contempt of Parliament' like the contempt of courts.

A journalist or editor can be punished with imprisonment or administered a warning, admonition or reprimand for the breach of privilege of the House. His privileges like facilities to enter the precincts of the House and cover its proceedings can be withdrawn. He can be asked to publish an apology. However, no fines are imposed.

There are a number of cases on privileges of the Houses. They include Karanjia Case (1961), Keshav Singh Case (1965), and Eenadu Case (1988).

In the Keshav Singh Case, the Speakerof Uttar Pradesh Vidhan Sabha, committed Keshav Singh to prison for contempt of the House for writing a disrespectful letter to him. On this an Advocate filed a petition in the High Court for his release. The Lucknow Bench of the Allahabad High Court released him on bail. Appraised of this order, the UP Assembly passed a resolution that not on Keshav Singh and his advocate had committed contempt of the House by moving the petition before the High Court, but the two judges were also guilty of contempt. The resolution directed that all these persons should be brought into custody before the House. Then the Full Bench of the High Court issued an interim order, restraining the Speaker and the Marshal of the Assembly from implementing the resolution of the House. After the interim order, the Assembly passed another resolution which made the previous resolution milder. At this stage the President of India made a reference to the Supreme Court for its opinion on the case.

In its opinion the Supreme court said that neither the two judges nor the Advocate had committed contempt of the House by moving or dealing with the petition.

Contempt has a wider sweep than breach of privilege. Contempt can be committed by an act or utterance which undermines the dignity of the House even without violating any particular privilege of the legislature.

But, it is not a breach of privilege to publish without malice a substantially true report of the proceedings of the House even if it is defamatory, seditious or obscene in nature. No civil or criminal proceedings can be launched in a court of law for publication of such a report even if it offends the laws relating to official secrets, defamation, sedition, obscenity or other offences under the IPC.

Q22. What do you know about press council of India?

Ans. The Press Council of India is a statutory, adjudicating organisation in India formed in 1966 by its parliament. It is the self-regulatory watchdog of the press, for the press and by the press, that operates under the Press Council Act of 1978. The Council has a chairman – traditionally, a retired Supreme Court judge, and 28 additional members of which 20 are members of media, nominated by the newspapers, television channels and other media outlets operating in

India. In the 28 member council, 5 are members of the lower house (Lok Sabha) and upper house (Rajya Sabha) of the Indian parliament and three represent culture literary and legal field as nominees of Sahitya Academy, University Grant Commission and Bar Council of India .

Justice Chandramauli Kumar Prasad is Chairman of the Council as of 2015. He has been appointed for a second term. The predecessor was Justice MarkandeyKatju (2011 – 2014)

The Press Council of India, which was first set up in 1966, under the Act of 1965, was abolished after the proclamation of emergency in 1975. However, the government enacted a new Press Council Act in 1978. Thus, the Council came into being again in 1979. Under this Act, the Council comprises a Chairman and 28 other members. Until now, only former Supreme Court judges have been selected for the Chairmanship of the council. The Chairman is selected by a committee consisting of the Chairman of the Rajya Sabha, the Speaker of the Lok Sabha and a person chosen by the members of the Council from among themselves.

Twenty members of the Council are nominated through an elaborate procedure from the panels of names submitted by representative bodies of working journalists, working editors, proprietors/managers of newspapers. and managers of news agencies. Of these, thirteen are nominated from among working journalists including six editors and seven other working journalists. Not less than three editors and four other working journalists should be from newspapers in Indian languages. Out of the six owners or managers of newspapers, two each should be from small, medium and big categories of newspapers. One person is nominated from among the managers of news agencies. The term of the Chairman and the Council is three years. While the members retire on the expiry of the term of the Council, the Chairman may continue in office until a new incumbent is nominated, but not for more than six months beyond the three-year term. A retiring member can be re-nominated for not more than one term. That is, a person can be a member of the Press Council for a maximum period of six years. Three persons having special knowledge or practical experience in respect of education and science, law and literature and culture are nominated, one each by the University Grants Commission, the Bar Council of India and the Sahitya Academy.

The Press Council of India has a two-fold objective; one, to preserve the freedom of the Press and two to maintain and improve standards of newspapers and news agencies in India. The Press Council has very wide functions in furtherance of its dual objectives of preserving Press freedom and maintaining and improving standards of print journals. However, the Council does not deal with electronic media. The Council has quasi-judicial functions and has, therefore, been vested with powers of a civil court. It can summon and examine witnesses, require the discovery and inspect documents, receive evidence on affidavits, issue commissions for examining witnesses or documents, or any other matter which may be prescribed. The Council holds open inquiries on complaints received both against newspapers and news agencies, and journalists as well as those made against the authorities, individuals, associations or groups of people. Based on its inquiries the Council declares its adjudications.

Q23. Explain the kinds of defamation.

Ans. When one person robs another person of fame than he/she is charged with defamation. Here the word does not automatically means famous. Also, fame is not a tangible object that someone can rob off physically. So, the best way to define defamation is when someone deprives another person a sense of their reputation. This reputation is in the eyes of other people who are in their right mind in and around the person. The reason for this is reputation is something that is very difficult to build, like a house of cards. Also, it can get over without even giving due notice.

Types of Defamation: There are two ways through which we can transmit the defamatory statement. One is through slander and another one is through libel. Libel is done through text or graphic and it is permanent in nature. Thus, it can be said that it will stay as long as the graffiti or statue or picture stays on.

Defamation can also be done through slander. Here, slander is referred to as transient or non-permanent in nature. Thus, in this case, the effect of defamation is considered to subsist for the time period of comment or action.

Constitutes an Offence of defamation-defamation is an injury to a person's reputation which is considered as his property. Let us now study the combined Section in the Indian Penal Code. Sec. 499 of IPC says: "Whoever by words either spoken or intended to be read, or by a sip or by visible representation, makes or publishes any imputation continuing any person intending to harm, or having reason to believe that such imputation will hand, the reputation of such person is said, except in the cross hereinafter excepted, to defame that pinned" There are four explanations and ten exceptions in this section. We will discuss them: later. Let us first examine the implications of the first part of this section. , It becomes clear from a reading of this part of the Section that an offence of defamation can be committed not only by spoken word or written statement but also by signs and visible representations. That means an offending cartoon or photograph may also give rise to an action for defamation. The ingredients of the offence of defamation. They are:

- An imputation concerning the person must have been made.
- Such imputation must have harmed, or there is reason to believe that it tends to harm, the reputation of the person concerning whom it is made.

Imputation means an accusation against a person and implies an allegation of fact and not merely a term of abuse or insult. To constitute the offence of defamation, it is not necessary that an injury to the reputation of the complainant must have been caused. It is enough if the offending statement is made to harm the reputation of the complainant or with knowledge or reason to believe that it will harm his reputation.

Not Constitute Defamation: Once an imputation is proved to be defamatory, it is for the accused to show that he is protected by any of the exceptions to Sec. 499. Therefore, let us now study the exceptions to Sec. 499 IPC.

- **First Exception:** It is not defamation to impute anything true concerning any person if it is for the' public good that the imputation should be made or published. Whether or not it is for the public good is a question of fact. The accused should establish two ingredients to avail the benefit under this exception. Both these ingredients are questions of fact. Therefore, he has to prove both ingredients strictly. The first one is to prove that the imputation is true. The second one is to prove that it is made for the public good.
- **Second Exception:** It is not defamation to express in good faith any opinion regarding the conduct of a public servant in the discharge of his public functions or regarding his character, so fat as his character appears in that conduct and no further. This exception, as is obvious, relates to the defence of fair comment.

The statement made by the accused is an opinion and not a statement of fact. It must have been made in good faith and public interest. When the comment is on the character of the aggrieved person it must be related only to his conduct in public and the function he is performing.

- **Third Exception:** It is not defamation to express in good faith any opinion regarding the conduct of any person touching a public question, and regarding his character so far as his character appears in that conduct and no further. This exception again is the one relating to fair comment. The only difference is that the opinion expressed relates to the conduct of a person touching a public question. So, as in the case of the second exception, the comment must have been made in good faith on a matter in which public interest is involved.
- **Fourth Exception:** It is not defamation to publish a substantially true report of the proceedings of a court of justice or the result of any such proceedings. This exception comes under absolute privilege. Only thing is that it should be a mere report of the proceedings without any comment. And it should be substantially true.
- **Fifth Exception:** It is not defamation to express in good faith any opinion regarding the merits of the civil or criminal case, decided by a court of justice; or regarding the conduct of any person as a party, witness or agent, in any such case; or regarding the character of such person, as far as the character appears in such performance and no further. This exception gives immunity to the publication oi comments on the merits of the case which has already been decided by a court or comments relating to the conduct or character of any party, agent or witness. Only thing is that the opinion or comment is expressed in good faith.
- **Sixth Exception:** It is not defamation to express in good faith any opinion regarding the. merits of any performance which its author has submitted to the judgement of the public or regarding the character of the author, so far as the character appears in such performance, and no further. This exception safeguards the reviews, critiques of any artistic work or public

performance. If the expression of the opinion is in good faith the newspaper or the journalist is not liable for action. The expression can either relate to the merits of such work or performance or the character of the author or performer in so far as such character appears in such work or performance. In this exception, the expression "submitted to the judgement of public" includes both expressed and implied submission. Publication of a book, public performance of a drama, music concert or release of a film is treated as an implied submission to the public judgement, suffice that such expression of opinion should be in good faith.

- **Seventh Exception:** It is not defamation if a person having authority over another, either conferred by law or arising out of a lawful contract, passes in good faith, any censure on the conduct of that person. This exception is not related to the work of a journalist and is related to an officer writing confidential reports about his subordinates.
- **Eight Exception:** It is not defamation to prefer in good faith an accusation against any person to those having lawful authority over that person, regarding the subject matter of accusation. Journalists do not make accusations against any person to higher officials. They publish whatever information they get expecting the lawful authority to act upon that. Therefore, the imputation must be made with due care after satisfying oneself with the truth about it. They must be able to show from the circumstances that there is a preponderance of probability.
- **Ninth Exception:** It is not defamation to make an imputation on the character of another, provided that the imputation be made in good faith for the protection of the interest of the person making it, or of any other person, or for the public good. Under this exception publication of matter concerning general public good are covered. If the public interest can be served by a private communication of the imputation, its publication is constructed by courts as indicating lack of good faith.
- **Tenth Exception:** It is not defamation to convey a caution in good faith to one person against another, provided that such caution be intended for the good of the person to whom it is

conveyed, or of some person in whom that person is interested, or for the public good. Here again, imputation published for the public good in good faith is excepted.

Q24. What is the meaning of public good and good faith?

Ans. A publication is said to be for the public good if it has rendered or sought to render some benefit to the public or a section thereof. A thing shall be deemed to be done in good faith when it is done honestly. A mere belief in the truth of an allegation itself does not amount to good faith. The belief must have a rational basis. That means before publishing a defamatory statement the journalist must make inquiries with due care and attention as is laid down by Sec. 52 of the IPC. Reckless statements will not get the protection of the plea of good faith. Similarly, imputation actuated by personal ill-will or malice or to scandalise the person against whom it is made, are also excluded. 'Good Faith' is also defined in Sec:3 (22) of the General Clauses Act. The Section states that a thing shall be deemed to be done in 'good faith' where it is done honestly, whether it is done negligently or not.

Q25. Explain journalistic defences.

Ans. There are four special defences available to journalists in an action for defamation. They are :

- Justification
- Fair comment
- Privilege
- Apology ground for exception is 'good faith' and 'public interest'.

In an action for defamation the complainant has to first prove :

- that the defamatory statement is published;
- that it refers to him, and
- that it is false.

The defendant in his defence can prove that

- the statement does not bear defamatory meaning;
- that it does not refer to the complainant or any other person on behalf of whom the complainant can initiate criminal proceedings under Cr.P.C.;
- that the statement is privileged;

- that the case is time-barred;
- that the suit is barred by res judicata. These defences are available to any person making an imputation against the other.

In addition to these, the special defences mentioned above are also available.

Justification: The defence that the statement is true is called the plea of justification. We have observed in the exception given in Sec. 499 IPC studied earlier, that truth of the imputation by itself is not sufficient in a criminal proceeding. A public good is also another ingredient that must have been involved. But in a civil suit, the truth of the defamatory statement is a complete defence. The burden of proof is on the defendant. If the impugned statement is provided to be substantially true it is enough. But if the plea of justification is taken in a criminal complaint, the evidence rendered should be such as would result in the conviction of the complainant for the alleged offence.

Fair Comment Fair comment on a matter of public interest does not amount to libel. In a plea of fair comment, three points arise

- The comment relates to a matter of public interest.
- It is only a comment and not a statement of fact.
- The comment is fair.

Any matter that affects the public at large is a matter of public interest. Conduct of persons in public office or sanitary conditions, public performances of dance, drama or publication of books or release of films for public exhibition etc., are all matters of public interest. Everyone is entitled to comment on such matters. Comment, being a matter of opinion, is enough if it is fair and honest. Others may agree with the comment but the commentator is not called upon by the law to justify it. The comment or criticism is said to be fair if an ordinary set of men with ordinary judgement, would think so. Criticism should not be actuated by malice. It should be a reasonable inference from the facts, which must be truly stated.

Privilege: There are some occasions when a person will not incur the liability even if the report or statement published ii defamatory. Such immunity is conferred by law for the protection of public interest.

A defence founded on such immunity is called the 'privilege'. Privilege is of two kinds:

- **Absolute Privilege:** On grounds of public policy no action is taken for the publication of reports or statements, however false they may be in cases covered by absolute privilege. Reports of parliamentary proceedings and coverage of proceedings of state legislatures are protected by Art. 361-A of the constitution itself. So no action can be taken for publishing statements made by members of either House of Parliament or legislature however damaging they may be to the interests of any person. But the report must be substantially true. This protection will not be available for publication of statements made by M.P.'s or M.L.A.'s outside Parliament or legislature, and also to the expunged portions of the proceedings of the House.
- **Qualified Privilege** used, counsels and parties in judicial proceedings are privileged and immune from liability for statements made even if they are defamatory. But newspaper reports of court proceedings come under qualified privilege in our country. Publication of statements relating to affairs of state and reports of public meetings are also given the protection of qualified privilege.

As far as reports of public meetings are concerned, care should be taken that:

- the meeting is lawful;
- the proceedings relate to matters of public importance, and
- the report is fair and accurate.

Q26. Who may file a complaint? Explain.

Ans. The Criminal Procedure Code, 1973, lays down the procedure for filing defamation complaints. Section 199 (1) says:

"No court shall take cognizance of an offence punishable under chapter xxi of the Indian Penal Code (Defamation) except upon a complaint made by the person aggrieved by the offence."

However, if such person is under the age of 18 years, or is an idiot or a lunatic or due to sickness or infirmity is unable to make a complaint, or is a woman who, according to the local customs, or manners ought not to be compelled to appear in public, some other on his or her behalf can make the complaint. From Sec. 199 (1) it is clear that normally only the aggrieved person can file a defamation complaint. This is at variance with the general rule which permits any person to file a complaint as to the commission of a criminal offence. A complaint about defamation filed by a person who is not the aggrieved person will not stand unless he is doing so on behalf of a minor, idiot, lunatic, infirm person or a woman observing "purdah", etc. The expression "aggrieved person" postulates that the person or persons defamed is or are identifiable. Persons who form part of an indefinite or unidentifiable body or group, cannot make a complaint unless he or they can prove that the defamatory statement has a direct bearing on him or them. That means if the spiritual head of a community is defamed his follower cannot make a complaint on the plea that he belongs to that community. B But there may be cases where a person is directly defamed by a statement and another person is indirectly defamed by the same statement. In such cases, both persons can file a complaint. For example, if an imputation of unchastity is made against the daughter of a person, both father 'and daughter can complain, an "aggrieved person".

Civil Suit: Any person who has been defamed is entitled to file a civil suit. An heir or legal representative cannot, in the ordinary circumstances, sue on behalf of the deceased person, except where the libel is also defamatory to the heir. A corporation can sue for defamation only when it affects its business or property. For example, where a libel charges the corporation with insolvency, or with dishonesty or incompetence, which tend to cause damage to business and property, the corporation can file a complaint. In other cases, individual members of the Corporation have to sue in their capacity only.

Damages depend on the assessment of the reputation of that person by the judge. There are certain principles laid down by case law. The number of damages depends on the nature of imputation, mode of publication, the social standing of a person defamed and mitigating circumstances. A person of high social position and the aggravating circumstances may call for exemplary damages. In cases such as loss of business etc., compensatory damages may be awarded. In other cases, general damages are awarded for the annoyance or mental pain caused to the defamed person.

Q27. What do you mean by working journalists act?

Or

Write a detailed note on working journalists act.

[June-2019, Q.No.-8 (c)]

Ans. The Working Journalists and Other Newspaper Employees (Conditions of Service) and Miscellaneous Provisions Act, 1955 is a welfare measure meant to regulate conditions of service of the people employed in the newspaper industry.

Its provisions relate mainly to (1) special provisions in respect of certain cases of retrenchment, (2) payment of gratuity, (3) hours of work, (4) leave, (5) fixation of revision of rates of wages, (6) enforcement of the recommendations of the wage fixation machinery, i.e., wage boards and wage tribunals, (7) Employees' Provident fund, and (8) recovery of money due from the employer.

In order to fix or revise rates of wages, separate Wage Boards for working journalists and other newspaper employees can be set up under the Act. The Wage Board for journalists shall consist of a chairman, two representing working journalists and two independent persons. In the Wage Board for non-journalist newspaper employees, two persons representing them shall be included. The Chairman of both the Boards is to be an independent person who is or has been a Judge of the High Court or the Supreme Court.

The Central Government may fix interim rates of wages (popularly called 'interim relief) in consultation with the Boards.

Money due to an employee under this Act can be recovered from the employer by the Collector in the same manner as an arrear of land revenue, and have it paid to the employee.

Question Papers

MASS MEDIA AND SOCIETY: JMC-02

December, 2017

Note: (i) Attempt any five questions. (ii) All questions carry equal marks. (20 each)

Q1. Discuss the historical perspective and practice of Caste System in India. How has it shaped the Indian society?

Ans. Refer to Chapter-1, Q.No.-2 and Q.No.-3

Q2. There has been a huge growth in media reach and access in India in the last one decade or so. What in your view are still the limitations for an average rural Indian? Discuss.

Ans. Refer to Chapter-1, Q.No.-21 and Q.No.-23

Q3. Define Development Support Communication. How can it help in addressing agrarian crisis in India? Discuss with suitable examples.

Ans. Refer to Chapter-2, Q.No.-10 and Q.No.-13

Q4. Media these days is blamed to promote consumerism and down play ethical values. What is your opinion on this? State with valid arguments.

Ans. Refer to Chapter-3, Q.No.-12 and Q.No.-13

Q5. There is a general criticism of stereotyping women in advertisements and entertainment media. Discuss with the help of relevant examples.

Ans. Refer to Chapter-3, Q.No.-3

Q6. What is the information imbalance debate international? Throw light on the concept of Free Flow of Information.

Ans. Refer to Chapter-4, Q.No.-8

Q7. Critically analyse how Reuters news agency became a monopoly and how AP broke its Monopoly?

Ans. Refer to Chapter-4, Q.No.-10

Q8. What is Defamation? Discuss the various kinds of Defamation citing examples.

Ans. Refer to Chapter-5, Q.No.-23

Q9. Media mirrors the society. Give your observations and views of how the changes in the society gets reflected in the content of the media that we see around us.

Ans. Refer to Chapter-1, Q.No.-10, Q.No.-11 and Q.No.-12

Q10. Write notes on any four of the following:

(a) Copyright Act

Ans. Refer to Chapter-5, Q.No.-6

(b) ITU

Ans. Refer to Chapter-4, Q.No.-4

(c) Non - aligned News Pool

Ans. Refer to Chapter-4, Q.No.-17

(d) SITE

Ans. Refer to Chapter-2, Q.No.-9

(e) Article 19 (1) (a)

Ans. Refer to Chapter-5, Q.No.-1

(f) Press Council of India

Ans. Refer to Chapter-5, Q.No.-22

(g) Parliamentary Privileges

Ans. Refer to Chapter-5, Q.No.-21

(h) Sustainable Development

Ans. Sustainable development is the organizing principle for meeting human development goals while simultaneously sustaining the ability of natural systems to provide the natural resources and ecosystem services on which the economy and society depend. The desired result is a state of society where living conditions and resources are used to continue to meet human needs without undermining the integrity and stability of the natural system. Sustainable development can be defined as development that meets the needs of the present without compromising the ability of future generations to meet their own needs. Sustainability goals address the global challenges, including poverty, inequality, climate change, environmental degradation, peace and justice.

While the modern concept of sustainable development is yet derived mostly from the 1987 Brundtland Report, it is also rooted in earlier ideas about sustainable forest management and twentieth-century environmental concerns. As the concept of sustainable development developed, it has shifted its focus more towards the economic development, social development and environmental protection for future generations. It has been suggested that the term 'sustainability' should be viewed as humanity's target goal of human-ecosystem equilibrium, while 'sustainable development' refers to the holistic approach and temporal processes that lead us to the endpoint of sustainability". Modern economies are endeavouring to reconcile ambitious economic development and obligations of preserving natural resources and ecosystems, as the two are usually seen as of conflicting nature. Instead of holding climate change commitments and other sustainability measures as a remedy to economic development, turning and leveraging them into market opportunities will do greater good. The economic development brought by such organized principles and practices in an economy is called Managed Sustainable Development (MSD).

♦♦♦

"A Man is like a fraction whose numerator is what he is and whose denominator is what he thinks of himself. The larger the denominator, the smaller the fraction." -Tolstoy

MASS MEDIA AND SOCIETY: JMC-02

June, 2018

Note: Attempt any five questions. All questions carry equal marks. (20 each)

Q1. Sadharanikaran is cited as the communication model emerging out of traditional Indian philosophy. Discuss in detail, with relevant examples.

Ans. Refer to Chapter-1, Q.No.-9

Q2. How have the Indian communication and media policies shaped up since independence, owing to various committees? Discuss in light of either the Chanda Committee or the Kuldip Nayar Committee.

Ans. Refer to Chapter-1, Q.No.-28

Q3. What do you understand by Development Communication? What role can media play in development communication? Cite a case study to elaborate media's positive role in pursuing a development goal.

Ans. Refer to Chapter-2, Q.No.-6 and Q.No.-8

Q4. What is Development Support Communication (DSC)? In what way can DSC benefit the formulation of communication strategies for the eradication of poverty in our country?

Ans. Refer to Chapter-2, Q.No.-10

Q5. State the role of media in popularizing methods to protect our environment. Write a 200 word speech by an environment expert, elucidating relevant actionable points to motivate listeners.

Ans. Refer to Chapter-3, Q.No.-7 and Q.No.-8

Q6. Define the concept of human rights. What is the role of media in bringing issues in the public domain?

Ans. Refer to Chapter-3, Q.No.-17 and Q.No.-19

Q7. What is the nature and function of a news agency? Talk about any two global news agencies.

Ans. Refer to Chapter-4, Q.No.-1 and Q.No.-2

Q8. Third World countries have been trying hard to bridge the information gap between them and the developed nations. List the initiatives taken by the NAM countries to become self-reliant for news gathering and dissemination.

Ans. Refer to Chapter-4, Q.No.-7

Q9. There is no formal section on Press Laws in the Indian Constitution, but Press Laws are inbuilt in various sections. Describe the substantive provisions of various laws relating to Press with suitable citations.

Ans. Refer to Chapter-5, Q.No.-16 and Q.No.-17

Q10. Write short notes on any four of the following:

(a) Voice of America

Ans. Refer to Chapter-4, Q.No.-3

(b) UNESCO

Ans. Refer to Chapter-4, Q.No.-4

(c) The MacBride Report

Ans. Refer to Chapter-4, Q.No.-12

(d) The Dominance Syndrome

Ans. Refer to Chapter-4, Q.No.-16

(e) Contempt of Court

Ans. Refer to Chapter-5, Q.No.-20

(f) Ombudsman

Ans. Refer to Chapter-5, Q.No.-4

(g) Working Journalists Act

Ans. Refer to Chapter-5, Q.No.-27

(h) Copyright Act 1957

Ans. Refer to Chapter-5, Q.No.-6

(i) Functions of Mass Media

Ans. Refer to Chapter-1, Q.No.-16

(j) PQLI (Physical Quality of Life Index)

Ans. An index of physical quality of the life index (PQLI), which emphasizes quality of life as evidenced by the state of literacy, life expectancy, infant mortality, etc. Yet another notion of development emphasizes freedoms, capabilities, and entitlements for better life, which could be expressed in terms of a scale, similar to the considered under quality of life.

♦♦♦

MASS MEDIA AND SOCIETY: JMC-02

December, 2018

Note: Attempt any five questions. All questions carry equal marks.

Q1. Discuss the oral tradition of communication in Indian society, with relevant examples.

Ans. Refer to Chapter-1, Q.No.-8 and Q.No.-10

Q2. Define media access and media reach. Analyze how media access leads to participation in democracy.

Ans. Refer to Chapter-1, Q.No.-20 and Q.No.-21

Q3. Discuss the concept of development. How have development issues changed over the last few years?

Ans. Refer to Chapter-2, Q.No.-1 and Q.No.-5

Q4. Design a campaign to motivate the rural community towards healthy eating habits.

Ans. Food environments in rural India have traditionally consisted of foods produced for self-consumption by smallholder farmers and foods purchased from small, local markets. In this context, food availability was largely dictated by agricultural seasons and the local agro-ecological environment, the 'thickness' of traditional trading and transport systems, and government distribution systems. For many rural Indians in immediate post-independence India, the food environment shaped diets towards traditional coarse grain cereals (such as sorghum and millet), rice, pulses and locally available fruits and vegetables.

Today, food environments in India are in the midst of a set of far-reaching changes that are impacting health and nutrition outcomes for rural populations. In the last two decades there has been a rapid expansion of formal food retailing in India, including supermarkets but also notably the proliferation of convenience stores. At the same time, the food processing sector has expanded across India, and continues to grow alongside a burgeoning modern wholesale and logistics sector. The result has been the massive penetration of processed and packaged foods into rural Indian food environments, where it is now often easier to buy a sugary drink or packet of processed snack food than it is to find fresh vegetables. As incomes have increased for many over time, so too has consumption of highly processed and energy dense snack and convenience foods, part of India's 'nutrition transition'. Adding to the complexity of changing food environments in rural India is the ongoing subsidisation of cereal grains through the Public Distribution System (PDS), and an ongoing policy debate about the efficiency and coverage of the PDS.

One of the key drivers of changing food environment interactions in India is shifting livelihood patterns among rural households. Rural livelihood patterns and lifestyles, as well as the composition and nature of the rural workforce, set the context within which rural people interact with their food environment. India's economic transition over the last three decades has increasingly created an urban-centric geography of growth, with a rapidly growing urban middle-class population. The nature of this growth, however, has led to dramatic shifts in the livelihoods of rural dwellers and been labelled an 'unusual' economic transition in rural India. This unusual transition is reflected in the slow percentage decline of the total labour force engaged in agriculture compared to the decline in the sector's contribution to India's GDP. According to the World Bank, India's agricultural labour force stands at 43% as of 2017, while its contribution to total GDP in India has declined to just 14%. These contrasting percentages reflect the slow growth of India's agricultural sector and the ongoing struggles of rural households for whom agriculture is still central to their survival.

The agricultural sector can influence food environment interactions in several ways. For example, agricultural policy regarding priority crops, price support and food price subsidies can have a strong impact on household nutrition. The diets of farming households are influenced both by the diversity of food crops being cultivated by the household, and the variety of fresh food available in the food environment. As a source of household income, agriculture can influence nutritional outcomes in terms of how much and which kind of food crops are grown for self-consumption, what crops are sold and which foods are obtained through transactions. The gendered labour roles in agriculture can affect the ability of women to provide nutritious food for their children and themselves.

As a result of the struggles of agriculture-dependent households, rural livelihoods in India are increasingly characterised by diversification. While the role of agriculture is critical to nutrition outcomes for many rural households, livelihood pathways are becoming progressively delinked from agriculture in many parts of rural India. For example, rural Indians are increasingly seeking employment in the non-agriculture sector through temporary and circular migration for meeting their income needs. These migratory patterns change the context in which rural Indians interact with their food environments. For example, as rural households move away from agriculture, they may acquire food via cash-based transactions in food environments that require them to make different decisions about diet. Returning migrants also bring with them new ideas and preferences about food. These fundamental shifts in rural livelihood patterns mean that rural people increasingly buy most or all of their food from stores and markets. If there is a diverse choice of nutritious and affordable foods in the food environment, then this may lead to improvements in dietary outcomes. However, given that food environments in rural India are now characterised by the increased availability of energy-dense processed foods, changing livelihood patterns may also result in poorer dietary outcomes.

Q5. Critically analyse the role of media in highlighting issues related to violence against women, with suitable examples.

Ans. Refer to Chapter-3, Q.No.-3

Q6. "Violation of human rights has become a cause of concern globally." Do you agree? Substantiate your answer.

Ans. Refer to Chapter-3, Q.No.-2 and Q.No.-3

Q7. Discuss the main recommendations of the MacBride Commission Report.

Ans. Refer to Chapter-4, Q.No.-12

Q8. Write a detailed note on any one of the following:

(a) Official Secrets Act

Ans. Refer to Chapter-1, Q.No.-23

(b) Law of Defamation

Ans. Refer to Chapter-5, Q.No.-23

(c) Contempt of Court

Ans. Refer to Chapter-5, Q.No.-20

Q9. Discuss the importance of 'Editorial Freedom' in the context of Indian media scenario.

Ans. Refer to Chapter-5, Q.No.-18

Q10. Write short notes on any two of the following:

(a) Ombudsman

Ans. Refer to Chapter-5, Q.No.-4

(b) UNESCO

Ans. Refer to Chapter-4, Q.No.-4

(c) Sadharanikaran

Ans. Refer to Chapter-1, Q.No.-9

(d) Press Council of India (PCI)

Ans. Refer to Chapter-5, Q.No.-22

(e) SITE

Ans. Refer to Chapter-2, Q.No.-9

It's possible to go on,
no matter how impossible it seems.
-Nicholas Sparks

MASS MEDIA AND SOCIETY: JMC-02

June, 2019

Note: Attempt any five questions. All questions carry equal marks.

Q1. What is sadharanikaran? Is it still relevant in today's times of technological interventions? Justify your answer.

Ans. Refer to Chapter-1, Q.No.-9

Q2. Discuss the major challenges that communication policy for India should seek to address in the present context.

Ans. Refer to Chapter-1, Q.No.-26 OR 25

Q3. Explain the theory of diffusion of innovation with the help of examples. Discuss relevance in contemporary times.

Ans. Refer to Chapter-2, Q.No.-12

Q4. Explain how communication strategies are formulated for development in health sector.

Ans. Refer to Chapter-2, Q.No.-14

Q5. Describe the role of media in protecting consumer rights with suitable examples.

Ans. Refer to Chapter-3, Q.No.-12 and Q.No.-14

Q6. While reporting environment, do you think media is sometimes biased towards the interest groups of the society? Explain.

Ans. Refer to Chapter-3, Q.No.-11

Q7. Discuss the need of self reliance in communication flow in developing countries.

Ans. Refer to Chapter-4, Q.No.-17

Q8. Write detailed note on any one of the following:

(a) Copyright Act

Ans. Refer to Chapter-5, Q.No.-6

(b) Freedom of Speech and Expression

Ans. Refer to Chapter-5, Q.No.-1

(c) Working Journalists Act

Ans. Refer to Chapter-5, Q.No.-27

Q9. "Self-regulation by media is the best regulation." Comment.

Ans. Refer to Chapter-3, Q.No.-15

Q10. Write short notes on any two of the following:

(a) Media access

Ans. Refer to Chapter-1, Q.No.-19

(b) Verghese Committee

Ans. Refer to Chapter-1, Q.No.-28

(c) Renters

Ans. Refer to Chapter-4, Q.No.-6

(d) Press Trust of India

Ans. Refer to Chapter-4, Q.No.-1

(e) Health Communication

Ans. Refer to Chapter-2, Q.No.-14

MASS MEDIA AND SOCIETY: JMC-02

December, 2019

Note: Attempt any five questions. All questions carry equal marks.

Q1. "Market braces use media to influence the audience. Do you agree with the statement? Justify your answer.

Ans. Refer to Chapter-1, Q.No.-23

Q2. Critically analyse the projection of women in a television serial of your choice.

Ans. Refer to Chapter-3, Q.No.-3

Q3. Define the concept of development. Explain any two theories of development which are relevant in the present context.

Ans. Refer to Chapter-2, Q.No.-1

Q4. Plan a development support communication campaign for farmers to promote organic farming.

Ans. Refer to Chapter-2, Q.No.-10

Q5. Define communication policy and underline its importance in the process of development and change.

Ans. Refer to Chapter-1, Q.No.-26

Q6. "Advertising is a powerful means to influence brand choice". Do you agree with the statement? Substantiate your answer.

Ans. Refer to Chapter-3, Q.No.-15

Q7. Why was the MacBride Commission set up? Discuss the main recommendations of the MacBride Commission report.

Ans. Refer to Chapter-4, Q.No.-12

Q8. Critically analyse the importance of the Right to Freedom of Speech and Expression in today's times with suitable examples.

Ans. Refer to Chapter-4, Q.No.-8

Q9. What is contempt of court? In what cases is it applicable? Explain with examples.

Ans. Refer to Chapter-5, Q.No.-20

Q10. Write short notes on any two of the following:

(a) Non-aligned news pool

Ans. Refer to Chapter-4, Q.No.-17

(b) UNESCO

Ans. Refer to Chapter-4, Q.No.-4

(c) Media access

Ans. Refer to Chapter-1, Q.No.-19

(d) Functions of news agency

Ans. Refer to Chapter-4, Q.No.-1

(e) Community participation

Ans. Refer to Chapter-1, Q.No.-22

Wondering who is Gullybaba?

© Gullybaba is a combination of two significant words **'Gully'** & **'Baba'**. The word 'Gully' comes from the ancient game played in Rural India–**Tip cat**. In Hindi, we call it **Gully Danda** (गुल्ली डंडा) which is a great **symbol of Focus & Fitness**.

The word 'Baba' stands for **Respect & Honour**. And these are the fundamental parameters for achieving success. **Focus & Fitness** are required to help one go a long way in life. This is all about achieving excellence in education and giving respect & honour to everyone, and thus, the name 'Gullybaba'.

To know more about why name GullyBaba visit: **GullyBaba.com/why-name-gullybaba.html**

- Syllabus covered as prescribed by Universities/ Boards/Institutions.
- Easily understandable language and format that help students prepare for exam in short period of time.
- Published with exam-oriented approach, hence prepared in question-answer format which provides students the instant understanding of a correct answer.
- Maximum solved previous year question papers included which help students to understand unique examination structure and equip them better for exam.
- Both semesters' question papers (June-December) are included with solutions.
- Instant updation of data as and when any change occurs.
- Use of recycled paper.
- Handy books and reasonable prices.
- For every book sold, we contribute for society/institution/NGOs/underprivileged

NOTES

NOTES

www.ingramcontent.com/pod-product-compliance
Ingram Content Group UK Ltd.
Pitfield, Milton Keynes, MK11 3LW, UK
UKHW021705190726
13853UKWH00001B/420